ANGELS
AT THE CROSSROADS

One Man's Story of
Redemption and Love

JERRY SHEPHERD'S
STORY

AS TOLD TO

ANN H. GABHART

Angels at the Crossroads
One Man's Story of Redemption and Love

Copyright © 2006, 2018 by Ann H. Gabhart

Previous ISBN-13: 978-0-595-38707-6 (pbk) ISBN-13: 978-0-595-83089-3 (ebk) ISBN-10: 0-595-38707-1 (pbk) ISBN-10: 0-595-83089-7 (ebk)

This Edition Print ISBN: 978-0-9983539-1-3

Printed in the United States of America

To Connie, Shayne, Christy and Tab who taught me
how to love and be loved.

—Jerry Shepherd

To my husband, Darrell, and all his fellow gospel
singers who stay on the road uplifting the name of Christ
and spreading the gospel through song.

—Ann H. Gabhart

A PERSONAL NOTE FROM
JERRY SHEPHERD

For many years while telling my life story after I was released from prison, people would come up to me and tell me I needed to have my story put into a book. I thought about it every now and then over the years, but then I would back off when I saw everything involved in getting a book together and getting it published. Well, it was too much for this old country farm boy to deal with, so things would cool off real fast and the thought of a book, let's just say, would be put on the back burner. I would give God another one of my excuses and leave it at that.

After I had been singing with the Patriot Quartet for four years, I came to another one of those crossroads that always seem to pop up in my life. With many hours and many miles on my body starting to take a toll on my health, I had to make a decision about continuing with the quartet or going into solo ministry to once again tell my story.

Then along came Ann who is married to Darrell Gabhart, the bass singer in the Patriot Quartet. Ann is a writer and she had heard me tell parts of my story. She took an interest. We got together and all of a sudden the big word, book popped up.

God never ceases to amaze me. God always has a plan. God always brings the plan together in His own time. Thanks, Ann, for letting God inspire you to pick up pen and paper and write about my life. I pray this book will touch and bless someone at a crossroad in his or her life.

CHAPTER 1

The chase was over. Jerry's car was running on fumes. He'd outrun them when they first pulled in behind him with their lights flashing as he headed home down U.S. 60. He floored the gas pedal, speeding well over a hundred, dodging other cars that spun off the road away from him and the police cars chasing him, and lost them. He might even have gotten away, found a place to fill up and gone on to Louisville and who knew where after that. Maybe California. He'd run there once. He could do it again. But he wanted to see his mom and dad one last time before he ran again or the police caught him.

With an eye on his rear-view mirror, he cut through the country roads to get back to his farm. He knew the roads. He could have made it if only his gas needle hadn't hovered on empty.

He had one last chance. He turned down a gravel lover's lane he remembered from his school days. Nobody would be there in the daytime. He pulled down among the trees and hoped they'd give up the chase. He didn't pray. No use of that since he'd long since gone beyond the mercy of prayer. He hunkered down behind the wheel and tried to be invisible.

But they found him. The car that pulled up behind him didn't have bubble lights, but its long antennas whipped in the wind. Without a doubt, police. It was time to pay for what he'd done.

Jerry kept his eyes on the car in his rearview mirror. They were bound to catch him sooner or later, but he had wished for later. He wanted, no needed to tell his parents goodbye, to see them one more time while he was still free. He'd been on the run for weeks. It was April 1969. Jerry was nineteen.

He'd thought about turning himself in. He'd done the crime. He was ready to pay for it, but he couldn't decide how to do it. Even now he wasn't sure what to do as he pulled the mirror down so he could see the men climbing out of the police car. One of them walked slowly toward Jerry's car. At least the car he was in. Never really his car.

Jerry didn't have a gun, but he could make them think he did. Or he could jump out of the car and take off across the field. They'd shoot. They'd shout at him to stop and then when he didn't, they'd shoot. He stared at the man in the mirror and tried to decide if he looked like a man who knew how to shoot. If Jerry ran, he wanted the man to be a good shot.

As his fingers touched the door handle to pull it up, he shifted in his seat and felt the Bible in his back pants pocket. Instead of opening the door, he reached around to take hold of the small serviceman's Bible the Gideons gave him what seemed like a lifetime ago while he was in basic training. He'd kept it with him through everything. He wasn't sure why. Courage maybe. Strength. Comfort. Definitely comfort. Now he knew he didn't want anybody else to get hurt because of him. Not even his parents, but it was way too late to be wishing that.

He didn't take the Bible out of his pocket, just curled his fingers around it. He watched the man in the suit and tie coming closer. The other man stayed at the car. The men watched for him to make some kind of move. Jerry's feet felt itchy and thoughts exploded in his brain like a lit string of firecrackers.

A calm voice bubbled up in his mind and pushed aside all other thoughts. *Peace be still. Peace be still.* He gripped the Bible tighter and waited, hardly daring to breath.

The officer leaned down to Jerry's open window. "Are you Jerry Shepherd?" His gray hair and wary eyes made the man look even older than Jerry's father.

"Yes, I am." It felt good to admit his name after using another man's name these past weeks. A man who was dead because of Jerry.

The officer's eyes swept over him and the front seat of the car. "Are you carrying any weapons of any kind?"

"No, sir," Jerry said.

"Keep your hands in sight and step out of the car, please." The officer kept his own hand near his coat. Jerry could almost smell the gun that was surely strapped to the policeman's chest. The other officer cautiously moved nearer. His hand was already inside his coat.

Jerry turned loose of his Bible, held up his hands, and eased out of the car. The top of the car was warm when he laid his hands there while the man searched him. The other man read him his rights and detailed the charges against him. Attempting to elude a police officer. Grand larceny. Murder in the first degree. Jerry didn't say a word as he did as ordered and put his hands behind his back. The handcuffs were cold on his wrists.

At their car, they pushed down his head so he wouldn't bump it as they put him in the backseat. Jerry wasn't very big. Five foot ten, but every inch muscle. He'd won all the performance prizes in basic training last fall. Running and pushups were easy. Living was what gave him trouble.

He shifted to find an easier way to sit with his hands pinned behind him. He could still touch the Bible in his back pocket. The peace stayed with him, but at the same time, he shuddered to think of what his mother would say. And how in the world would he bear his father seeing him in handcuffs? He wanted to disappear, just vanish into thin air before his parents could see him like this.

It wasn't the first time he'd felt that way. He'd even managed to make it happen a few times. The disappearing. And there had been plenty of times he'd thought his mother would be happy if he did disappear forever. Ugly memories of times he'd failed to live up to her standards poked at him from all sides. He shut his eyes and tried to blank out all thought, but a long ago memory slithered out to torment him.

"Gerald Warren Shepherd, you're worthless. You can't do anything right. You can't even get up to go to the toilet." His mother shouted at him as she yanked back the covers on his bed. The smell of urine was strong. "Six years old and still needing diapers."

"I'm sorry, Mama. I won't do it again.". Jerry would have given his every toy to stop wetting the bed, but no matter how hard he tried not to, it just happened. Then he felt worthless. And bad. But mostly he felt lost.

Everything at the new farm they'd just moved to was so different. He missed the tree he could climb at the old house. He missed Ginger, his cat they left at the old barn. His father said Ginger would be happier there. Jerry wanted to be at the old farm with Ginger. He'd been happier there too. Every time he got used to a place, every time he got used to people, something happened to change everything. He didn't have a place to belong.

"I'm sorry." He despised the whine in his voice as he begged for his mother's forgiveness. It never did any good anyway. He couldn't even do that right.

She slapped a diaper against his chest. "Here, put this on. If you're going to act like a baby, you can dress like a baby."

He blinked hard to keep from crying as he took off his wet pajama bottoms, put the folded diaper between his legs, and let her pin it on him. He wanted to crawl under his bed and just hide back in the dark corners. He didn't want anybody to see him in the diaper. Especially his father.

Jerry tried to remember if his father was home or out driving his Greyhound bus route. He was probably gone. He was nearly always gone. Jerry wished he was on the bus with him, sitting in the first seat behind him, staring at his father's ramrod straight back. He didn't want to hear what his mother would say five hundred times all day. "Look at the big baby."

Now in the police car, Jerry shook his head to get rid of the memory. But dozens more were ready to pop up in its place. He'd never been able please his mother. Not when he was six. Not when he was sixteen. Not even when he was singing and leading the music at church revivals. Certainly not now, arrested and on his way to jail. That would be the ultimate shame for her.

Maybe she would wash her hands and be done with him. He was never going to be the perfect child she wanted. Nobody in his family had ever gotten so messed up they were arrested. And nobody had ever tried to just disappear forever.

But Jerry had. When he was seventeen. The year he was a senior in high school.

CHAPTER 2

Your senior year in high school was supposed to be the best year of your life. It was a given. Finally you got to reap the rewards of all those long years of homework and tests. Senior year. Homecoming games and dances. Proms. Graduation. Jerry looked forward to all that in 1967 as he finished up his junior year at Oldham County High School. Another whole year of fun with his friends before they went off to college, found jobs, or perhaps got drafted and shipped out to be shot at by some faceless enemy in the jungles of Vietnam.

And then his parents dropped a bombshell. They were moving. His father had sold their farm in Oldham County as if it didn't make the least bit of difference where they lived. His father said it wasn't like they were leaving the country or anything. The new farm was just over the county line in Shelby County.

For a few foolish moments, Jerry had hope. He could drive back to Oldham County High to go to school and be with his friends. He'd make sure to get all A's and B's so he wouldn't be grounded because of bad grades the way he'd been most of his junior year.

"I'll keep up with my homework and get the grades." Jerry promised his father. "All A's. Even in math. Just let me go back to Oldham County High. You said yourself it isn't that far."

His father frowned. "I might need my truck, son."

"I can make some money working for other people this summer to buy my own car or I could even ride my bike that far," Jerry pleaded. "Remember how in the seventh grade I biked to baseball practice. Fourteen miles round trip. It wasn't so hard. No problem at all."

"You can't be riding a bicycle that far on those roads. It wouldn't be safe." When his mother spoke up, Jerry's hopes withered. "And the weather. Try to think straight for once in your life, Jerry. You couldn't be riding that old bicycle in the rain and cold."

"You could take me when the weather was bad."

It was hopeless. His mother had never been willing to drive him to anything, not even to Louisville to be part of the Lawrence Welk show the year before. He could have been on television, but his parents said the only place he needed to be was helping them on the farm or singing at the church. But he had to ask. He didn't want to go to school in Shelby County. He wanted to go to school with his friends in Oldham County. When his mother's eyes flashed at him, he cringed and braced for what was coming.

"You never think about anybody but yourself, Gerald Warren Shepherd. It's always what you want. You're the most selfish child I've ever had the misfortune to be around, never grateful for anything your father and I have done for you, the sacrifices we've made for you. You should get down and kiss your daddy's feet for the way he's provided for us and always kept a roof over our heads."

Jerry switched off his ears. He heard her talking, but he wouldn't let the words come into his head. Enough of her hurtful words already floated around in there poking him at unexpected times, making him want to run off to the woods with a tube of glue or a can of gasoline to sniff. A good buzz helped him forget how he couldn't do anything right.

He started listening again when his father spoke up. "Shelby County High is just as good a school as Oldham County. You'll do fine there."

"My friends won't be there," Jerry protested.

"We're moving and that's it." His father rarely told Jerry what he could or couldn't do. He left that up to Jerry's mother, but when he did speak, that was it. No arguments allowed.

Jerry tried one more time anyway. "I could live with Billy's family. They wouldn't mind. I could help them do chores and stuff and still help you on the weekends."

His father frowned, and Jerry wanted to put his hands over his ears to keep from hearing what he knew he was going to say. "That's not going to happen. You're our son and you can't live with anybody else. You're going to Shelby County." His father's face softened the barest bit. "You'll do fine, son, once you get started there."

For a minute Jerry thought his father might touch his shoulder, show him he knew this wasn't easy for Jerry. But he didn't. His dad wasn't much for showing affection. Some days Jerry wasn't sure his father knew how to smile, but then his dad worked so hard. And he'd seen bad times. Times that might make a person forget how to smile.

When his father was only a couple of years older than Jerry, he flew bombers in the South Seas during World War II. He didn't talk about it much, but his planes were shot up. More than once he'd landed with some of his crew dead in the plane. Every time his plane was slingshot off the carrier, he didn't know whether he might be next.

The war wasn't the only time he faced death. He'd been nearly killed in a barn construction accident when Jerry was thirteen. The memory still made Jerry's heart squeeze tight in terror. His father had been standing to the side watching some men remodel a barn when a nail ricocheted off a piece of metal and split his eye wide open. If the nail hadn't bounced off his nose, his father would have died right there. Killed by a nail out of a barn builder's nail gun after surviving all those Japanese bullets.

Jerry had come home from school that day to an empty house. He looked on the table for a note, but no note. No one there. It felt funny. While he was never sure what his mother might say to him when he got home or if he'd do enough right things to keep her from yelling at him, he still expected her to be there.

When his mother finally called to tell him what had happened, he barely made it out to the porch to throw up. He was that worried. He worried even more after he saw his father bandaged up in the hospital bed, looking ready to take a short step on into eternity. His mother looked just as concerned, but at least she couldn't blame Jerry for the accident since he'd been at school.

While his father was in the hospital, Jerry couldn't sleep. What would he do if his father died and left him alone with his mother? During the day he went to school and did the farm chores, but he couldn't shake the terrible dread of being left alone with his mother. That couldn't happen. No way could he stand that.

He explained that to the Lord in desperate prayers. When no clear answers came down out of heaven, Jerry stepped closer to pure panic at the thought that his father might die. His father might not say anything whenever Jerry's mother tore him apart for doing something wrong, but he was there.

Late at night, in his darkest moments, Jerry decided if

the worst did happen, if his father did die, he would simply have to kill his mother. It was that simple. That would be the only way he could survive.

His father finally came home from the hospital, but with one eye blinded. His Greyhound bus driving days were over. The family had to depend on farming for all their needs now, and one of the ways his father and mother made money was by buying farms, cleaning them up, and then selling them. Jerry didn't mind moving as long as they stayed in Oldham County the way they had when they'd moved the last time. He thought his parents liked it in Oldham County. They knew Jerry did. They had to know Jerry wanted to graduate with his friends at Oldham County High. Why couldn't they wait a year to buy another farm? Just one year. That was all Jerry asked. After that he wouldn't care.

But somebody had offered his father a good price for the farm where they were living. His father found a new place in Shelby County. He said it didn't matter where they lived as long as they were together. After all, God was everywhere. His dad understood Jerry had friends in Oldham County, but Jerry could make new friends. His father waved away Jerry's protests, and his mother said he was being silly, immature, and difficult as usual.

From the day they told him, Jerry began planning. He was seventeen. Not a kid anymore. He could go wherever he wanted to go. But first he needed money and a car.

School ended in May and they moved. The new farm wasn't a terrible place even though they had to live in a trailer while they fixed up the old house. Whenever his father didn't need his help, Jerry worked for other farmers in the area. He liked farm work. Liked the plowing and planting and watching crops grow in the sunshine and rain.

He even liked putting in hay, rising to the challenge of keeping up as the hay bales fell off the conveyer belt in the dusty haylofts. He made every move count as he lifted and stacked the bales while hayseeds stuck to his sweaty arms. The farmers bragged about how fast he worked. Finally something he could do right.

On the weekends and sometimes during the week, churches asked him to lead the music at their revivals. He sang specials, directed the church choirs, did whatever they asked. Sometimes they paid him.

So he worked on the farms during the daytime and at night and on Sundays, he sat on this or that pew listening to a preacher exhort people to turn away from their sins and live for Christ. Everybody thought Jerry did that when he was thirteen and walked the aisle to profess Jesus as his Savior. But it hadn't been right. He walked the aisle to please his parents, his Sunday school teacher and the preacher. They wanted him to join the church. Be baptized. Be saved.

Jerry did it all, but it hadn't meant anything to him. He was pretty sure the Lord was up there in his heaven somewhere, but Jerry rarely consulted him on what to do. Jerry was going to church, singing and reading the Bible, but he hadn't surrendered anything. He just kept doing what he'd always done while thinking about doing some new things that didn't have anything to do with living for the Lord.

Besides, his mother was always telling him he couldn't do any of it right anyway. If he couldn't please his own mother, how in the world could he expect to please the Lord? Not while he was sniffing glue with his friends, and for years he hadn't been able to stop doing that. Not until he started passing out all the time and got scared his mother might find out.

He watched people get saved at the revivals. He shook their hands and welcomed them into the family of God, but he didn't feel part of that family. It didn't bother him. He read the Bible, went to Sunday school, sang holy songs, but the day he joined church was the day he began walking away from God.

He didn't think about what the words of the songs he sang in the churches said. Instead he thought about how he sounded, how he could make his voice go up and reach the high notes. He liked the way his songs made the church people get teary-eyed, and how they'd give him money for doing something so easy. It didn't matter that on the way home his mother told him over and over what he could have said or done better. He didn't care about anything except the money he could add to his stash in his sock drawer.

In June his father unknowingly gave his escape plan a big boost when he told Jerry about the 1964 Dodge Dart on a car lot in Louisville. It was perfect. Only sixteen thousand miles. Good gas mileage. The car dealer might even have told the truth when he said a little old lady owned the car and only drove it to the grocery store and church.

Jerry thought about how that was going to change as he polished the car's baby blue top and sides until they glimmered in the sun. This car was going places.

CHAPTER 3

When the first day of school rolled around the end of August, Jerry drove his Dodge Dart to Shelby County High. Maybe his parents were right and he would make friends. But the Shelby County seniors had their tightly knit groups with no welcome for Jerry. Everybody talked around him, but not to him. If anybody did notice him it was to point a finger and laugh. He hated every minute he was at school. He wanted to be at Oldham County hanging with his friends and flirting with his old girlfriends.

He went to class, but didn't care what the teachers said about homework. Doing homework didn't add to his stash of money, and he didn't plan to be around long enough to get a report card. Chorus class wasn't too bad, but the teacher wasn't like Mrs. Owens at Oldham County. Nothing was like Oldham County. His friends back there helped him get through things. Like the time he wrecked his father's new truck last spring.

Somehow Jerry's dad had talked his mother into letting Jerry drive the truck even though his grades weren't up to her standards. Jerry tried. All spring he tried to pull up his grades, but he blew a couple of tests. And no matter how much he studied, he couldn't keep that math stuff in his head. He kept a copy of the multiplication table in the top of his notebook for a cheat sheet.

He could remember the words to hundreds of songs. He could give a speech that would knock a person's socks off, had even won speech competitions, but math rules and formulas slid right out of his head without leaving a trace. The teachers would give a test and Jerry would stare at the paper without the first idea of what to do.

His mother was good at remembering. She could remember everything he'd ever done wrong, every bad grade he made, every note he hit off key. That day as he drove home from school, he dreaded the thought of getting his next report card. His teachers expected too much. Everybody expected too much. He couldn't do it. He'd even messed up at chorus practice after school. Forgot the words of his solo. He hated that. It made him mad. Mad at everybody. Mad at himself. He was always letting people down, not doing things right.

The madder he got, the harder he pressed on the gas pedal. When the truck tires began slipping as he went into a curve, Jerry decided it was a sign.

"Why don't you just get it over with and end it all?" he muttered out loud. "That way you won't be a bother to anybody anymore."

Jerry turned the steering wheel until he was heading straight for a tree and mashed the gas pedal all the way to the floor. The truck hit a bank, slid to the side and crashed into the tree at an angle. His head cracked the side window. A huge goose egg popped up on his forehead, but he was okay. He couldn't say the same for the truck. It was smashed. He felt sick. He hadn't thought about being around to pay the consequences for messing up his father's truck. He'd expected to be dead.

His parents didn't understand. They accused him of wrecking the truck on purpose so he would get to drive the family car to date his girlfriend. But he didn't intend to hurt the truck. Just himself. He loved that truck.

His friends didn't understood either. At least not what he had really tried to do, but they rallied around, did stuff to cheer him up, gave him rides to chorus practice. Now here in Shelby County, he didn't have any friends.

But he would be away from it all as soon as he earned a little more money.

Then one Saturday morning he got up, pulled the covers up on his bed, and knew he wouldn't be pulling them down to sleep there that night. After breakfast, he went to the field with his parents to put in hay. With only one load to go, Jerry asked to go to the house to fill up the water jug.

He felt funny stepping into the kitchen, knowing he was leaving. The house was so old the people who sold it to Jerry's dad said President Truman's great great grandparents got married there. Jerry wondered how many other people had packed their bags to leave the place forever.

After he stuffed his roll of money deep in his pocket, he jammed all his underwear in a paper sack. He swept the clothes out of his closet still on hangers and threw them in the trunk of his car. After a last look around his room to make sure he had everything, he grabbed the pillow and a blanket off his bed and stuck his Bible under his arm. In the kitchen he filled that jug of water and grabbed a jar of peanut butter and a loaf of bread. He could live on that a while. He didn't plan to spend his money on anything but gas to get him far away from here.

He considered writing a note. *So long. See you later. I'm out of here. You won't have to be bothered with me anymore.* None of that seemed exactly right, so he headed outside without writing anything. When the door shut behind him, all he felt was relief. This part of his life was over. He was going west, maybe all the way to California. His spirits lifted. He couldn't wait.

No need worrying about his parents. He was more of a bother to them than anything else anyway. Except when they needed help on the farm, and they could hire somebody for that. They'd probably be happier with him gone. He sometimes felt like they weren't really his parents anyway, just these two people he lived with and tried to please. And he was nothing but a failure at that.

This would be better for everybody. He was sure of that as he drove away from the farm. When he pulled out on the interstate going west, his heart beat faster. He was free. On his own. Nobody would yell at him. Nobody would even know which direction to yell.

As he sang along with his radio, he wondered when they would realize he was gone. Really gone. They would think he'd slipped off to get out of work. They'd never guess he was headed for California. The thought made Jerry smile as his little car purred along. His gas tank was full, and he had peanut butter for when he got hungry.

He wondered how long it would take to get to California. Maybe he'd do some sightseeing on the way. See the Grand Canyon. He had the rest of his life. California wasn't going anywhere. He was the one going somewhere.

He glanced up in his rearview mirror and saw a truck gaining on him. Not his dad. This truck was tan, an old Chevy. Jerry's heart didn't even start beating harder. His dad wouldn't come after him. At least not right away. He'd tell his mother not to worry, that Jerry would come home. He'd tell her there was no need running all over the country hunting the boy. Where could he go anyhow?

Jerry smiled as he thought about them talking about where he'd gone. They wouldn't call anybody till dark. Then they might go look in his room, but he'd shut the door to his closet. They wouldn't see all his clothes gone. He had at least three days before they started looking and by then he'd be so far west they'd never find him.

He should put a sign in his back window. "Go west, young man. Go west." He'd heard that all his life. It sounded like a good plan to him.

He turned the music on his radio down and began singing one of his favorite songs. "The Impossible Dream." That's what he was living this very minute.

CHAPTER 4

The first time Jerry stopped to fuel up and take a whiz, he was sure people were eyeing him and wondering what a kid from Shelby County, Kentucky was doing so far from home. He kept a smile on his face and acted as though he was headed to choir practice. In Arkansas or somewhere. As he turned back out on the road, he bit into his peanut butter sandwich. Maybe next stop he'd buy some jelly. That wouldn't cost much.

He tried to figure out how far his money would take him, but that made his head hurt. He wasn't good with numbers. Not like his mother and father who didn't need pencil and paper to know how much to pay a farmhand for a day's work or how much something was a pound or gallon or whatever. Gas was thirty-two cents, around three gallons for a dollar. If he got twenty-three miles to a gallon the amount of gas he had money to buy would take him how many miles? Maybe not enough. California was all the way across country. He'd need a lot of gas.

By the time he stopped the second time to fill up in Memphis, he was already worrying a little. His roll of bills was nice and thick, but each time he peeled one off, it was gone with no way to replace it.

He drove on into the night until he started nodding off behind the wheel. As he slowed to pull into a rest area, a Greyhound bus zoomed past him. People on the way somewhere. When he dad drove the Greyhounds, he'd sometimes talked about where his passengers were going. Some would be on long trips and others just riding to the next town. Jerry fluffed his pillow and settled down in the back seat of his car. His back seat was empty whenever he was driving. He could be a bus for a couple of people if they were going his way. West.

At sunrise the next morning, he was at a Greyhound Bus Station watching people line up to buy tickets. He studied the people for a while before picking a couple, not too old, not too young. The man looked a little worried as he jingled the change in his pocket. The woman's eyes were droopy and she was yawning. Maybe she'd sleep and not talk the whole way if they rode with him.

Jerry had changed his shirt, combed his hair and washed his face in the bus station restroom. He wanted to look clean cut and trustworthy. He even practiced a smile in the restroom mirror. Not too big. Not too small. The kind of the smile he used when he met preachers for the first time before he sang at their revivals.

The practice must have helped. The man smiled when he walked up to them. "How you doing, folks? I'm Jerry Shepherd and I'm on my way west. You happen to be going that direction too?"

The man nodded. "As a matter of fact, we're going to Arkadelphia just the other side of Little Rock."

"How about that? I'm heading right for Little Rock.

Tell you what. I'll give you a ride for half whatever your bus ticket would cost. That sure would help me with my gas money." He stretched his smile a little wider without looking too eager.

The deal was easy to make. Even the woman smiled at him. Of course a lot of the women he met at churches thought he was cute. It was the girls his own age and his mother who kept knocking him down. Jerry gave his head a mental shake. That was all in the past. This was now. This was on the way west.

Jerry piled the couple's suitcase in the front passenger seat while the couple climbed in the back seat. The man was a talker. His words slid around Jerry who nodded now and again to make the man think he was listening. Jerry even came up with a half true answer when the man asked what he was doing out on the road by himself.

"After I got out of school last year, I worked all summer to save up some money. I figure I'll have to get a steady job and stuff soon enough. Probably even get drafted. But first, I wanted to see the country." Jerry glanced in the rearview mirror at the man. "You know any neat places to see in Arkansas?"

The woman spoke up. "'Bout the most interesting thing to see in Arkansas is a dead armadillo on the side of the road."

Jerry laughed. "I've never seen an armadillo. Might be interesting."

As soon as he dropped them off, he hunted another bus station and picked out another couple. He liked the short trippers best because they didn't have time to get too curious about him. Each time he added another bill to his roll of money he felt better. Whenever the riders wanted to stop at a restaurant, Jerry stayed in the car and ate peanut butter even when the riders offered to buy him something.

He didn't know why his mother always made such a fuss about eating vegetables anyway. So what if he was a little constipated? That was heaps better than being the other way when a fellow was on the road.

Things couldn't have been going better. His car was running like a top. His tires still had plenty of tread. It was hot, but he rolled all the windows down to let the air blow in on his sweaty skin. He saw that dead armadillo in Arkansas. He passed through mile after mile of flat land in Oklahoma. He went through Oklahoma City where nearly everybody in Oklahoma must live. As he drove across the Texas panhandle, he wondered how a cow found enough to eat to stay alive there.

Then just when he thought the landscape couldn't get any more different, he drove into the canyon lands. He imagined cowboys and Indians up the gullies and riding across the dry plains looking for water. He sang along with the Beatles and Elvis when he could pick up a radio station. He was alone now. He dropped off his last passenger just west of Albuquerque and didn't pick up anybody else.

Arizona was hot, really hot, so folks were ready to pay for Greyhounds' air conditioning. He didn't care. He was glad not to talk for a while, and maybe if he got out of the car and walked around some that might help with the no vegetables problem. On top of that, a sign about the Grand Canyon being up ahead made him remember reading in Psalms about God making the mountains and the valleys. It would be almost sinful to pass by one of the Lord's most amazing creations without taking a look.

Out here away from the cities, everything moved in slow motion and gave Jerry time to think about the big things—the world and God. At night, the stars practically dropped down to surround his car while he was sleeping, and the deep silence was unbroken except by a bird now and again or a coyote. No motors. No tractors. No trains. Nothing but the natural sounds of the country.

Things were going good. Better than good. He could handle things. He had a direction. His gas tank was full and not a soul but him on the road. He pushed the speedometer up to seventy-five. The speed limit was seventy but the roads were so straight and flat he could go ninety without the first problem as long as a cop wasn't around.

The thought had barely crossed Jerry's mind when he spotted a car in the distance coming toward him, moving fast. He had a bad feeling about it as if he'd conjured up a policeman just by thinking about one. The other car was still a good distance away when he made out the bubble lights.

Jerry groaned. "I'm in trouble now."

He backed his speed down to sixty-five just in case his speedometer was off a few miles. He kept his eyes on the road and pretended he wasn't the least bit concerned about the state trooper, but the trooper slowed down anyway and stared straight over at Jerry when he passed him.

Gripping the wheel, Jerry was almost afraid to breathe. He'd passed troopers on the interstates where he was just one car among dozens. Here he was the only one on the road, and his Kentucky license plate made him stick out like a sore thumb. His parents probably had some kind of APB out on him. His goose was cooked.

The trooper went on past. Jerry kept his speed steady as he watched the taillights of the trooper in his mirror. He was beginning to breathe easy again. Another minute and the trooper's car would be out of sight. All at once the trooper's taillights flashed red and he made a U-turn.

"Oh, no." Jerry's heart sank. "This is it. They've got me and I didn't even get to see the Grand Canyon. Looks like I could have made it to the Grand Canyon."

The trooper came up behind him fast, then slowed down and followed him. He didn't turn on his lights or siren. If Jerry had been sweating buckets because of the heat before the trooper came on the scene, now his t-shirt and the waistband on his pants were soaked. The cop followed him for about a mile before he switched on his lights and siren. Almost relieved, Jerry pulled over.

The trooper stopped behind him and got out. He peered into Jerry's window and asked for his driver's license and registration. The policeman studied them for a moment. "What are you doing out here, kid?"

Jerry said the first thing that came to mind. "I thought I'd do some sightseeing. See the Grand Canyon and stuff, you know."

"This says you're seventeen. Don't you go to school?"

"Not now. I quit."

The trooper frowned a little. "That's a bad thing to do, young man."

"I know." Jerry started to smile then thought better of it as he rubbed the sweat off his forehead with the back of his hand.

"Where you headed?"

"California. After I check out the Grand Canyon."

"California, huh. What are you planning to do out there in the big state of California?"

"Just see the sights and sounds." It seemed as good an answer as any.

The trooper looked him straight in the eyes. "Do your parents know you're out here?"

"No, sir." Jerry groaned inwardly. What an idiot! He should have told the man that sure, his parents had let him come. That they thought he should see the country while he was young. Before he had to go to the army and maybe Vietnam. That he was going back home as soon as he saw some things. But no, he was stupid and told the truth.

"Are you on the run?" The policeman's gaze didn't waver on Jerry's face.

"No, sir. I'm driving." Now he'd been a double idiot. Saying a smart aleck thing like that. The cop would probably haul him straight off to jail.

The trooper twisted his lips to the side. Jerry wasn't

sure if it was to keep from smiling or because he was mad. "Step out of the car, please."

"Sure." Jerry opened the door and got out. He felt like a limp rag.

"Would you open your trunk for me?"

Jerry didn't ask what he was looking for. He just opened up the trunk where all his clothes lay in a jumble with the peanut butter and bread he'd bought that morning.

"Appears you might have loaded things kind of fast."

"Yes sir," Jerry said.

"So you didn't tell your parents you were taking off across country?"

"No sir." No need to start lying now.

"Are you going to call them?"

"Eventually," Jerry said.

The trooper stared at him a long minute. "You do anything wrong?"

"No sir, not except running away from home." He might as well keep telling this guy the truth. He was busted already anyhow.

The trooper nodded. "I'm calling to check you out. You stand right here and wait."

Jerry leaned on the car and let the hot Arizona sun bake the sweat out of his t-shirt. It was a different hot out here than at home. Lots of things were different out here, but he wasn't sure the policeman would be different. He'd take him to his station and make him call his parents. Jerry had no idea what he'd say.

He felt sick by the time the patrolman got out of his car and came back toward him. Jerry wanted to crawl under the car and hide, but his father said a man had to face up to whatever he did. So he stood up straight and kept his head up.

The trooper smiled the barest bit. "Everything's clear. You're not wanted for anything, but you get on to the nearest phone and call your parents. Let them know you're all right."

Relief flooded through Jerry, but he kept his face straight and serious. "Yes sir. I'll do that, sir. Just as soon as I get to a phone."

Late that afternoon he sat on the lip of the Grand Canyon and ate a peanut butter sandwich while the sun went down. Then he kept sitting there. After all the other people went back to their cars and he was alone, he sang "For the Beauty of the Earth." He'd led that song in churches dozens of times, but he'd never sung it the way he sang it this night with the Grand Canyon spilling away from him.

What other wonders was he going to see? His promise to the state trooper poked him, but he wasn't anywhere near a phone. And eventually hadn't gotten here yet.

CHAPTER 5

He crossed into California in the middle of the day. The land didn't look any different from Nevada, but the "Welcome to California" sign proved he'd made it. All the way to California. Kentucky was forgotten, back in a different universe as he drove on toward the Pacific Ocean.

But what now? His money wasn't gone but it was dwindling. He spotted a sign that said 256 miles to San Francisco. He had enough gas money to get that far so he took the turn. He needed a plan and driving helped him think.

When he saw a man with his thumb up on the side of the road, he put on the brakes. He didn't know why. He hadn't picked up a hitchhiker all the way across country, hadn't even slowed down when he passed them along the road. Hitchhikers could be trouble, maybe psychos like in the movies. But this time he pulled over. The man looked almost as old as Jerry's father, but he lacked a lot being military neat the way Jerry's dad always was. This guy needed a haircut and looked a little grungy, but then so did Jerry.

"Hey, fellow, you want a ride?" Jerry yelled out the window.

"You bet." The man threw his duffel bag in the back seat and wasted no time climbing in the front. "Where you headed, kid?"

"Nowhere special. Just wherever the road takes me."

"Did I see right on your license plate? Kentucky?"

"Yeah, you saw right, but I'm in California now."

"You're a long way from home."

"Just about long enough." Jerry smiled. "Where are you going?"

"Now don't laugh, but fact is, I'm headed home to New Jersey."

"New Jersey?"

"Yeah." The man looked at him without saying anything for a couple of minutes. "You ever been to Jersey?"

"Nope."

"I guess not. Jersey's not exactly a vacation hot spot or anything."

Jerry kept his eyes on the road and didn't say anything.

After a minute the man went on. "You might not want to hear this, but California can swallow a kid like you whole. You'll end up in trouble for sure. Tell you what, if you take me back to Jersey, I'll pay half the gas and food and once we get there you can stay with me at my mother's house until you get on your feet. I'll even help you get a job."

"You look like you could use a job yourself." Jerry glanced over at the guy. New Jersey? He had never once considered going to New Jersey, but he had wanted a plan. This hitchhiker might be a sign.

"Guess that's the truth, but I never had any trouble

getting jobs. Keeping them is a little harder for me. I may look old to a wet behind the ears kid like you, but I've never felt old enough to settle down."

"What's your mama think about that?"

"She gave up on me a long while back." The man laughed. "So what you say? You game to drive back across the country? It's not like you don't know the way. You just head east instead of west."

East? Why not? Here he was west, but with no particular reason to stay. This was a reason to go. So he turned around and started watching for signs that said east now instead of west.

The man's name was Pete Harmon. He'd been bumming around for a year or two, but now he was ready to go home and see his folks again. He might even settle down this time if he found a job that didn't drive him totally crazy.

They took turns driving and sleeping and made good time back to the flat section of the country where Jerry sometimes wondered if they were moving at all with the way the cornfields alongside the road looked the same hour after hour.

During one of Jerry's drive times, Pete noticed the Bible in the backseat. He reached back and picked it up. "What you doing with this?"

"I don't know." Jerry shrugged as he glanced over at the Bible. "I read it some. To pass the time at night or whatever."

Pete opened it up. "Presented to Gerald Warren Shepherd by Hazel and Dewey Shepherd. Your folks, I guess."

"That's right." Jerry wanted to grab the Bible and stuff it under the seat, but he didn't want to upset Pete or anything. So far they'd been pretty good traveling companions.

Pete leafed through a few more pages. "Your parents

religious? Churchgoers?"

"Every time the doors are open. As long as the ox isn't in the ditch."

"Oh, yeah. You said they were farmers." Pete turned a few more pages in the Bible. "Here's one of my favorite stories about Joseph going off a slave and ending up the main cheese of everybody."

"You go to church?" Jerry couldn't keep the surprise out of his voice.

"When I'm at home. It makes my mother happy."

"You have a hard time doing that? Making her happy?"

"Well, I guess she'd probably be a lot happier if I'd settle down and raise a family instead of knocking about all over the country, but she doesn't give me too hard a time." Pete let out a short laugh. "She's a great old girl who always lets me back in the house whenever I show up at the door."

Jerry watched the road a minute. "You think she likes you?"

"Yeah, sure. She's my mother." Pete sounded like he thought anybody would know the answer to that.

Jerry gripped the steering wheel and stared at the road. "I've never been all that sure my mother liked me. I don't hardly ever do anything to make her happy."

"Is that why you ran away?" Pete kept his eyes on the Bible as he leafed through it.

"I didn't say I ran away." He flashed a worried look over toward the man.

"But you did, didn't you?" Pete didn't wait for an answer. "It's okay if you did. I've been running away all my life."

"I just left. I didn't like school." Jerry relaxed his grip on the steering wheel. Pete couldn't make him go home.

"Me neither. I did get my high school diploma. Even went a little to college, but going to class was optional. So I flunked out."

"Was your mother mad?"

"Nah. She knew I wasn't a nose in a book kind of guy anyway. Least ways not school books."

"She sounds neat. What are you going to tell her about me when we get there?"

Pete laughed at little. "Maybe that I brought home a stray. She's always had a soft heart for strays. She'll probably especially like one who has a Bible."

And she did. Mrs. Harmon took one look at Jerry and said he could stay as long as he wanted to. Then she cooked him meat loaf, apples, and green beans and told him to leave his peanut butter in the car. When she talked about getting his system back in order, it didn't sound as bad as when his mother talked about it.

It was different in New Jersey. The weather was cool already and there were people all around them. No wide-open spaces to take a walk or sit and watch the sun go down. No tractors in the fields. Pete got him a job at a factory. The work was boring but not too hard. And even if it had been, Jerry had never been afraid of working.

He sometimes thought about what his father would be doing on the farm. He was probably sowing the cover crops or putting in the last cutting of hay. If the weather had cooperated, he might be stripping the tobacco to get it ready for market. With winter coming on, he'd start feeding the cows and checking for new calves.

Sometimes at night before Jerry drifted off to sleep in the Harmon's spare bedroom, he'd wonder if his folks missed him. His mother was probably relieved he wasn't there to be such a bother anymore, but his father might miss his help on the farm. Then he'd whisper a little prayer for them.

"Bless Mom and Dad."

CHAPTER 6

It drove Mama Harmon crazy—the fact that his folks didn't know where he was. She took Jerry under her wing and treated him like family. She introduced him at church as Pete's friend and everybody made him feel like he belonged. He liked belonging. He liked going days without anybody telling him he was doing things wrong. He wasn't a bit sorry he'd picked up Pete and left California behind for New Jersey.

He told Mama Harmon the truth about running away without leaving a note or anything. She didn't fuss at him, but she did tell him he should call his parents.

"I'll call them eventually." That was what he'd told the Arizona patrolman too, but he just wasn't ready yet. He looked at Mama Harmon. "I don't want you to call them or write them either."

"I won't, honey," Mama Harmon promised him. "But I just can't keep from thinking how worried your poor mama is bound to be, you so young and all, and her not having the first idea where you are. It tears me up inside knowing how she must be feeling."

"You don't know my mama," Jerry told her.

"No, but she has to be worried. I've been praying for her every night and for your daddy too."

It took her a while, but finally she talked him into calling home. He didn't practice what to say. He just dialed the number and sent up a little prayer that his father would pick up the phone. He decided to hang up without saying a word if his mother answered.

But it was his father saying hello. Jerry's voice deserted him and he had to swallow a couple of times before he could force out some words. "Hey, Dad, it's me. I've got a job." He mashed the receiver up against his head so hard his ear hurt.

His father started talking fast. "Jerry. Are you okay, son?"

"I'm fine, Dad. Doing really good and stuff."

"Where are you?"

"I can't tell you that right now, but I'm safe. In good hands. I've got a roof over my head and a job."

"But can't you tell us where? We've been worried sick about you."

"I'm sorry, but I'm not coming home. Things are going good here. How's things on the farm?"

His dad told him about Jerry's cows, which ones had new calves, which calves he'd sold. "I'm saving the money for you. I'll send it to you if you'll tell me where."

"I don't need it. I told you I had a job."

Silence stretched between them. Finally his father said, "Your mother misses you, son. We've been praying every day that you'd call."

"I've been praying for you too. I'll call you again." Then he hung up before his father could hand the phone to his mother.

Mama Harmon was so proud of him she baked him a chocolate cake. After that it didn't seem so hard to call. The next time he even talked to his mother, and she didn't sound mad, just worried. So when she asked for Mama Harmon's address for the tenth time, he gave it to her after she promised they wouldn't come after him.

Jerry didn't want to go home. He liked it in Jersey. Mama Harmon was always hugging him, bragging on him for doing the littlest things like helping clear off the table and wash the dishes or sweeping the snow off the steps. When she heard him singing in his room, she asked him to sing her favorite, "Amazing Grace" At night Mama Harmon read her Bible at the kitchen table before bedtime. Sometimes Jerry sat down with her and she'd read the Scripture out loud.

One night she looked straight at him. "I know you've got a job, Jerry, but that's not what you want to do the rest of your life. The Lord has something special in mind for you. I just know it."

Jerry laughed a little. "My mother used to tell me that too, but if he has, the Lord isn't letting me in on the plan."

"He will, honey. Maybe he's waiting for you to be ready. To finish school. At least high school. Even Pete got his high school diploma. Didn't help him much since he can't decide what he wants to do with his life, but you're not like Pete. You can be somebody. But you need to get your education first."

"Have you been talking to my mother?" Jerry frowned at her.

"I did talk to her last week. She cares about you and so does your father. They want you to come home."

"Don't you want me to stay?" The kindness radiating off Mama Harmon's face made tears come to Jerry's eyes. She was like a special grandmother who would love him no matter what he did, but at the same time, he didn't want to disappoint her.

Mama Harmon reached over and laid her hand on his cheek. Her blue gray eyes were sad. "You know I love you and I'd be happy if you stayed with us forever. But I prayed about it and that's not what the Lord wants. He wants you to give your mama and daddy another chance. He wants you to go home and finish school."

"I'm not sure I can." Jerry blinked back tears. "You just don't know how my mother is. I can't do anything right when I'm there."

"She may be different now. She loves you. I can tell she does by the way she calls and writes. You don't have to decide right away. Just think about it. That's all I'm asking."

The very next day Jerry got a package from his parents with a batch of chocolate fudge, some new white socks and underwear, a pair of leather gloves, a jar of his favorite dill pickles, and an envelope with a twenty-dollar bill stuffed in it. It seemed like another sign.

He cried the day he packed his stuff to go home. He looked around the little room that had started feeling like home. All because of Mama Harmon. He hugged her and promised to write as soon as he got home, but she shook her head.

"That's not a good idea, honey. This is killing me to see you leave, but it's time you get on with your life back home. You need to put all your thoughts on going to school and patching things up with your parents. You can't be thinking about us up here."

She stood on the front walk and waved. When he couldn't see her anymore, he wanted to turn around and go back, but he kept driving. Soon he crossed the New Jersey state line headed west again. He thought about just going back to California, but he'd promised Mama Harmon. Maybe she was right and it would be better now. Christmas was coming up. A person ought to be at home on Christmas.

He wished he'd gotten Mama Harmon a present before he left. He couldn't get her anything now. She didn't want him to write or send her anything. But she promised she would pray for him, and he could pray for her.

When he turned down the road toward Shelbyville, his throat got tight. His hands were sweaty on the steering wheel. In a few minutes he would see his father. His mother. He told himself things had to be different now. He had gone all the way to California and then back to New Jersey. Things would have to be different because he was different.

As he drove up his driveway, his dad came out of the house in his shirt sleeves and ran across the yard to meet him. He didn't act as if he even noticed the cold as a smile stretched all the way across his face. Jerry's mother was in the doorway waiting. He couldn't see if she was smiling or not.

CHAPTER 7

Maybe he wasn't different enough. Things were just the way they'd always been. At least some things were. His dad was happy to have him home. He talked nonstop about the farm and all the things Jerry missed while he was gone. He wanted to hear about what Jerry had seen and done while he was away, but he didn't push Jerry to talk if he didn't want to.

But things weren't different with his mother. She kept harping on how running away was the dumbest thing he'd ever done.

"A person has problems, he fixes them," his mother told him. "He doesn't just up and run clear across country while his parents go crazy with worry. If you don't learn to think, Jerry, you're going to be the death of your father and me."

Even when she wasn't lecturing him, her disapproval

hung heavy and black over his head. She expected him to earn her forgiveness and he could start by catching up on his schoolwork.

Somehow his mother talked the principal into letting Jerry come back to school to finish out his senior year. As long as he made up the missed assignments.

Jerry stared at the stack of books and papers and thought about New Jersey. It would have been way easier to stay up there working at the factory, but he was home now. And he'd promised Mama Harmon he'd try. She said he needed his diploma. She was praying for him. So he did the worksheets while his mother hovered over him to make sure he didn't mess up this second chance.

Christmas morning came, and they got up, fed the pigs and cows, and opened presents the same as any other year. Out at the barn, his father pulled him aside to say having him home was the best present he could have gotten. Jerry was glad his father was happy, but he couldn't help wondering what Christmas was like in New Jersey.

At church, everybody acted as if he'd simply been away to camp or something. He even sang "O Holy Night" at the Christmas service. They told him nobody could sing that song like he could and how proud they were he was using his talent for the Lord.

School wasn't much better than before he ran away, but this time he had to stick it out and get that all important piece of paper. He started hanging out with some guys at school. Nobody like his friends at Oldham County. These guys didn't care about anything but partying. Jerry tagged along with them, but he stayed away from the booze. He had to keep his grades up.

He turned in his assignments, but the teachers were always after him to do more and more. He decided they were mad he'd been allowed to come back to school after missing so many days and wanted him to fail. Mr. Chester, his chorus teacher, wasn't like that. He wanted Jerry's voice in the a cappella choir to help win awards at the state competitions. Mr. Chester told Jerry his voice was a gift and if he didn't waste it, he could go far.

Janice, a girl in some of his classes, thought so too. She said he'd make the big time someday. They started dating right after Christmas on and off. They'd go on a few dates, break up over something silly and then get back together. She kept saying if he really loved her he'd let her wear his class ring. So one night he slipped it off his finger and put it in her hand. Janice kissed him till he was dizzy, but the next morning his mother hit the ceiling.

"You did what?" She slammed his plate of eggs and bacon down in front of him, then leaned down to stare in his face.

Jerry slid his eyes to the side.

"Look at me when I'm talking to you," she yelled.

"Yes ma'am." Jerry shrank back in his chair to get as small as he could. He looked straight at her face but in his head he pulled down a black shade to block her out.

The words came through anyway. "Why do you keep doing the dumbest things? You weren't thinking again, Jerry. You've got to start thinking. Your father didn't pay his hard earned money for that ring so you could throw it away on some girl. If you aren't the most ungrateful son a father ever had. Giving your ring to that girl. Janice Crossfield of all people."

"I'll get it back."

"Today," his mother ordered.

So Jerry got his ring back and broke it off for good even though Janice didn't think he really meant it. Not for good.

He hoped breaking up with Janice would mollify his mother. He needed to do something to make her happy, because she wasn't going to be pleased with the way his grades were sinking. When the last grading period started in the spring, he quit studying. If he was going to flunk out, he might as well do it with flying colors. If that was possible.

Then Mr. Chester recruited him for the senior play. "The Crucible" by Arthur Miller was a serious drama, not a musical, but Mr. Chester said presenting a song with feeling was part acting and hadn't he won some speech contests? He kept on until Jerry agreed to audition.

Nobody was more surprised than Jerry when he got the part of John Proctor. He'd never been in a play before and now he got a starring role. Acting was exciting. His lines were way easier to remember than math formulas, and the director, Mr. Riddle, pushed them to become whatever part they'd won. Jerry knew about pretending anyway. He'd been doing it for years. But this was more fun.

The play was set back in the 1690's during the Salem witch hunts. It sounded crazy people blaming babies dying and crops failing on witches, but then Jerry had sometimes wondered if somebody put a curse on him when everything kept going wrong.

If his parents ever heard him say a thing like that, they'd be horrified. They'd tell him his only curse was one he brought on himself but not trying hard enough, not studying or paying attention. Not making the grade.

Thinking about report card time made his throat so tight he could hardly swallow. What if he didn't graduate? His mother would die of shame. Especially after she'd talked the principal into letting him back into school after his "little trip across country." And Mama Harmon would be disappointed too. Jerry didn't see how she could know about it, but if she did somehow find out, she'd be disappointed in him. He always let down everybody.

Then he flubbed his lines at play practice. Totally forgot them. Nobody yelled at him or anything, but messing up made him want to bash his head against a wall. He'd felt the same way earlier that day when Mrs. Smithers told him about his bad Government Studies grade. She hated him. She was happy he was failing. She wanted to grind him into the ground and never let him up. She expected too much. Just like his mother. That's all he could think about as he drove home from school.

As he went around a curve too fast, his wheels squealed. But instead of slowing down, he mashed his foot down on the gas pedal. He didn't want to make the curve up ahead. He knew that curve. He kept it in his head as a place to end it all. If he hit the big trees there, he would die. That would be better than failing.

He slid into the curve. He wasn't going to make it. All at once one of the scenes from the play was in his head. Next week was the first performance. He had to stay alive for that. He yanked the steering wheel hard to the left to get back on the road, but too late. The car banged into a tree on the passenger side.

Metal crunched. The windshield shattered and showered glass on him and the seat. Then it was quiet. So quiet it hurt his ears. Stunned, he kept his grip on the steering wheel for a long moment. He took a deep breath. He was alive. He uncurled his hands from the steering wheel and flexed his fingers. They still worked. He felt his head, wiggled his toes in his shoes. He wasn't even hurt. He sat there in a cocoon of safety in the battered car. Dread soaked through him as he thought about telling his parents. They'd take his driving privileges away. They'd say he couldn't do anything right. And they'd be right. He couldn't even kill himself.

He slung open the door of the Dodge Dart and jumped out. He grabbed a big limb and slammed it into the car. He couldn't even kill himself. Any idiot ought to be able to kill himself. He banged the limb on the roof of the car and let out a victory yell when it caved in. He pounded on the car until he couldn't lift his arms.

Totally spent, he sank down beside the car, leaned up against the wheel and cried. He'd gone all the way to

California and then back east in this car. Now he'd ruined it. He always ruined everything.

His parents did take away his driving privileges. Of course, he didn't tell them the whole truth about the wreck. He said he slid off the road and bounced off a few trees. They said he could fix his car whenever he earned the money to pay for it. Until then, he'd have to find his own way to wherever he wanted to go. He could ride the school bus, walk, whatever. They were too busy to haul him around. If he couldn't find a ride to play practice, he'd have to drop out of the play.

He found rides. His friends came through. Being in the play was all that held him together as the school year wound down. He took tests, even passed some of them. He was going to fail Government Studies for sure. He didn't know about his other classes, but he was on the edge of disaster in everything except A Cappella Choir and Advanced P.E. He could sing and he could do pushups.

And he could act. Everybody said so. People loaded him down with compliments after the first performance.

Jerry replayed all their words over and over in his head. Maybe he'd found something he could do. He should have stayed in California and gone to Hollywood. When his parents saw what he could do, they'd be proud of him at last. They were waiting for the last performance when Jerry's aunt and uncle could come with them.

That last night, the curtains pulled back the same as the other nights, but things started going wrong from Scene I. His mother being in the audience seemed to jinx him. He flubbed his lines and missed a couple of cues. The crowd didn't give them any encouragement, and everybody up on the stage quit acting. Everything was flat as they walked through their scenes, not living them the way they had the night before.

After the final scene and they'd done curtain calls to polite applause, Jerry's parents and aunt and uncle told him they had enjoyed the play. Jerry wanted to scream at them how they weren't supposed to enjoy the play. They were supposed to be moved by it, bothered by the fact that he as John Proctor had been hung as an innocent man. Instead he smiled and let them talk.

Before the cast left, Mr. Riddle gathered them together for a parting word. "You all did a fantastic acting job. This was a serious play, not some piece of fluff everybody would forget before ten o'clock tonight. You've done something real and professional and your performances will have people in Shelby County thinking for weeks to come."

As Jerry was picking up his duffel bag to leave, Mr. Riddle pulled him aside. "You were a great John Proctor, Jerry. One of the best I've ever seen."

"I flubbed my lines."

"Don't worry about that. You can't have perfect performances every night. You should consider acting in your future. You have a gift. Of course, it's hard to get started, but you never know. Everybody was an unknown at one time."

"I'm about as unknown as they come."

"Well, you don't have to head to Hollywood today. In fact maybe considering your history, I should tell you definitely not to head to Hollywood today." Mr. Riddle laughed. "Now get out of here and go have some fun. You wait until you read the paper next week. You'll see that they thought you were great."

"Come on, Jerry. Let's go," Jacob yelled at him from in front of the stage. Jacob had helped with the lights and had been one of the guys who ferried Jerry back and forth to practices after his wreck. "Everybody's waiting."

Jerry jumped down off the stage and Jacob threw his arm around his shoulders. "Waiting? What for?"

"To party. You close down a show, you party. It's tradition. Even Mr. Riddle says so."

"Where? Here?"

"Nah, not here. You can't have fun at school," Jacob said. "And we intend to have some fun tonight."

"I'm in. Lead the way."

"It would be an honor to lead such a renowned actor to my car. After you just walked off to be hung, this is your second chance at life." Jacob punched him in the arm and Jerry laughed. He was glad his parents had gone home. Glad he was with a friend.

Jerry followed Jacob out of the gymnasium. He'd always turned down the beer the guys pushed at him. Tonight he wouldn't turn down anything. Maybe that could make him forget that look in his mother's eyes when she'd talked about him forgetting his lines. The look that said he might as well forget trying to do anything right. Ever.

The beer tasted better than he'd thought it would. He drank three bottles straight before he came up for air. By then, he was feeling fine.

CHAPTER 8

He didn't know why it had taken him so long to discover beer. His friends were right. It did solve a lot of problems especially if he popped a pill or two to go along with the booze. His head pounded a little after a night out with the guys, but he managed to hide it from his parents. He'd never been extra cheery in the mornings anyway. And he sweated out most of the alcohol in P.E. or doing chores on the farm.

His English and Anatomy teachers both told him he still had a chance to pass if he studied for his semester exam. Jerry carried his books home, but going out with the guys and drinking beer was loads easier than studying.

The hardest thing about the beer was getting it, at least until he got a job fixing fence on Mr. Abram's farm one Saturday. Mr. Abram's farmhand, Harvey Smith told him getting beer was no problem.

"Not for you now." Jerry looked up from working the posthole digger. "But how did you get it when you were in school?"

"Everybody always knows somebody who's twenty-one."

"Yeah, you're twenty-one, aren't you?"

"And some." Harvey grinned at him as he dropped a post in the hole. "You give me the money and I'll get you all you want. You're eighteen, ain't you? Had to sign up for the draft already, I reckon. If you're old enough to get drafted and sent off to be shot at in 'Nam, you're old enough to drink a little beer."

"Gee, that'd be great, Harvey." Jerry pulled a couple of fives out of his pocket on the spot.

Harvey folded the money and stuck it in pocket. "Just don't tell your folks. If your mama found out, she'd come after me with a hoe."

Overnight, Jerry's stock rose with his friends. Now they had a reliable source for their beer. So when Senior Day arrived, their one day reward of getting to skip school after twelve long years, they had plenty of booze thanks to Jerry and an empty house thanks to Bennie's parents being at work.

They aimed to have a little fun together, but they didn't expect so many people to show up. It wasn't supposed to be a riot scene with everybody so drunk they were either passed out or punching holes in the wall just because they could. A neighbor must have called Bennie's father because he came home early and caught them there. Bennie was passed out on the floor, so his dad lit in on the rest of them, yelling so loud it hurt Jerry's ears.

Jacob grabbed Jerry's arm and yanked him out the door. Jacob jumped in his car and hit the gas before Jerry got the passenger door shut. The car fishtailed and almost hit a mailbox. Jacob didn't slow down. He left black marks on the road as sirens wailed in the distance.

Jerry spent the night with Jacob. Jacob's parents never fussed when he came dragging home late after a party. His father could put away the booze himself. He seemed almost proud Jacob was following in his footsteps. But Jerry's mom and dad wouldn't be proud if he showed up there drunk. They would make him sleep with the pigs once they got through yelling at him.

At school the next day, his buddies ratted on him. As if everything that happened at Bennie's was his fault. He didn't know why. He hadn't punched the first hole in a wall. But he had brought the beer. Plenty of it.

Graduation was only a day away, but Jerry figured it might as well be twenty years when he was called to the principal's office. He stood in front of Mr. Harrison's desk for what seemed like an hour before the principal looked up from the papers he was working on to skewer Jerry with his stare.

"Jerry Shepherd, I'm disappointed in you. You have let down your parents, your school, your teachers, and your friends. And me. You've let me down. All the good you've done over twelve years in school undone in one day. And for what?"

Jerry started to say something in his own defense, but the principal held up his hand to stop him. "I don't want to hear any stories you've made up about what you did or didn't do. I know what you did. I talked to Bennie's father. You're lucky you aren't behind bars."

"Yes sir." Jerry stared down at his feet and mumbled, "Things got out of hand."

"That has to be the understatement of the year." Mr. Harrison leaned back in his chair and tapped his pen on the desk.

Another uncomfortable minute went by. Over the tapping of Mr. Harrison's pen, Jerry heard his classmates out in the hallway going to the gym for graduation practice.

"What are you going to do?" Jerry finally asked when

he couldn't stand the silence another second. He looked the man in the face. "You going to tell my folks?"

"Your folks. Do you know how hard your mother worked to get you back in school after that stunt you pulled last fall? She practically camped on my doorstep until I promised her I'd give you another chance. But how many chances do you deserve?"

"I don't know, sir. One more, I hope."

The principal shook his head. "I can't imagine what your mother is going to say. And your father. He's a good man, an asset to our community."

"I promise I won't do it again. I didn't think things would go so crazy."

"That's the trouble, Jerry. You didn't think. When you get to be a senior in high school, you're supposed to think about the consequences of your actions. You're not a child any longer. You have responsibilities to your parents and your school."

"Yes sir." Jerry stared down at the scuffed toes of his shoes. "Am I going to graduate?" He peeked up at Mr. Harrison.

"I don't know. I should just kick you out of school and be done with it, but your mother would take to her bed." A strange look crossed Mr. Harrison's face as if he were thinking about the calls Jerry's mother would be making to him when she found out Jerry wasn't going to graduate. After a minute he cleared his throat. "I just don't know. When you get your diploma, you'll just have to open it up and see if it's signed. Now get out of here. I'm sick of looking at you."

The next night, Jerry's stomach was in knots. He put on the cap and gown. He walked in with the rest of his classmates. Some of them wouldn't meet his eyes. Probably the ones who'd put the blame on him for the party, as if they hadn't popped the tops of the beer bottles themselves.

They always gave out the awards first, so he had a long

wait to find out if Mr. Harrison had decided to sign his diploma. He didn't even want to think about what he'd tell his mother if he unrolled it and there wasn't a signature. Maybe he could fake the principal's signature. He'd doctored a few grades on report cards more than once. Of course he'd always gotten caught and ended up in worse trouble.

He wasn't half paying attention as the principal droned on about the awards. Joseph Phillips got the math award. Everybody knew he would. Everybody knew who would get all the awards. That was practically decided by the time you hit your sophomore year. If he'd gotten to stay at Oldham County he might have gotten some kind of award. If he'd stayed at Oldham County a lot of things might have been different.

People were clapping as Rebecca Jackson climbed up on the stage to get the English award. No surprise there. She was always carrying around some book by an author with a name nobody could pronounce.

He was all primed to hear them announce Marianne Matthews as the National Choral Award winner. He was rolling his neck to get the kinks out of it when his own name slammed into his ears. "Jerry Shepherd, National Choral Award."

He was stunned. He must have heard wrong. April Sanders, sitting next to him, poked him with her elbow and whispered, "You have to go get it."

He stood up and his feet worked. Mr. Harrison almost smiled at him when he handed him the award. Jerry looked over at his parents as he went back toward his seat. He barely had time to sit down when Mr. Harrison announced that Jerry had won the Drama Award. As he headed back off the stage to his chair, Mr. Harrison told him to wait that he'd also won the Best Actor Award. Jerry couldn't quit smiling. At least not until they started going up to receive their diplomas from Mr. Whitson, the superintendent.

Cheers and raucous cries greeted some of the names as if their family and friends never thought they'd actually make it through school. Jerry could hardly swallow by the time his name was called and he took the rolled up diploma from Mr. Whitson who shook his hand and congratulated him. He had to wait until he got back to his seat. He couldn't unroll it while he was walking. While they called out the W names, he peeked inside his diploma. He'd never been so glad to see William Harrison's name in his life.

"Thank you, Lord," he whispered, putting his hands together in prayer. "And thank you, Mama." Sometimes a demanding mother paid off. Even Mr. Harrison hadn't wanted to deal with her again.

By the time the principal presented the class of '68 to the world, Jerry was almost laughing he was so happy. He yanked off his cap and slung it so high it hit one of the gym lights. He'd done it. He'd graduated.

CHAPTER 9

"So what are you planning to do now that you're out of high school, Jerry?"

The people at church and in town who kept asking him about his plans for the future had no idea what a firestorm that set off inside Jerry. He wanted to study music or drama. That's what he was good at, but his parents said no. Music was fine for a sideline but not for a career.

He could just stay on the farm, but with no end in sight to the Vietnam War, he faced the draft if he didn't go on to school somewhere. So he enrolled in the Spencerian Business School in Louisville. He didn't have much choice since his parents wouldn't pay the first bit of attention to what he really wanted and he didn't have the money to go to school without their help. He needed the money he was making at revivals and hiring out to farmers to fix his car. Thank goodness, his dad let him drive the truck until he saved up enough.

His mother mostly stayed off his back. He'd graduated. He didn't have a serious girlfriend, and he had a plan for school. She went to business school herself and worked as a secretary for Greyhound before she'd married his father. She claimed the business field was one where he could get a job just about anywhere. His father didn't look as sure, but he didn't say much about it as they worked on the farm through the summer.

On Sundays Jerry sang in the churches and on Friday and Saturday nights, he went out with his buddies. As Jacob was always saying, if God hadn't intended for man to drink beer, he wouldn't have made it taste so good. Jerry wasn't real sure where God was that summer anyway. Sometimes in church when he was singing, he almost felt something. Then the service would be over and he'd feel empty inside.

He tried to fill up that emptiness with beer and pills. And it took a lot of beer to do it. Even Jacob got on his case a couple of times.

"Slow down, man," Jacob told him when Jerry came to after passing out from drinking too much. "You don't want to kill yourself. You just want to get drunk."

That was all Jacob knew about it. Jerry wanted to do more than get drunk. He wanted to go to some place where he didn't have to think, where he didn't have to worry about going to business school, where he didn't have to hear his mother telling him he was doing it all wrong. He already knew he was doing it wrong. He didn't need her to tell him that.

With September getting closer, Jerry's feeling that it was all wrong kept getting stronger. The only time he didn't feel the nervous little ants crawling around inside his skin was when he was smashed. One night he was supposed to get with the guys, but he started drinking early. Maybe Jacob was right and he could drink enough that he could pass out and never wake up. That would be an easy way to go. Or another wreck.

He chugged down a whole case of beer, but he didn't pass out. So he kept driving. His wheels slipped off the road on first one side and then the other, but he wasn't all that worried about staying on the road. He just wanted to find the right curve, the right tree this time. He felt a little guilty since he was in his father's truck, but his father could get it fixed. Once Jerry was gone, his father wouldn't have to pay for this crazy business school idea. He could use that money to fix the truck.

Jerry didn't really know what happened. One minute he was driving fast, weaving back and forth, waiting for the curve to end it all. The next minute the truck was crashing into a tree. He was thrown clear, out in the middle of a field. He hit hard, but he didn't feel any pain. He tried to stand up, but his head was spinning and his muscles felt like wet noodles. He tried to push up off the ground again and sat his hand down on a piece of glass. He picked the broken beer bottle up and looked at it a few seconds. Then he tilted it up and held it over his mouth in case a drop or two was left inside it.

Somebody must have called his father, because he was there before the police. But Jerry heard sirens. They were on the way.

"What in the world, son?" his father said as soon as he saw Jerry wasn't bleeding or anything. "The whole field smells like a brewery."

Jerry held up the broken beer bottle, sniffed, and then laughed. "It does, doesn't it?" His tongue felt thick, but he thought the words came out okay.

"How much beer did you have in the truck?"

"I don't know." Jerry felt suddenly near tears. "Are all the bottles broken, sir?"

"I hope so." His father stared down at him. "How much have you drunk tonight?"

Jerry tried to stand up, but fell back. "Not so much, sir.

Just a case."

"A case? Twenty-four beers?" His father looked over at the sheriff's deputy who was coming down from the road toward them. "You'd better call an ambulance, Harold."

"Is he hurt, Dewey?" The deputy flashed his light on Jerry's face.

Jerry groaned and threw his arm up to shield his eyes.

"Not that I can tell, but he's got way too much alcohol in his system," his father said.

"This isn't the first time your boy's been out drinking. You know that, don't you, Dewey? We done caught him with some of his buddies and warned them all a couple of times."

"He's just a boy, Harold. You remember how it was when you were a boy."

"Yeah, I know, Dewey, but I'm going to have to write him up. I can't just look the other way this time," the deputy said.

"Do whatever you have to, but call the ambulance. The boy's going to be sick."

The deputy flashed his light around them. "Well, if the alcohol don't get him, the poison ivy might. Did you ever see such a healthy stand of the stuff?"

Jerry ended up in the hospital for a week. Once they decided he wasn't going to die from an alcohol overdose, he broke out in poison ivy. He thought he might die from that. His eyes swelled shut and they had to tie his hands down to keep him from digging at his arms and legs. His mother said it served him right. That he was nothing but a drunk.

The word pierced through him. He wasn't a drunk. He'd been drinking, but he wasn't a drunk. After that, September and the start of school couldn't come fast enough. He wanted to be out of his mother's sight. At the same time he didn't want to go to the school. He wanted to stay on the farm and work with his father.

His father knew the drinking was nothing but a mistake, like the time when he was fourteen and his father had caught him inhaling gasoline fumes out in the tobacco patch. Jerry could quit. He'd quit the glue as soon as he started passing out when he sniffed it. He'd quit the gasoline fume sniffing. He could quit the beer and pills if he wanted to. His dad didn't call him a drunk. He just told him to work harder on the farm.

Jerry could do that. He was good at farm work. He couldn't imagine being good at business. Didn't a person have to know math for that?

He kept on a brave face as his mother helped him pack. They took him to Louisville and unloaded his stuff in a room at the YMCA. They paid for a week. After that they promised to send more money. They said business school would be good for him. And he wouldn't be drafted. The last wasn't said out loud, but it was in all their minds.

He went to classes the first day and knew it wasn't going to work. The teachers were going to expect too much out of him. Stuff he couldn't do. It was stupid to sit through a bunch of dull classes to fail again.

The next day he stayed in his room and slept through the daylight hours. He wandered around some at night. He didn't know anybody. He stayed the full week in the room since it was already paid for, but he didn't go back to classes. At the end of the week, he had to move out. No way could he go home, but he had to go somewhere.

He clicked the back of his class ring on the telephone receiver as he tried to think of somebody to call. The ring made him remember his old girlfriend. Janice was a senior this year. Older, cuter maybe. Back at graduation, she'd hugged him like she still liked him, and her parents were nice. Maybe if he came up with a good enough story, they'd come get him and let him stay with them until he decided what to do. If Janice asked them to.

Janice sounded excited when he called her. He told her maybe they could go steady again, but that his folks were mad at him for quitting school and he needed a place to stay till they got over it. It was all true. His parents would be mad at him when they found out he'd quit school. They just didn't know yet. They thought he was in Louisville, sitting in class, learning to be who knew what. Certainly nothing he could be.

Janice talked her dad into picking Jerry up at the school. He gave Janice his class ring. It was the least he could do. Things went good for a week, but then her father caught them necking on the back porch. Janice cried and said she loved Jerry, but that just made her father's face turn even redder.

Mr. Crossfield took a deep breath and ordered her inside so he and Jerry could have a man-to-man talk. When the door slammed behind her, he stared at Jerry. "This isn't going to work out. You need to go home."

"But, sir, we were just kissing a little." Jerry pleaded his case.

"That may be true, but I was young once. Things like this can get out of hand in a heartbeat. I'm not saying you and Janice can't date, but the two of you are way too young to be living under the same roof. I understand you have problems with your folks, but they're good people. You go home and work things out with them. Then you can give Janice a call."

"Yes sir." What else could he say?

"Get your things together and I'll take you home."

They dropped him off at the end of the driveway. Janice was still crying when she waved goodbye to him. He watched their car drive out of sight. He wished he'd gotten his class ring back, but it hadn't seemed the best time to ask for it.

He looked up at the house. Nobody saw him to come meet him. He started up the driveway that suddenly seemed a mile long. With every step he felt a little sicker. He should have warned them he was coming.

Maybe they wouldn't be home. Maybe he could just slip inside up to his room and hide out a few days without them knowing he was there. Sometimes he felt as if they lived in separate rooms anyway. That they never actually lived together. He lived in his own little room and they in theirs.

But of course they were there in the kitchen, just finishing up supper. They'd done the evening chores and were planning the next day the way they did every night. He could see them through the window before he opened the door. He felt like he'd swallowed twenty-five bumblebees. He pushed open the door and set his suitcase down. "I'm home."

They both looked as if they were seeing some kind of apparition. Finally his father said, "Well, where have you been?"

"I've been here and I've been there." Jerry tried a grin but it died on his face.

"I don't think that answer is good enough, son," his father said.

"Why aren't you at school? That's where you're supposed to be," his mother said.

"School didn't work out. I couldn't do it, so I left."

"You can't just keep running away from things." His mother raised up from her chair to glare at him. "You'll never amount to anything if you don't start facing whatever problems come your way."

Jerry's dad held up his hand to stop his mother's tirade. "Where have you been, son? Out on the road again?"

"Janice and her folks came and got me. I've been at their house a few days. They just dropped me off."

"At Janice Crossfield's house?!" His mother's voice went up a few decibels. She sounded ready to explode. She kept talking, but Jerry quit listening. He'd learned to do that a long time ago when she got this mad. He didn't know how long it lasted before his father spoke up again.

"Go on to bed, son. We'll figure out what to do after we get the hay in this week."

The next morning Jerry got up and went down to breakfast like always. His mother had quit yelling, but she hadn't quit frowning or fussing. She just couldn't understand why he hadn't come straight home instead of going to Janice's house, and Janice's folks were going to hear it from her for not letting them know Jerry was there.

Jerry was relieved when he and his father left for the hayfield. It was easy out there. Just load up the bales and carry them to the barn and stack them up in the loft. He liked building walls of hay around him. The cows wouldn't get hungry when the snow started to fly. Better than that, his mother never worked in the loft. She always drove the tractor when the wagons were being loaded, so he didn't have to hear her.

That night when he came in from the barn, his mother had been in his room. She'd found everything that had anything to do with Janice and had taken it and stuffed it in Janice's mailbox. Jerry didn't understand why she was so mad at Janice. Janice hadn't done anything. He was the one who had quit school. He was the one who couldn't do anything right.

After they got the hay in, Jerry went down to the recruiting office and joined the army. His father said that was the only thing to do. His parents were scared to death he'd be shipped right out to Vietnam if he was drafted, but if he volunteered he could go to some kind of training school and maybe stay out of the fighting.

His daddy knew what it was like being shot at from serving in World War II, and he wasn't anxious to see Jerry follow in those particular footsteps.

CHAPTER 10

He had to report to Fort Knox for basic training right away. His father said October would be a good time to do basic. The weather would be cooler than if he'd signed up in July. His mother didn't say much. Jerry figured she didn't think he could make the grade.

All his buddies warned him basic would be awful, but it wasn't all that bad. Jerry was used to getting up at sunrise and working hard every day. During training, his body got even tougher and stronger, and he won every award they gave, including an Expert in Marksmanship. Targets were easier to hit than the squirrels and rabbits he hunted out on the farm. For the first time in he didn't know how long, he was proud of himself. Even his mother sounded pleased in her letters.

Late December, he finished up basic and went home for Christmas before being sent to a different post. When the army said his aptitude tests showed he could be an electronic instrument repairman, Jerry had some doubts.

"I don't want to be an electronic repairman, sir," Jerry told his training officer when he found out his assignment. "I don't know whose tests you've been looking at, but it couldn't have been mine."

"The Army doesn't make mistakes, Private," the officer said.

"But my math is bad, and I'm pretty sure you have to know math to do electronics." Jerry's voice was shaky as he tried to get the man to listen. "Can't you assign me to something else? Anything else. There's an M.P. school down there, isn't there?" He thought he might do okay in M.P. school. He could shoot and he was strong and quick on his feet.

The officer fastened cold eyes on Jerry. "You're in the army now, soldier. You'll go where you're assigned when you're assigned and that's all there is to it."

That hung over Jerry like a black cloud all through Christmas. His father tried to make him feel easier about the assignment. "Give the school a chance, son, and if it doesn't work out, they'll assign you to something else. Just enjoy your time off. It's Christmas and your mother and I are both so proud of you."

The training school wasn't ready when his leave was over, so he went back to Ft. Knox for a few weeks until they shipped him out to the Ft. Gordon Electronics School in Georgia. He tried to get them to test him again. He still had the feeling he'd make a good M.P. They heard him out, but the army needed electronic repairmen. He couldn't switch his assignment.

The first week he went to the classes and tried to make sense of what the teachers said. Then they started expecting him to put wires together to make things work. The others around him could do it, but Jerry stared at those wires and cords and had no idea what to do. The instructors might as well have been speaking Japanese. For a week he twisted wires together and tried to look as if he understood Japanese.

When weekend came, somebody always had plenty of beer and pills. Some of the guys took the uppers, but he stuck with downers. They went with the booze better.

He wasn't sure what made him decide to walk away from it all. He'd thought they'd teach him a job, and if he couldn't do that job, they'd transfer him to something else. But they kept saying he had to be an electronics repairman. Even the sound of the words made him sick at his stomach.

He was ready to be a good soldier. He didn't speak the first word of disrespect or dissent to Lieutenant Roberts or anybody else. He jumped to do whatever they said, but when he saw that forty-five on his grade sheet, he knew it was hopeless. He begged Lt. Roberts to let him go somewhere else, even to Vietnam. At least if he died over there it would be for his country. But Lt. Roberts said he couldn't transfer. He had to stay in the electronics school until he learned the job.

Jerry stood up straight and said, yes sir. He went back to class, but he knew his next grade wouldn't be any better. This time he'd not only let down his parents, he'd let down Lt. Roberts and his other commanding officers, his unit, the whole army. He would be booted out of the service, sent home in disgrace. All his achievements in basic would be for naught. They didn't care that he could run and shoot. He had to twist wires together.

His parents told him to pray and ask the chaplain for help. Jerry didn't know he had to go through special channels to see the chaplain. If they had told him that, he didn't remember it. Sergeant Harrod let him have it for going over his head to the chaplain. Made him do extra duty. Pushups. Polish everybody's shoes. Called him a shirker, a liar, and worse.

And not just the sergeant. The guys in his unit were on him too. "Aw, Shepherd needs to pray about his grades. Shepherd can't tell a red wire from a white one. Shepherd's a wash out."

So before he punched somebody in the face to shut them up, he got up one morning and walked off the base. He had no idea what he was going to do. He didn't have much money and nothing but the clothes on his back. Thank goodness he had his coat. He tried to pray as he kept putting one foot in front of another to see if the Lord would point him in some direction, but he just felt blank inside.

That first week, he hardly knew where he was as he spent most of his money on beer and pills. But then the money ran out and he woke up in a junky old Mercury on the back of a car lot. He was hungry. He fingered the change in his pocket. Some quarters and a few nickels. He could try to get a job, but this close to Ft. Gordon, they'd catch him for sure.

He remembered the prodigal son story in the Bible. His daddy was like that father. He had hired hands. Jerry could go home and work for him until they decided what to do. His mother would feed him. She might yell at him but she'd feed him. He went back out on the road and hitched a ride with a guy in a pickup truck. He said he was on leave, going home to see his folks. It was mostly true. When that ride ended, he got another.

A cold rain was falling when an old guy in a Chevy dropped him off just across the border into Tennessee. He wanted to ask the old man if he could go home with him and warm up, but instead he said thanks and got out of the car to start walking.

It seemed forever before a salesman picked him up. The man had a whole rack of clothes hanging across his back seat. "Poor kid. You look about froze," he said when Jerry got in. "Where you headed?"

"To Kentucky to see my folks."

"Well, how about that? That's where I'm going. To Louisville." The man shifted his car into gear and pulled back out on the road.

"That sounds about perfect." Maybe the Lord was watching over him a little after all, because Jerry wasn't sure how much longer he could have made it before he fell in front of a truck. He had no idea how long he'd been on the road. Seemed like weeks. He wanted to be home.

"Are you in the service? On leave?"

"Yeah, on leave," Jerry said. "Hitching home. You care if I go to sleep?"

"Nope. You look about done in. Tell you what. I'll turn the heat on high to warm you up." The man flicked a knob and the heater fan roared louder.

"Thanks. That's feels great." Jerry was already half asleep. "Are you an angel?"

The man laughed. "That's the first time anybody's accused me of that since I was a little squirt on my grandma's lap. She thought I was the greatest thing since sliced bread."

With no trouble at all, he caught a ride in Louisville to get to the farm. Nobody yelled at him when he got home or if they did, he didn't hear them. He hardly knew where he was. The world was blowing up around him, and he was just standing there letting the debris fly past him. He wasn't even sure he was really in his kitchen.

The next morning things were clearer. After he ate breakfast, his mother went out to feed the animals and left him alone with his dad. Jerry told his dad what happened, how Sergeant Harrod had called him a liar. He might be a failure and no use to anybody, but he wasn't a liar.

"I know you're not a liar, son," his dad said. "That wasn't a good thing to tell you, but army sergeants aren't known for their sweet tempers. They're ready to bash you over the head about just about anything."

"I told them I couldn't do math" Jerry hung his head. "Why didn't they listen?"

"I guess they thought they could teach you." His father put his hand on Jerry's arm. He was silent a few minutes before he said, "What are you going to do now?"

"I want to go back, do my duty. I never aimed to run away from my responsibilities, but I just can't do that school. Can you talk to them, Dad?"

"I've been talking to the lieutenant down there ever since you went off the base."

"What did he say? Will they put me in the stockade?" Jerry shifted uneasily in his chair. He didn't like to think about being locked up.

"I don't think so." His father patted Jerry's arm. "He said it was a minor disciplinary problem, but if you went on back, they'd work it out with you."

"You never had this kind of trouble when you were in the service, did you, sir?"

"No, but they let me do something I wanted to do."

"Do you think I could fly bomber planes?" Jerry thought he could do that.

"Not in the army. Maybe we should have tried for the Air Force or Navy, but I didn't think your grades were good enough for that."

"I like the army okay. Do you think they'd let me go to Vietnam?"

His father winced a little. "Let's not look that direction just yet, son. You don't want to go over there if you can keep from it."

"It'd be better than the electronics school." The sick feeling woke up in Jerry's stomach. "So they said I could come back?"

"Lieutenant Roberts told us to send you back as soon as you got home and he'd take care of everything. Are you sure that's what you want to do?"

"Yes sir. They'll have to transfer me somewhere else

now, won't they?"

"Maybe. You talk to them when you get back and I'll talk to them too. Could be you might need some extra help, some counseling. They will have good counselors down there."

Before his father put him on a plane to Atlanta, he called the base to get somebody to pick Jerry up at the airport, but they said he'd have to get back to Ft. Gordon on his own. Jerry told his father not to worry. He could take a bus. Even if he had to walk, he'd get there. But he didn't know about the military police at the Atlanta airport.

CHAPTER 11

A man in a uniform grabbed Jerry in the airport before he could find a bus.

"You look like a soldier going where you aren't supposed to go." The man clamped his big hand on Jerry's shoulder and stared at him with cold, dark eyes.

"Hey, let go of me." Jerry tried to jerk away from man, but it was like trying to push a five hundred pound boulder off him. "I'm on leave and headed back to my base."

"Yeah, and I'm on the next rocket to the moon." The guy clapped a pair of handcuffs on Jerry's wrists.

"You can't do that."

"I just did. Now shut up and don't give me no problems. A few days in the cage will get you in a more truthful frame of mind."

"Call Ft. Gordon. They'll tell you I'm on the way back there."

"We'll check it out. When we get the time. No sense

getting in no big hurry. Other deserters just like you are out here begging us to catch them."

"I'm not a deserter," Jerry said, but the man didn't even glance around at him.

They put him in a cage, a freestanding cell made of metal bars. There wasn't even pallet for a bed. Another guy, in the same kind of cage on the other side of the room, kept his gaze fixed on the floor. He waited until they were alone before he looked up and in a voice not much above a whisper said his name was Paul and that he'd been there two days. Locked in the cage.

"I wouldn't treat a dog like this," the guy said.

"Are they really MP's?" Jerry asked.

"Who knows what they are." Paul looked even younger than Jerry. His face was pale under the faint shadow of a two-day growth of beard. He sneaked a peek at the door. "Other than scary."

"Shut up in there," somebody yelled from the next room.

"Hey, I've got to go take a leak," Jerry yelled back.

"Well, you should've thought about that before you got yourself all locked up," the man yelled back.

"If you keep hollering long enough, they'll finally let you go." The guy named Paul rubbed his hands up and down his legs. "But you have to get hoarse first."

"They have to let us call somebody. They can't just stick us in here and not let us call somebody."

"They haven't let me call nobody yet. I'd even call my sergeant who hates my guts and let him make me do pushups till I puked to get out of here." Paul kept his voice low "If I have to sit here much longer, I'm gonna go clean off my rocker."

"How about food?" Jerry's stomach was growling.

"They pitched me a couple of hotdogs yesterday. Not cooked, but they weren't bad. Better than the stale crackers and cheese the day before."

"This can't be happening. Not in America." Jerry stared at Paul who just looked back at him. "Can it?"

"We ain't both in the same nightmare. Then again maybe we are. A wide awake nightmare."

The nightmare went on and on. Jerry jumped up and down and shouted and yelled, but it was still two hours before they let him out to go to the john. After that, he sat down on the floor in the corner and wrapped his hands around his knees. He wouldn't let them break him. He whispered every Bible verse he knew. Then he sang songs in his head until he fell asleep sitting up.

The days and nights ran together. More men were shoved with them into the cages. They talked a little, but not much. There wasn't much to talk about. They took Paul out first. Then they came for Jerry on the third or fourth day. He wasn't sure which.

They put him in an MP van and drove him to Ft. Gordon. Jerry was almost glad to see the place, to see any place besides where he'd been for the last few days. He was hungry. He hoped they'd let him eat before they disciplined him.

Lt. Roberts met with him when he got to the school. He said he was giving Jerry another chance, to go back to his barracks, and clean up. He didn't want to hear about where Jerry had been or what had happened to him in Atlanta. He didn't want to hear about Jerry wanting another assignment. He didn't want to hear that Jerry would like to talk to the chaplain. All he wanted to hear was yes sir. So that's what Jerry said.

When the sergeant and the other guys in the barracks got through making fun of him that night, Jerry wrote his parents after lights out by the moonlight filtering through the window. He told them about what had happened in Atlanta and how the lieutenant wouldn't listen. He wrote that he loved his country, but he couldn't do what his officers wanted him to do. He'd rather die than go back to school. He told them he thought dying sounded like the best plan he'd made for days. Then he signed it *your loving son.*

He folded the letter, put it in an envelope, and stuck it in the mail slot the next morning. He ate breakfast at the mess hall. Then he walked off the base instead of going to class. Maybe the MP would find him again and this time Jerry would fight him. He'd let the big guy mash him into nothing.

He headed home, hitchhiking again. He would be safe at home. His father would help him. He was hungry, half out of his head. He had a few cold medicine pills in his pocket and he took them to keep his feet moving up the road. He tried to sing, but the words of songs he'd sung a hundred times kept slipping away from him. He got some rides but he didn't remember much about any of them.

Then he found himself in a town that looked familiar, and he shook away his brain fog long enough to know where he was. He used to visit his grandparents here. They were dead now, but his aunt and uncle still lived there. It was late and spitting snow. He didn't have a ride and he was freezing. He found the house and slipped into the basement. They never kept their doors locked. He'd hide out until morning. They'd never even know he was there.

The next morning when he woke up, the house felt empty. He was so hungry all he could think about was his stomach, so he crept up the basement steps. His aunt Betty would have some peanut butter he could swipe. He could almost smell the peanuts. No need for crackers or bread. He'd just dig the peanut butter out with his fingers and lick it off.

He was tiptoeing across the living room when he heard his aunt humming in the kitchen. He ducked down behind the couch. He wasn't sure why except he didn't want her to see him like this—dirty, needing a shave, so hungry he was ready to steal. He pulled the collar of his coat up to cover part of his face. He'd hide there quiet as a mouse until she went down to the basement or upstairs. Then he'd slip away. He thought regretfully of the peanut butter, but he couldn't stand up now and say hello, Aunt Betty. Not and scare her like that.

He had a bad feeling when she got out her sweeper, but maybe she'd only hit the high spots. He should have known better. Not his aunt Betty. She had to poke the sweeper everywhere. She screamed when she saw him just the way he'd known she would. He jumped up and held his palms out toward her to make her hush.

"Don't. Don't scream!" he begged.

In two minutes he was out the door. She never knew it was him. It was better that way. She thought he was a good boy, doing whatever he was supposed to be doing, not going AWOL from the army. But he couldn't do that electronics stuff. He could scrub toilets, anything, as long as it didn't take math.

His mind went into idle as he ran past barking dogs through backyards and over fences. His aunt would call the police. He had to get away. It felt almost like being home when he got back out on the highway. And he got a ride right away. The guy even let Jerry have a handful of the chips he was eating.

It took him three days to get home, the same amount of time Jesus was in the tomb. Jerry felt like he was in a tomb but he didn't think he could come out.

The night was cold with snow falling. He stood in the driveway and stared at the dark house until snow covered his coat. Then he went to the barn and started up the old farm truck. Maybe the barn would be tight enough to keep the fumes in. Carbon monoxide poisoning wouldn't be a bad way to die. A person just went to sleep and didn't wake up. He didn't want to wake up.

But he did. The truck ran out of gas. The cold crept back and shook him awake in the pitch black of the night, long before daylight. Jerry climbed through a window into the garage and found an old heater. He wanted to be warm. More than he wanted to eat. More than he wanted to sleep somewhere soft. Almost more than he wanted to breathe.

The next morning when his father went out to feed, he spotted Jerry's footprints in the snow and found him in the garage. His father didn't fuss at him. He didn't even look mad as he put his arms around Jerry and pulled him into the warmth of the kitchen. His mother didn't yell at him either. Instead tears rolled down her cheeks. He wanted to tell her things weren't that bad, that she didn't have to cry. He opened his mouth, but no words would come out of the empty dead place he was in.

He ate and he slept. His parents talked to him. He wasn't sure what they said, not in words, but they wanted him to go back. They said he couldn't stay AWOL. So he told them he wanted to go back. Didn't he always do what people wanted him to do? He was an obedient son. A soldier ready to do his duty. He didn't lie. He knew the Ten Commandments. Honor your father and mother. Stop failing at everything you do. Be tough. Stick it out in the army.

Sunday morning, his parents skipped church to drive him back to Ft. Gordon. They talked about the farm, about how Jerry could partner with them after he got out of the service. They told him he might do well in the army. They didn't talk about him going back into the electronics school. It was as if that couldn't happen.

The army didn't agree. His father waited out in the hall while Jerry reported back to Sergeant Harrod on Monday morning, March 3.

Jerry tried to explain. "Sir, I've been mixed up in my mind, but I went home and talked to my parents and they've helped me see things straight now. I enlisted. I want to serve my country. But I can't stay in the school. I don't know how to do what they want me to do, sir. So I'm respectfully requesting a transfer. I'll serve anywhere else. Do anything else. Go anywhere. Even Vietnam."

"Vietnam?! A lily-livered sorry excuse for a soldier like you wouldn't last two days in Nam and while that might be a favor to the army and the country in general, you're so pathetically inept, you'd take half your unit down with you."

"No sir, I wouldn't do that. I could handle it, sir."

The sergeant let out a long line of curses. Jerry tried to shut his ears, but the words barked through until he wanted to curl up on the floor and put his arms over his head. Instead he stood ramrod straight. His father was out in the hall. His father had been a soldier. His father had said to do whatever they told him to do and he'd get by.

The sergeant paused in his rampage and Jerry shouted, "Yes sir."

"And not only that, you're a liar, Shepherd. You can do the work at this school. Your tests show you can. You just aren't giving it the effort the army demands. So stop lying and running away and do your duty."

"Yes sir," Jerry shouted again.

"Now get your contemptible, sorry face out of my office, go draw your billet supplies and get an assignment to a billet in the quarters. And don't let me ever catch you trying to run away from your duty again."

Jerry told his father goodbye and did what the sergeant said.

Everybody was on him. The ridicule circled him like buzzards over a dead possum. Even after the mouths of the men around him quit moving and they all went to sleep, the horrible things they said echoed in his ears all night.

In the morning he wrote something upbeat on the birthday card he had for his father and stuck it in the mail slot before he went to buy some cold pills. The clerk looked at the three packages of pills and then Jerry.

"Expecting an epidemic, soldier?"

Jerry managed a smile before he wiped his nose on the back of his hand. "Need extras for some of my buddies. A bad cold's going around our barracks."

The barracks was empty when he went back to his bunk. Everybody was at the school learning to twist wires. It took a long time to get all thirty cold pills out of their foil squares. He'd push out five and swallow them, then push out five more. After he'd taken them all, he said a prayer for his mother and father and lay down on his bunk. It felt good to go to sleep.

CHAPTER 12

L etters from home:

March 6, 1969
Dear Jerry,

As usual our regular guests (the Bertrams!) were here so I couldn't get a letter mailed. We also had to go to Shelbyville to finish setting up the loan for the dairy. The cistern is almost finished. They won't work tomorrow because it's snowing hard now.

Monday, we got to Mary's at 7 p.m. She wanted us to stay over Tuesday so we left there Wed. morning and got home about 7 p.m. I saw nothing in the Carolinas that I want, but Virginia is O.K. and some of Georgia. Dewey says your Base is beautiful.

Jerry, I hope your card to your Dad means what

he thinks it does, that things are working out good, that you got your February pay.

We told you exactly how things were, Jerry. Dewey fought hard to see that you had a good home and love. We both deeply regret that we didn't realize long ago that we were making a mistake by not telling you. None of the things that happened before Dewey and I met was yours or Dewey's fault. You have nothing to regret or be ashamed of. We are proud of you.

And we are not mistaken! You do have a good mind and ability. Talk to your Sergeant or Lt. If you stay in school, give it all you've got. If you and the Army decide on something else, put the past behind you—forget it. Look ahead.

Can't write another page. It won't go in the envelope. Call once a week and write when you can. Remember—we never have nor ever will, turn our back on you. Take care of yourself.

Love always, Mom

◆ ◆ ◆

Dear Jerry,

Your birthday card and money came in the mail today. Do you think I should spend all the money on our special gal, or keep it and spend it on a big milk cow? Son, I hope you're back on regular status by now. We got home at 7:00 p.m. Wed. We had a nice trip. Everything here was just like we left it except the snow was gone. Yesterday and today were pretty days, but the snow is falling out there right now. We went into Shelbyville today and left your car at Mr. Shaddocks so he could sell it for you. So, I hope it will sell right away so you will have a little money for your bank account.

The pigs insulted me this morning, from the way they acted, they didn't even miss me. I believe they liked Harvey just as well. Everything is just set and ready to build the milking parlor when the weather lets up.

Jerry, we miss you around here very much and we are looking forward to the day you can be back and try your hand at milking cows. Your ma will have plenty of good old cold milk to make homemade ice cream.

Son, we love you with everything we have got and we hope that with your help and God's help we have been able to explain enough about your life as a child, that you can overcome this empty feeling you have had so long. Son, I hope you will be able to get things straight in the army. Please don't let things get you down in the dumps. When you are in the dumps your pa is in the dumps and I don't like it in the dumps.

Jerry, I know this sounds crazy, but we are very close to each other. The distance we are apart in miles don't mean a thing as far as the way we feel about you. We are where we will be waiting for you when your Army enlistment is over. Jerry, you are just as much a part of our lives as any son could be, you being in the Army and away from home don't have anything to do with the way we feel about you, or affect the place you fill in our home, yours, your ma's and mine.

Right now our greatest hope is for you to be satisfied and happy in the Army for the duration of your enlistment. Son, I am looking forward to hearing from you soon.

Love, your Dad

Letters returned to sender due to soldier going A.W.O.L.

CHAPTER 13

He didn't die. Suicide must have something to do with math. That's why he could never do it right.

He woke up in the infirmary. They pumped his stomach and said he was okay to go. Back to duties. Back to school. He didn't report back anywhere.

He went straight to the chapel. His head was spinning. It was all he could do to lift one foot in front of the other. He wished the pills had worked and he was still asleep. He wished he were dead.

No one was at the chapel, not even the chaplain. Jerry held his head and tried to think. He wasn't supposed to see the chaplain without asking permission. But he couldn't remember who to ask.

He sat down in the back of the chapel to let his head clear a little. He softly sang the Lord's Prayer. He hadn't forgotten everything.

The chapel was quiet, peaceful. The Lord was there and hadn't a Sunday school teacher somewhere sometime told him that Jesus loved him no matter what he did? Jerry needed somebody to love him, but he doubted right then that even Jesus could. He'd done everything anybody could do wrong.

It was probably even wrong to fall asleep in the chapel, but that's what he did. He lay on the very back pew and went to sleep. A door opening somewhere woke him. Without thinking why, Jerry rolled off the pew and silently hit the floor. The feet moved past him toward the front of the church. They looked like regular army issue shoes. Jerry didn't know if chaplains wore special shoes or not. Then the man was kneeling at the front, saying a prayer.

Jerry crawled under the pews and slipped out into the side rooms.

"Who's there?" a voice called from the chapel.

Jerry slid into a supply closet and huddled down between some brooms. He didn't actually decide consciously to stay in the chapel. He just did. Nobody ever saw him. They came in and out, but nobody ever looked under the pews. The hours passed.

At first he was too sick to even think about food, but after a while—he had no idea how long—his stomach began growling. After dark, he sneaked outside to look for food. He found the telephone first. He ignored it, but then he saw another phone and another until it seemed like a sign. He dialed his parents' number. When his mother said hello, he tried to sound normal as if everything was okay.

"I've been sick. I had a fainting spell and the doctors want to check me out to be sure I didn't have a stroke or something." He didn't know why he said stroke. People his age didn't have strokes except maybe heat strokes. And it was winter now. He wondered if the doctors had said something about a stroke or if that had just floated up from nowhere. If only some food would float up from nowhere.

His mother was asking questions. He tried to think what happened to somebody when they had a stroke and remembered a man at church was paralyzed on one side by a stroke. Jerry felt half paralyzed now, so that's what he told his mother.

"I've been a little paralyzed, but I'm okay now." Saying he felt paralyzed wasn't as much of a lie as saying he was okay. They talked for a few minutes. He had no idea what else he said. Words came out of his mouth, but it was noise with no meaning.

He wandered around the base for half the night, staying away from lighted areas. Toward daylight, he spotted some workers going into the PX. He waited a few minutes and followed them in. The only food in easy reach was candy on the counter by the door. He grabbed two chocolate bars and hustled out before anybody saw him. Five minutes later he was in the chapel. Somebody had left a candle burning. Jerry stood by it and looked at the candy bars. He'd never stolen anything before. Ever.

Thou shalt not steal. The Lord might strike him down for eating stolen candy bars in the chapel. Jerry pulled back the wrappers and ate the candy bars one after the other. Nothing happened. He went into the restroom and drank out of the sink.

The sun came up and went down. People came in and out of the chapel. They didn't see him. He stole more candy bars. He slept. When he woke up, he lay still as stone and stared up at the bottoms of the pews. Some of them had chewing gum stuck on them. He didn't try to peel it off. He didn't want to move. He thought about the chaplain finding his bones under the pews five years from now.

He didn't think about what he should do. He couldn't think. Everything was in a confusing fog. He tried to reach into the fog and come up with a plan but then his hand just got lost too. A few times he came to himself enough to wish he was at home working on the farm with his father and eating whatever his mother had cooked that day, but he couldn't go home. They would just tell him to come back, to do what the army said he had to do.

At first, he kept count of the times the sun came up and went down, but after a while he quit noticing the sun and drifted in a timeless void. Then the hunger became a mighty roar inside him he could no longer ignore. He had to get something to eat no matter what. After he cleaned up as best he could in the restroom, he headed to the mess hall. He still had his meal ticket. He could get breakfast.

Nothing had ever looked as good as those eggs and bacon strips. He ate one of the biscuits on the way to a table back in the corner. He should have stuffed the food in his pockets and walked on out the door. He hadn't even finished the eggs before Sergeant Harrod and another sergeant nabbed him. Jerry shoveled in a few more bites as fast as he could before they made him leave the food.

They took him out of the dining room to another area and assigned a soldier to watch him. The specialist looked kind so Jerry asked him if he could have another glass of milk. When the man told Jerry to go get it himself, Jerry just walked on out the back door. It was that easy. He didn't stop walking until he was off the base. He hid out for a while in some trees till it was almost dark. Then he started walking again.

He needed a car. The first place he passed was a dry cleaning store with a garage beside it. It was closed down for the day, but he found a jack handle on the ground and broke out the window in the back door. He fished a few coins out of a jar on the counter before he tried to break through the door into the garage. He pushed his shoulder into it, but it didn't budge. He kicked it with no luck.

He couldn't open the door. He should be able to break open the door. He couldn't do anything right. In a rage, he grabbed what looked like a broomstick off the floor and began beating everything in sight. Things crashed off the shelves and broke. Racks of clothes in plastic bags tumbled to the floor. He kept swinging the stick until there wasn't anything left to break. Then he went outside, found the jack handle again and beat on the garage door till it finally popped open.

The keys were in the 1963 Chevy inside the garage. It started, but ran rough. But it ran and the fuel gauge showed a full tank of gas. That would get him on down the road. Where he didn't know. Anywhere away from here.

He hadn't gone far when he spotted a hitchhiker. He slammed on the brakes before he thought about what he was doing.

"Where you going?" the hitchhiker asked him as he got in. The man had a shaggy beard and looked like the kind of guy Jerry's mother would tell him to keep away from. But it didn't matter what his mother thought now.

"Just traveling." Jerry shrugged. "How about you?"

"Yeah, me too. Wherever the road takes me."

They rode a ways before the guy said he was thirsty and that if Jerry would stop, he'd buy them both a beer. Jerry should have asked for something to eat instead. The alcohol exploded in his system. He couldn't see straight, much less drive straight, so he told the hitchhiker he needed to stop and grab a few zzz's. The guy pointed out a motel where they could park awhile.

The hitchhiker told Jerry to call him Butch and he'd call Jerry Buddy. He claimed names could get a man in trouble and that Jerry looked as if he had enough trouble already without piling on more.

Jerry didn't care. He didn't need a name. He needed a plan. A what to do next idea. Something besides heading home again. He wasn't some kind of homing pigeon. Hadn't he run off to California and disappeared in New Jersey for weeks?

Jerry pulled the car into the motel parking lot. He

barely got it between the white lines before the motor wheezed and died. Just for the heck of it, Jerry tried to start it again, but the old Chevy had had enough.

"Piece of junk," Jerry muttered. Maybe when he sobered up, he could get the car running again. But it was almost out of gas anyway and Jerry didn't have any way to fill it up.

"Don't worry about it, Buddy." The hitchhiker peered out the window as if looking for something or somebody. "Cars are everywhere. The parking lot is full of them."

Jerry was half dozing when the hitchhiker poked his shoulder. "Come on. Let's go over there where that old guy is carrying in his bags. I need to use the john."

The man used one of his bags to prop open the motel door while he headed back to his car. Jerry followed the hitchhiker into the room. While the hitchhiker kept watch, Jerry stumbled back to the bathroom, used the john, and splashed some water on his face. He couldn't get his head straight. Black balls kept popping up in front of his eyes.

When Jerry opened the bathroom door he heard a bunch of screaming and hollering. His heart began pounding hard. He didn't know what was going on. All he knew was that he had to get out of the room. He tried to run for the door, but the old guy stepped in front of him and started screaming. His spit sprayed Jerry's face.

"Please move and let me out of here," Jerry begged. "I don't want to hurt you. Please."

But the man kept yelling at him. Jerry's heart was crashing madly back and forth in his chest and he couldn't get enough air. If he didn't get to the door, he was going to die. He had to get out. He started swinging his fists. He had to get out of the room and away from the man screaming at him.

All at once, the face in front of him shifted, became his mother's face. Jerry kept swinging, kept pounding his fists into the face. Over and over.

CHAPTER 14

When Jerry came to himself, he was on the floor beside a man he'd never seen before. The man wasn't breathing. His eyes were wide open, but he wasn't breathing.

Nobody else was in the room. The hitchhiker was gone. The door was closed. Jerry had blood on his hands. With horror, Jerry stared at the man's bloody face and willed him to breathe, but the man's chest refused to rise and fall. Jerry squeezed his eyes shut and wished to be somewhere else. Back in the chapel hiding under the pews. At home in his bedroom waiting for the sun to come up so he could go work in the fields. Out on the road running three miles. Anywhere but here. He eased his eyes open. The man was still there. Stiff. Not breathing.

No use asking the Lord for forgiveness. How could the Lord forgive this? *Thou shalt not kill.* But he did whisper the

23rd Psalm as he pulled the red and gold striped spread off the bed to cover the man's body. That made things easier. Not having to look at him. He hoped the man's family wouldn't grieve for him too much. He was old. And alone. Maybe nobody would miss him.

In the bathroom, Jerry threw up in the commode. Then he scrubbed his hands until his skin was red and raw. He rubbed off his shoes with one of the towels before he went back out to stare at the shape of the man's body under the cover.

Sitting down on the bed, Jerry tried to think. The black balls came in front of his eyes again and he felt faint. He breathed in and out slowly until the room came back into focus. A car started up outside. That's what he needed. A car. He had to get away.

The man's wallet and keys were on the table beside the bed. Jerry opened the wallet to look at the man's driver's license. Edward Baylor from New York. Seventy-three. That might be easy enough to change to twenty-three. He checked for money but the back pocket of the wallet was empty. Maybe the hitchhiker took the man's cash. The vinyl picture pockets were filled up with credit cards instead of pictures. Jerry was glad. He didn't want to see a wife or kids smiling up at him.

He stuck the wallet in his pocket along with the man's keys. He picked up the suitcase off the luggage rack. The man was bigger than Jerry, but some of his clothes might fit well enough. He started to go through the man's clothes right then and there. Change into something without blood on it, but he had to get out of there. Get away from the body under the bedspread.

He eased back the heavy window curtain to peek out. The parking lot was empty. No sign of the hitchhiker. No sign of anyone. It was dark. Everybody was asleep.

Jerry opened the door inch by inch in case somebody was waiting to get the drop on him, but the shadows weren't hiding anybody. He hung the "Do not disturb" sign on the outside doorknob and pulled the door shut. The man's car was nice. A gray 1969 Grand Prix.

After another glance around to be sure no one was watching, Jerry bent down and fumbled with the keys until he found one to open the door. The car started up at the first turn of the key and Jerry felt safer. But he didn't turn on the headlights until he was pulling out of the motel parking lot.

He listened for sirens behind him, but the night was quiet. Almost too quiet. He breathed easier when he pulled out on the interstate headed south. He wondered again what had happened to the hitchhiker. Maybe there had never been a hitchhiker. Maybe no dead man was back at the motel. But then where did he get the car?

The thing that bothered him most was how he kept slamming his fists into the man while he saw his mother's face in the dark.

He couldn't think about that. Not without getting sick. So he shoved it away. Right now he had to concentrate on driving. He had to get far, far away from Richmond Hills, Georgia.

He needed a place to get lost. He already felt lost. He could never go home now. Not after what he'd done. He was lost in every way a person could be lost. So he headed south to Florida.

◆ ◆ ◆

On the beaches, people soaked up the sunshine even though it was still March. Nobody paid much attention to one more guy sleeping on a towel on the sand. After he bought soap and a razor, he took a shower in the beach house and felt almost like a real person again. He sat in the sun and ate powdered doughnuts with no idea what to do. He watched waves come in and go out and listened to the sea gulls and sandpipers. He couldn't be any place more different than home.

The second day out on the beach, some guy plopped down beside Jerry.

"Hey, what's up?" The guy looked about the same age as Jerry but had long hair. No soldier for sure. "You from around here?"

"Naw. I'm from up north. Still cold up there."

"Yeah, tell me about it. I'm from up north, too. New Jersey. It's always cold up there," the guy agreed with a grin.

"New Jersey? Sure enough. I used to know some folks up there. Harmons." Jerry wished he could talk to Mama Harmon. She might help him know what to do.

"Never knew anybody by that name. I'm Richard Chiles." The guy stuck his hand out toward Jerry. "Friends call me Rich."

Jerry shook his hand. "Ed." His tongue tripped a little on the name even though he'd practiced saying the man's name. He cleared his throat. "Eddie Baylor from New York."

"The big city?"

"No, New York state." Jerry had found the man's town on the New York map in the car. He changed the subject. "But who wants to talk about the frozen north when we're soaking up rays here?"

"Not me." Rich gave Jerry a long look. "You got a place to stay?"

"Nope. Just got out of the service a few weeks ago and I've been bumming around ever since. Not in any hurry to go back north. I'm a little short on cash, so I've just been hanging out here." Jerry pulled his fingers back and forth through the sand.

"You don't say."

"It's not too bad during the daytime." Jerry smoothed his finger trail out of the sand and turned his face toward the sun.

"I saw you getting out of a pretty nice car there a while ago. I've got this friend down in Coral Gables. If you give me a ride down there, we can crash at his place for a while. I even know a place where you might make some cash doing some modeling over at the college there. You've got an interesting face and good muscles."

"I'm not taking off my clothes for nobody to draw me." Jerry narrowed his eyes on Rich.

"No, no. Not like that." Rich held up his hands as though to bat down that idea. "You get to keep your clothes on. I've done it. It's easy money."

It seemed as good a plan as any. Turned out good. Once they got to Coral Gables, Rich and his buddies had beer and dope. Jerry turned down the marijuana and cocaine, but he was glad to swallow the beer and downers. When he passed out, he didn't have to think. And not thinking was good.

Then one day Rich said, "Hey, how about we drive to Jersey? It won't be snowing there now."

"You sure about that?"

"No, but we can give it a try."

They drove straight through. Jerry used the credit cards from the man's wallet for gas. Nobody ever gave him a suspicious look. Up in New Jersey, they stayed with Rich's folks. When Rich got out his guitar and Jerry sang a couple of songs for him, Rich got all excited and got them a gig at a lodge in the next town. Jerry sang and Rich played his guitar while the people drank and talked. Sometimes they listened to the music and clapped a little. It didn't matter how much they listened. It was just more easy cash money like the modeling had been in Florida.

Being in New Jersey kept Mama Harmon on Jerry's mind. She might hug him and tell him what to do. He couldn't keep running forever. Sooner or later the police would catch up with him. He almost wished they would.

He thought about turning himself in. Just walking up to some policeman and confessing.

He even practiced what he'd say. "Hello, my name is Jerry Shepherd. I think I killed a man in Georgia. No, change that. I did kill a man in Georgia. I've been driving his car, using his credit cards. You need to lock me up."

He could do it. Confess. Then he'd think about his days in Atlanta after the MP's had picked him up. He couldn't stand being locked up like that. Not forever. Maybe he'd just let the police shoot him on the spot. But they wouldn't do that if he gave himself up.

Mama Harmon might help him make sense of the stuff happening to him. She could read him something out of the Bible to fill up the empty hole inside him. The beer and pills weren't doing too good a job of that anymore.

He went to the right town. He remembered the stores, the church, but nobody he talked to knew Mama Harmon or Pete. Some of them said they thought the last name sounded familiar but if they had ever lived there, they didn't now. How could that be? The whole family couldn't have just disappeared. Maybe instead of being real, they'd been angels the Lord had put there to help him and then they'd just disappeared. Gone somewhere else to help some other poor sucker.

That was stupid. Of course they were real people. Then where were they? Thinking about it made his head pound as he drove back to Rich's house.

He was glad when Rich said he was ready for Florida sunshine and they headed south again.

But it wasn't any better in Florida. Warmer, but no better. Jerry crashed one night in Coral Gables, but he didn't want to bring trouble to Rich and his buddies. The police might catch up with him any time. So the next day he dropped Rich off at the college to do some modeling.

"I should be through around six, Eddie. I'll pick up my pay and then we can go get some weed." Rich grinned as he got out of the car. "Tomorrow we can check out the clubs around here to see if they need some music."

Jerry pushed a smile across his face and waved. When he pulled back out on the highway, he turned the Grand Prix north. He had no idea where he was going. He just kept driving. He stopped at a motel in Jacksonville to get some sleep. The next morning he went to the restaurant beside the motel for breakfast. After he ate, he gave them Edward Baylor's credit card. They told him it wasn't any good.

"Gee, I can't imagine what the problem could be." Jerry tried not to look worried, but his heart started pounding. "Look, I've got some cash out in my car. I'll go get it and be right back."

He didn't have cash in his car. He didn't have any money at all. Without looking over his shoulder to see if anybody was watching, he got into the car and drove away. No sirens followed him, but it wouldn't be long. He had one credit card he hadn't used. Maybe he could use it to make it to Kentucky before the police caught up with him.

He kept the tires rolling north. He was going home one more time. Maybe for the last time.

CHAPTER 15

All the time Jerry was driving north, he planned to drive straight home, but then with the green Shelbyville exit sign in front of him, he couldn't do it. He drove on to Oldham County instead, back to where he'd lived before Shelby County and everything had gone bad. Their old farm didn't look the same. The barn roof was sagging. The cows looked skinny. They weren't their cows. It wasn't their farm any longer.

He drove to Billy's house. Billy used to be a good friend. He might let him crash a couple of days while Jerry worked up courage to face his mother and father after what he'd done. He'd have to tell them. But how could he tell them that he'd killed a man? He could hardly believe it himself. There had to be two Jerry Shepherds. Him, the real Jerry Shepherd who wouldn't hurt anybody, and the other Jerry Shepherd, the one who did that horrible thing in Richmond Hills, Georgia.

He told Billy his folks had bought him the car for a late graduation present, but they were upset at him for getting booted out of the army. He promised to go home after they had a few days to cool off. Billy acted as though he believed him, but now and again, Jerry caught Billy staring at him with an odd look on his face.

On Wednesday night, the third day he was back in Kentucky, Jerry drove over to his folks' house. They'd be at church. They were at church every time the doors were open. He knew that, but he thought it might be easier to go in the house if nobody was home. He didn't expect to see a note stuck on the door. He stared at the square of white paper. He could see writing on it, but he couldn't read what it said from the car.

Maybe the note wasn't for him. Maybe they were expecting company after church. They wouldn't be expecting him. Not unless somebody had spotted him driving around town. Or Billy's folks had called them. That might have happened.

He got out, but left the car running with the door open. He didn't pull the note off the door. It was his mother's handwriting.

> Dear Son,
> If you see this, please don't leave without talking to us. We can't help you if we can't find you.
>
> We love you so much, Jerry, and this is tearing us to pieces. So I know what it's doing to you. We will help you straighten this out however you think you should. We know a good lawyer.
>
> We love you, so please don't refuse to let us help you.
> Mom & Dad

Jerry gasped as if somebody gut punched him. He stumbled off the porch and ran back to the car. He couldn't go in. He couldn't let them see him. Not after what he'd done.

As he drove away, the words on their note kept running through his head. They wanted to help him. They loved him. They knew a lawyer. Did they already know about the man in the motel or were they talking about the Army? He had to think. Figure out what to do.

He drove around a while before finally heading back to Billy's.

"Are you sure you're all right, Jerry? I mean you'd tell me if something bad was going on, wouldn't you?" Billy sounded worried.

"Sure I would. You're my buddy." Jerry punched Billy's upper arm lightly. "It's just my folks and all. You know how it is."

"Yeah, well, you need to talk to them. You can't keep putting it off."

"Right. I'll go tomorrow." Maybe by morning, he could work up his courage.

That night Jerry stared up at the ceiling in the dark room and rehearsed over and over what he was going to say to his parents. Once or twice he touched his Bible on the table beside the bed. When the sun came up, he whispered, "Please don't let this be too hard on my folks, Lord."

So he headed home. The police lights came up behind him as soon as he crossed the line into Shelby County. Somebody must have tipped them off.

He didn't stop. Instead he mashed down on the gas. He might have outrun them if he hadn't been low on gas.

But they tracked him down and now he was in the back of the police car hearing the crackling sound of the police radios. Other sirens wailed in the distance. All because of him.

If only he could slip his hands free from the handcuffs. He needed to block out the noise by covering his ears. His head pounded. If only he had made it home. His mother would have given him an aspirin and let him rest a while before they called the police.

Jerry answered yes sir or no sir whenever the policemen in the car spoke to him. He told them he was sorry about the cars he'd run off the road and that he hoped nobody got hurt. He was relieved when they said the only casualties were some bent fenders.

"The Lord must have been protecting them," Jerry said.

The police detective stared over his shoulder at Jerry. "Must have been protecting you too. They clocked you over a hundred miles an hour."

"Yes sir, that was way too fast. I should have stopped, but I was scared. And I wanted to see my folks."

"You'll get to see them."

"Yes sir." Jerry didn't want to think about seeing them from inside a jail. "Where are you taking me?"

"LaGrange."

The name hit Jerry hard. That's where the penitentiary was. His father had worked there for a year after the accident that blinded his eye. Nobody ever said anything good about LaGrange and now he might end up there for the rest of his life. Even if that was what he deserved, he could hardly bear to think about it. So he didn't.

Instead he thought about the Bible in his pocket and how the voice in his head whispered, *Peace, be still.* Was it possible the Lord still cared about him after all the commandments he'd broken?

Jerry slumped against the seat. He was tired, bone weary, but he was almost glad the running was over. He prayed for his parents. They did their best to bring him up right. Took him to church. Made him read the Bible. Pray. Taught him the value of honest labor and provided his needs through the years. That note on the door written by his mother even said they loved him. What was wrong with him that he'd never been able to feel that love?

Now he was letting them down yet again. He was a total mess up. Had always been a total mess up. Maybe he'd get the death penalty for what he'd done to that man in Georgia. The idea didn't bother Jerry. The only thing that bothered him was that it wouldn't be soon enough. He'd have to face his folks first.

They took him to an interrogation room at LaGrange. They told him he had the right to contact a lawyer, but he didn't know any lawyers. He remembered his mother's note about knowing a lawyer, but what was the use? He'd done the crime. He had to pay for that. All he wanted to do was get it over with, so he confessed everything. About how he'd walked away from Ft. Gordon. About sneaking into the motel room, hitting somebody and waking up beside a dead man. About stealing that dead man's car and using his credit cards. They wrote it all down.

The room was so hot it sucked all the oxygen out. He had a hard time breathing. He needed a drink. They gave him water, but he needed a beer. Or a pill. His head pounded, and the black balls kept jumping up in front of his eyes.

Nobody cared. They went on asking question, but his mind was too fuzzy to know the answers they wanted. He didn't know exactly what happened. He remembered hitting somebody, then seeing his mother's face and continuing to pound with his fists. Then he must have passed out because he woke up beside a dead man. He didn't tell the police about seeing his mother's face. He could barely stand to think about that, much less say it out loud.

They took him to the Oldham County jail to wait for the Georgia sheriff to come after him. They said he had to be tried where the crime happened. He didn't care. He wished he could go right then before his parents found out he was there.

It didn't happen that fast. The sheriff or somebody told his parents. They came to the jail to see him. When the jailer opened the cell door for them, the man kept his eyes on the floor as if he didn't want to witness Jerry's father's shame. Jerry wanted to sink back into the walls and disappear.

His mother started crying when she saw him. Not just a tear or two, but sobs. Jerry didn't remember ever seeing her cry like that. Crying never helped anything, she said. She believed most anything could be fixed with the right effort and she didn't mind giving that effort. But this time Jerry had done something she couldn't fix.

His father's face was grim with tears in his eyes too. "Son, what they're telling us can't be true. What did they do to you to make you say you'd done such a thing?"

His mother wiped her face with a white handkerchief and jumped in with her own disbelief. "We know you couldn't have done anything like that. You're a good boy. You wouldn't steal a car. And this other…" She let her voice trail off unable to say the word murder. She pressed her lips together and pulled in a breath. "Why would you make up something like that?"

Jerry didn't want to hurt them, but they should know he always messed things up. He held up his hand to stop them talking.

"I'm sorry, Mom, Dad, but I did do it. I don't know why. It just happened. I was in there and I couldn't get out. Somebody kept yelling at me, in my way. I had to get out. So I hit him. I know I hit him more than once, but I don't know what happened after that. I must have passed out. All I know for sure is that when I woke up a dead man was beside me. I tried to get up but big black balls came in front of my eyes and I kept falling back on the floor. Over and over."

New tears ran down his mother's cheeks, and his dad looked as if he'd just been hit by a train.

His father rubbed his face with both hands before he pulled in a deep breath and let it out slowly. "All right, son. Start at the beginning and tell us exactly what happened after I took you back to Ft. Gordon."

So he tried to tell them. He didn't lie about anything, but he wasn't sure they really listened. They didn't want to hear what he was saying. But he kept talking. They had to understand why he couldn't go back to the school, why everything had happened. He'd tried. He hadn't intended to shirk his duty. His father had gone to war and put his life on the line for his country. Jerry would have done the same.

He looked straight at his parents and tried to keep his voice from shaking. "Mom and Dad, I'm not a deserter. I didn't run away from the army. I ran away from the school. I just couldn't do the school, but I'm not a deserter. I like the army. I begged them to put me in the infantry or send me to Vietnam or anything but to please take me out of the school. But they wouldn't. I told them my head was all mixed up, but nobody cared. They all made fun of me. Said I was a deserter. I told them it wasn't that way. I wanted to do my duty. But they wouldn't listen. I got so mad I thought I was going to burn up inside."

"It's okay. We know you tried," his father said.

Jerry shook his head. "It's not okay. But I want you to understand. I really liked Lt. Roberts, but he wouldn't help me. Nobody would help me. But I'm not a filthy deserter the way they kept saying." He wanted to get down on his knees and beg them to believe him. "You have to believe me."

They said they believed him, but they didn't. They promised to help him. They'd pray about it. The whole church would pray for him. First, they would get him a lawyer. They'd take care of things for him the way they'd always done.

But he'd already told the police what he'd done. Now he had to pay for his crime. Even the Bible said that. An eye for an eye. A life for a life. After his parents left, Jerry searched for that passage in his Bible. He couldn't find it. Instead his Bible kept falling open to Psalms. Somehow as he read the words King David had written centuries before, he felt calmer until he was able to fall asleep.

CHAPTER 16

Those first few days in jail, Jerry thought he was going to die. Then when he didn't, he wished he would. He wanted to close his eyes and never have to open them again. He needed some booze or a pill, but nobody cared. He'd have to go cold turkey. They said a kid his age shouldn't be addicted to anything and that if he was, he needed to get off the stuff. They wouldn't call a doctor or give him anything. They said the d.t.'s wouldn't kill him.

He screamed and banged his head against the wall, but he couldn't knock out the pain. Clawed hands grabbed the inside of his stomach and tied his gut in knots. Every muscle in his body shrieked in protest when he moved. When he did manage to sleep, monsters came into the jail cell and tormented him. He fought them, but they ate him alive and then spit him out to lie in the bunk sweating and heaving.

The demons were still chasing him when the men

showed up to transport him to Pembroke, Georgia where he'd be tried. His parents kept trying to find a way to keep him from going to Georgia, but Jerry had waived his rights. He'd confessed. They couldn't change that.

Even the lawyer they hired said Jerry had to go to Georgia. Mr. York was nice enough, but the best lawyer in the world couldn't clean up the kind of messes Jerry made.

Jerry's dad was still talking with the Army, going up through the chain of command. He got some promises that they'd give Jerry a medical discharge and take over the criminal case. They might get Jerry straightened out and back home. Down deep, Jerry knew it wouldn't happen. The Army hadn't done anything to help him while he was at Ft. Gordon. A soldier who wouldn't fit in the hole they wanted to pound him into wasn't worth helping. But Jerry couldn't quite squash the hope his father might make it happen.

"You can come home and go back to helping with the farm. We'll get you counseling for all this other stuff," his father told him. "Being back on the farm will help as much as anything. You need to be working. Using your head and your hands."

That sounded good to Jerry. Sometimes when the pounding in his head eased up, he would stare at the jail wall and imagine the farm. He'd think about walking across the fields to check on the cows or plowing the long rows of tobacco. The smell of fresh cut hay filled his nose. He even thought it might be good to feed the pigs again, and he hated pigs.

But the Georgia sheriff showed up to get him while the Army was still deciding what they could or couldn't do. Jerry didn't mind going back to Georgia. He didn't like being in the Oldham County jail and thinking about his friends out on the street, free as birds. Plus, he hated how his mother came to visit with written list of dozens of questions. She was determined to find some other explanation for him waking up beside the dead man in the motel.

She refused to believe he'd done it. Not something so horrible. She could accept that he'd run away from the school, but he had to be mixed up on the rest of it. She kept talking about the hitchhiker until Jerry wished he'd never told her there was a hitchhiker. She even brought in a newspaper clipping about another man found murdered in a Texas motel room. Whoever had murdered that man, she said as she poked her finger down on the newspaper, could have been in Georgia. He could have been the hitchhiker. The one who killed Edward Baylor because she knew Jerry couldn't have done it.

Jerry could hardly bear the look in his mother's eyes when she asked her questions. She always brought two things of cookies or brownies so she could leave one bunch in the sheriff's office. She did her best to anticipate his every need, to find a way to help him. She was the Martha type, the one always busy about something instead of the Mary type who could sit peaceful and calm while waiting for a spiritual revelation. She knew Jesus said it was better to be a Mary, but she couldn't help it. She had to be doing something. She couldn't simply sit and wait for whatever was going to happen next. Especially not if that was her son going to prison.

If there had been a way, she would have broken down the jail walls and carried him home on her back. The thought of what might happen to Jerry in prison brought pure panic to her eyes. She promised to spend her every waking moment either praying for Jerry or hunting the right person to keep him out of prison. But they took him back to Georgia to be tried before she found that person.

The Georgia sheriff, Harry Montgomery and his deputy, Rudy Hackett, were nice enough guys. They didn't even make Jerry wear handcuffs. They were barely out of Oldham County before Sheriff Montgomery said Jerry wasn't at all what they were expecting.

"We came up here to get a criminal. You're not a criminal." The sheriff stared back at him for an extra long moment. "What they say you did and what we see of you, there's no way we can put you there in that motel room."

They talked about all sorts of things as they crossed out of Kentucky and through Tennessee. Jerry was carsick. And his head was still pounding when the demons came after him.

After they'd been riding for a few hours, the sheriff asked him about Mr. Baylor. Mr. York had told him not to talk to anybody about what had happened unless a lawyer was with him, but sheriff kept asking. Jerry had to say something, and he couldn't see what difference it would make. He'd already told the whole story to the first bunch of policemen at LaGrange.

Jerry didn't want Sheriff Montgomery to think he wasn't being cooperative. Being cooperative was important when you were a prisoner. His dad told him that. They did read him his rights before he left Kentucky. He had the right to remain silent, but Jerry wanted the sheriff to like him. So he answered his questions.

The day after he got to Pembroke, Deputy Hackett took him to a hearing. His father along with his uncle Milton and his lawyer, Mr. York, came too. Jerry was glad his dad was there. He didn't think he could have stood in front of the judge and heard the charges against him if his dad hadn't been there with him. Murder in the first degree. Grand larceny. Robbery. Jerry heard the words, but it was as if they were talking about somebody else.

The deputy gave him some time to visit with his dad and uncle after the hearing. They didn't talk about the charges. They talked about the farm. His dad said the house needed painting. Jerry jumped at the chance to think about something besides being in jail and he promised to paint the house if he got home before summer was over.

After his dad and uncle left, Deputy Hackett took him to be fingerprinted. He'd been fingerprinted in Kentucky, but he had to do it all over here in Georgia.

Then the deputy said they needed to interview him again, and he took him into a room where an FBI agent and a state policeman were waiting. They told him their names, but Jerry was too scared to keep them in his head. As soon as he went in the room, it was like somebody was playing back a movie he'd already seen. His heart began racing and his stomach wanted to heave. He'd seen these men before. Not in real life, but in a dream.

Jerry took a few deep breaths to keep from throwing up while the FBI guy read him his rights again. Then the man said, "We just want some answers about what happened, Jerry. So we'll have it all straight."

"I would like to remain silent." This time Jerry remembered his rights. The right to remain silent.

"That's fine, Jerry." The FBI man actually smiled. "But why don't you listen and see if you can answer some of things we need to clear up. Okay?"

They made Jerry sit down at a table. At first, Jerry kept saying he didn't want to talk, but then Deputy Hackett told him to answer. That it might help him. He smiled and said it was all routine. So they could be clear on what happened.

The FBI man sat down at the table and stared straight at Jerry. "You look like an honest boy. It's not like you haven't already told your story. You came clean up there, but we need to hear it firsthand from you. To see if they got it right. They might have missed something that might make a difference for you."

Jerry wanted to be honest. So he answered them, and all the while it was like an echo in his head. In his dream he had answered the questions too. He'd been in this room, talking to these men. That scared him more than anything they said. He'd dreamed the future.

It wasn't until they were through with their questions

that he saw the tape recorder. It was all on tape. He must have missed that part in his dream.

CHAPTER 17

He was still upset when the deputy locked him back in his cell. They brought him supper but nothing tasted good. He paced the cell. The place was filthy. It smelled and bugs ran races across the floor. He stepped on a roach, but plenty of others took its place. He tried to read a book, but the words ran together and didn't make any sense. He sang a couple of songs and felt a little better. If he couldn't do anything else, he could sing. Even his mother thought he could sing.

He remembered the letter she tacked to the door at his house before the police caught him. *We love you so much.* He had never believed his mother loved him. He was just somebody she wanted to mold into a decent human being even if it did seem an impossible task. But she wrote the words on the note. *We love you so much.* She'd been distraught when she came to the jail and not only because his arrest might make people talk. She was concerned for

Jerry. She wanted to help him.

Jerry picked up the spiral notebook and pencil the sheriff had let him have. His mother wanted him to keep a record of all that was happening now or had happened to land him in jail. She said that would help Mr. York defend him.

He wrote two and a half pages to his lawyer about what had happened since the sheriff picked him up in Oldham County. He explained how the sheriff and deputy had kept asking him questions on the ride down to Georgia. He told him how he'd tried to keep busy that first day after he got to the jail working a jigsaw puzzle and thinking about plans for his dad's farm. He wrote about being nervous at the hearing but how glad he was to see his dad. Thinking about talking to his dad made him smile while he wrote, but his smile slid away as he started writing about the police interview after the hearing. He even put in how he had dreamed about being questioned by those men before it happened and how that scared him.

He folded up the pages and shook the writing cramp out of his hand before he picked up the pencil again. He couldn't send the lawyer's letter without writing his mother and dad too.

April 30, 1969
8:25 p.m.
Dear Mom & Dad,

Been trying to keep myself busy by working the jigsaw puzzle and reading and singing. I'm also thinking up plans for the farm which will make it better.

Mom, I don't know if Dad told you about my plan on how to paint the house. If he hasn't he can tell you about it better than I can explain it in the letter. I was pretty happy about that plan cause Dad thought it was a pretty good idea.

I was a little upset this afternoon, when they had me down for an interview. When I was sitting in that room talking with those men, I remembered that I had been in that same room before with the same men talking to me. I had really dreamed about this interview taking place earlier this year, and now it had really come true! It's almost like really reading the future! So this little bit got me upset, but I guess it would get anybody upset.

I have also enclosed some information to my lawyer of my day to day experiences. I want to help in any way I can, and I want to help Mr. York.

Well, I hope to hear from you soon.
Love, Jerry

The days were long in jail. He worked more jigsaw puzzles. He wrote pages to his lawyer. He read his Bible. He sang songs, and he slept as much as he could to make the days pass. On Sunday, he would have given anything to be home going to church with his folks.

Since they wouldn't let him out to go to church, he did his own church service by reading some Psalms and singing hymns. He ended by praying for his folks and Mr. York and the sheriff. He just kept going, praying for everybody he could think of until they brought him his dinner.

The food wasn't bad, but he wanted double portions. He hadn't had enough to eat for months, and now that he was off the booze and pills, his appetite came back full force. He couldn't wait till his folks could visit and bring him food. What he'd like to have marched through his head. Chocolate chip cookies, chocolate cake, blackberry pie, pork and beans, crackers, tuna fish, Vienna sausage, potato chips, sour dill pickles. He wanted to pile up food in the corner of his cell and never be hungry again.

But he couldn't keep his mind occupied all the time thinking about food or working puzzles. The jail walls kept closing in on him, smothering him. His head felt heavy and sort of numb. His eyes hurt. Sometimes it was like an elephant was sitting on his chest. What he'd done tormented him every minute of the day.

His mother told him to write it all down for Mr. York. He had to do something or his head was going to explode. So he picked up his pencil.

> <u>May 5, 1969</u> I got tired of working the jigsaw puzzle, so I decided to rest for a bit. I then got to thinking about what I had done. I'm trying to forget it, but when you're not a killer, you just can't let it drop and forget about it. It's the hardest thing that I have ever tried to live down. It's with me in the day, it's with me when I go to bed, it's with me when I get up in the morning. It's just glued to me.
>
> I've cried myself to sleep a few nights asking myself, why did I do this, why did I do that, and why did I kill that man. I know no reason, no reason at all. I've searched and searched for an answer. Maybe it was the overdose of all those pills that I had taken that last week. Maybe it was all the tension and strain that had built up inside of me over the past years.
>
> I do know one thing and one thing only. There are two Jerry Shepherds. I don't know the other Jerry and I don't want to know him. But let me tell you this, <u>the real Jerry Shepherd did not kill that man</u>.
>
> If I was a murderer, I wouldn't have gone home to try to get money. If I was a murderer, I would have jumped someone and taken his money or I would have robbed a store. If I was a murderer, I would have killed again. I'm not

a murderer. I couldn't have jumped and robbed somebody if I wanted to and I know I couldn't kill anybody. I'm just like my dad. I'm too soft and tenderhearted to hurt anyone. I'm always helping people, not hurting them.

There is one thing I wish I could do. During my court date I wish I could stand up in front of everybody and sing one song that would tell them what kind of person I am, and how I really feel. I really believe in this song with all my heart, mind, body, and soul because it shows my feelings of what I believe in. The name of the song is "Impossible Dream." And if you don't believe me, read the words to the song or listen to someone sing it. Then you will know.

This is a true statement written by Gerald Warren Shepherd

Jerry read back over his words. Then he stood up and sang the song all the way through as though rehearsing for his appearance in court. They'd never let him sing in court, but just in case he was wrong, he wanted to be ready.

The days dragged by. Others came in for little stuff like drinking too much. They'd stay a day or two and be out. Then it would be quiet again until the next arrest. Jerry paced his cell. He talked to the deputy. He talked to the guy who brought his food. He read his Bible and prayed. He sang until he was hoarse. He wrote his folks and asked them to bring his guitar when they came to visit. He couldn't play very well, but now he'd have plenty of time to practice. He stayed so hungry he got worried he might have a tapeworm. He dreamed about food.

He wrote his diary of his day-to-day activities for Mr. York. The second Sunday he was in jail in Georgia, he wrote his life's story for the lawyer.

I was real shy around people for a long time. I guess being the only child had a lot to do with that. I liked to be alone with myself. I didn't care for crowds and I still don't. I liked going places and doing things by myself cause I felt better that way.

I always had a big problem with school, cause I always had trouble with my math which has always been hard for me and still is. I always wanted to please my parents in everything I did, but when I brought bad grades home I knew it didn't please them and it hurt me cause it didn't.

For some odd reason Mom and Dad didn't seem like my parents. They were just two people I was living with which I was always trying hard to please.

My freshman year at Oldham County was the best living year I had since I was born. Everything was going great. I made the honor roll two or three times that year and I was making my parents proud as punch of me. The best thing I liked was music. I was in the choir and I really liked the music teacher. I can sing pretty good which is a God given talent. Our music teacher was taking us everywhere to sing and all the time I knew I was pleasing my parents.

After that one great year, the curtain fell. I had just turned 16 and these three years of high school and living at home were the worst years of my life. I was already 16 my second year in high school and I couldn't drive until I brought my grades up. Well, I didn't get to drive that whole year.

He stared at the wall a long time before he started writing again. He wrote about driving his dad's truck into a tree and how he'd run away but he didn't mention Mama Harmon. The lawyer didn't need to know about her. He wrote about thinking he was going to fail when he was a senior and then about being chosen to star in the senior play and getting depressed and wrecking his car. He scribbled the words fast, putting down whatever came to mind.

The big week of the senior play came. We were to put it on three times. My parents and an aunt and uncle were coming to our last performance. The first two performances were really good. The night my parents were there was a flop. So I thought I had let everyone down including Mr. Riddle, the director. That night, the cast and crew, we all went out and had a party of our own. This was the first time I ever did drink. I thought I could drink all my problems down but it just caused me more trouble. I almost didn't graduate because of the trouble at school I got into for drinking.

I worked with dad all summer on the farm and in Sept. I was to go to a business college which I didn't want to go to but I thought it would please my parents. All I wanted to do was stay on the farm and work. But if I did that, I would soon be drafted into the Army.

I withdrew from college and my parents didn't know where I was for a week. I stayed at my old girlfriend's house cause I knew I would be accepted there. I knew Janice loved and needed me and I needed somebody to love. I decided to go back home and face the facts. After that I went back to drinking again. I thought I could drink all my problems away. I got to where I was drinking heavy and one night on my way back home I had a wreck. Well, I really let my parents down this time. Mom & Dad were very upset over this and Mom called me a drunk. Well, I decided to enlist in the army. I wanted to be just a foot soldier and go to Nam cause I felt like I was needed there and if I died, it was for a cause. But Dad wanted me to go to an army school, so I wanted to please him and I entered into an army school. I took basic training at

Fort Knox and enjoyed every bit of it. I also was drawn closer to my parents. After basic, I then had to go to Fort Gordon for my school and after I was there a few weeks I felt like I had lost complete contact with my parents and I felt like I wasn't needed here. All I wanted to do now was to be home with my parents and work with Dad on the farm. I hadn't really known my parents at all for 19 years. I felt like they were in one room and I was in another, but those few weeks at Fort Knox had brought us closer together.

As for the rest you know about it. I just wish I could forget it but I can't.

True statement written by Gerald W. Shepherd

Jerry read it over but he didn't change anything. Then he wrote his mother and dad that they could read what he had written for Mr. York before they sent it on to the lawyer. He wanted them to understand too. He just wasn't sure what he wanted them to understand.

That's how he was when he prayed too. He wanted to ask the Lord for help, but he didn't deserve any help. His mother and dad told him the Lord loved him no matter what he'd done, but how could he? Jerry didn't deserve anybody's love, especially not the Lord's, but he did want it. He wanted everybody to love him. He just hadn't ever been able to do enough of the right things to earn that love. Now here he was in jail. He didn't deserve anything but punishment for what he'd done. He needed to accept that truth.

A Bible verse popped up in his mind. *The wages of sin is death.* That's what he deserved. Death. He'd been chasing after death for years. Maybe at long last he'd found the way to catch it. He had committed murder. His punishment could be, maybe should be, the death sentence.

CHAPTER 18

The days passed. Each morning when he woke up, he tried to think of something to look forward to. Maybe about finding the jigsaw puzzle piece he searched for the night before or what they might bring him to eat. They were giving him an extra meal every day, but he was still hungry.

He couldn't wait for his parents to visit him. In Oldham County he'd dreaded their visits, but not now. They hadn't turned their backs on him. Instead, they were working to get him out of this cell and home again. They thought it was possible. Sometimes when Jerry read their letters, he almost believed it too.

Then reality would set in. The four walls would close in on him. His trial date was six months down the road. Six months he'd be stuck in this cell with the bugs and whoever else the sheriff dragged in to lock in there with him.

He spent hours in his bunk wondering how this could be happening to him. Then he'd think about what he'd done and want to bang his head against the wall the way he had when the alcohol demons were after him. He would pray and his prayers bounced off the ceiling and slammed back in his face. He'd open the Bible and the words would be nothing but a black blur. He feared he might be going mad.

Then he'd have easier times when he sang songs and wrote poems. He'd draw some pictures and write out detailed plans for things he could do on the farm when he got out. He'd get a letter from his folks, or Deputy Hackett would come in and ask him to sing a song for him. He'd open the Bible and a verse would jump out at him as if the Lord was saying, "Here, read this. It will help." *For to be carnally minded is death; but to be spiritually minded is life and peace.*

Somehow hope stayed alive. The middle of May Jerry got a letter from Mr. York.

> *May 15, 1969*
> *Dear Gerald:*
>
> *Your mother and father have delivered to me all of your recent fine letters which you have composed, addressed to me. I thoroughly enjoyed reading all of your communications and I am so happy to learn that all the town people of Pembroke, and the authorities, are taking excellent care of you while you are with them. They are all real fine people and very much concerned over your welfare and that a good solution can be found for you, that you can be properly treated and assisted in finding out the answers to some of the things that have bothered you.*
>
> *Keep up the good work and trust in your fellowman and keep your faith in God and I*

can assure you that in the time to come you will find a complete peace of mind and adjust your life to making the best of your surroundings wherever they may be. As I have pointed out to you, mankind only knows part of the answers, but people everywhere are concerned and basically gentle and want to help each other. As the modern saying goes, "Keep your faith."

Your father and your uncle were here at the office yesterday and we have requested the authorities, through Mr. Cheney, the Solicitor General, to make arrangements for you to have complete medical examinations at the earliest possible date. This will perhaps give you a new surrounding and different people to work with and talk to for a period of several weeks. When they start these examinations in Georgia, you are to have complete confidence in your doctors and to cooperate to the fullest extent and give them all of the fine details of your life as you have related them to me. We are seeking the best of help for you and can assure you that medical science, with all its wisdom, can give you the outline for understanding your mental processes.

I encourage you to continue to correspond with your parents, your friends and myself, and you must be reassured that everyone, and I emphasize "everyone," is working in your behalf. This is the greatest country on earth and it isn't our wealth and material possessions that make it great, but it is our feeling for the individual as the most important thing on earth that gives the American people this real value. Our government and laws are based upon this feeling for the individual and you must remember that in time medical science will find the answers for most of our illnesses. Be patient and continue to take care of yourself.

With kindest regards, I am,

Sincerely,
William F. York

The lawyer's letter lifted Jerry's spirits and made him think things were going to work out. Nothing about it prepared him for Central State Hospital in Milledgeville, Georgia. That was just as well. If he'd known what the hospital was going to be like, he'd have found a way to escape. He'd have run forever before he would have allowed them take him to that place.

Deputy Hackett drove him over. When they turned in through the gates and drove up to the stark gray building, the deputy looked over at Jerry. "Just remember you can take whatever happens and after a while you'll be sent back to us at Pembroke. Only a few weeks here. Anybody can take anything for a few weeks. Right, kid?"

The deputy's words and the very aura of the building caused a cold fist of dread to grip his insides even before Jerry was ushered to the ward for the criminally insane. They took his clothes away and gave him tan pants and a shirt to wear. Then they told him the facility was overcrowded with no open bunks in the dorms. They shut him up in a cage something like the one he'd been in when the MP's picked him up at the Atlanta airport, but this time he didn't have to worry about yelling till somebody let him out to the restroom. They supplied an empty coffee can for that.

That night as he lay on the mat in the cage, the Pembroke jail began to seem like a luxury hotel. He couldn't believe his parents had requested he be sent here. He wasn't crazy. At least he hadn't been when they brought him in. No telling what he'd be by the time he got out of this place. He wasn't even sure he could get through the night with his sanity.

The guards let him out in the morning to eat with the other inmates, patients, whatever they were. Jerry was trembling inside, but he tried to hide it. All around him were men who may have done terrible things, and they were eyeing him to decide what they should do to him. The guards didn't look much better. Jerry wasn't sure some of them hadn't just exchanged their inmate uniforms for a guard uniform for the day.

Jerry wanted to jump up on a table to announce to everybody sane enough to understand that he wasn't one of them. He didn't belong there. But instead he stayed in his spot and tried to take up the least amount of space possible. It might be better if nobody noticed him.

After breakfast, the guards herded them out into a bare dirt lot. Some of the men plopped down on the ground as if they didn't even notice the hot sun beating down on their heads. Others prowled the area hunting shade the way lions in the jungle might hunt good resting spots, ready to kill if another animal got in the way. A few men bounced a basketball in the hard dirt in front of a basketball goal. The bent metal rim didn't have a net. Here and there a man pulled out a deck of cards. Other men gravitated to the sound of shuffling cards.

Jerry stayed back against the metal building alongside the lot and prayed to be invisible. If only he could disappear. Even the cage with the stinky coffee can started looking good. At least then that man staring at him with cold, blank eyes couldn't get to him.

The guards came out in the yard and grabbed first one man then another to hustle back inside. Jerry started to sit down, then decided against it. He might need to move fast if one of the crazies came after him. Crazy wasn't so bad. He was half crazy himself, but that wasn't the same as being criminally insane. Thinking about what that might mean gave him chills.

Across the way he spotted a man who looked as uneasy as he felt. The man stared straight at Jerry before heading across the yard toward him. He dodged in and out of the other inmates.

When he stepped up beside Jerry, he looked him in the eyes. "What are you in for?"

The man was tall with an ample belly pushing out against his loose shirt. His slicked back brown hair was streaked with gray. His greenish gray eyes looked worried, but not weird.

"Evaluation," Jerry said. "How about you?"

"Same here. I wish they'd done it by mail."

"Can they do that?"

"I don't know, but it would have been better than this. These weirdoes aren't just crazy, they're crazy mean. And I ain't necessarily talking about our fellow guests. The guards are just weirdoes in uniforms, but then I guess you have to be crazy mean to take a job working here." The man looked out at the men around them. "But some of us like you and me are just here because some idiot judge wants them to pick our brains. See George over there and Junior." The man nodded toward two men off to themselves across the way. "We hang together and watch out for one another. It's a way to survive out here."

"Sounds good. Surviving, I mean."

"My name's Jack. Jack White."

"Jerry Shepherd."

"You look like a kid. How old are you?"

"Nineteen."

"What'd you do?" The man took back his question before Jerry could answer. "No, don't tell me. I don't want to know. Whatever you did, you don't look crazy mean, so we'll watch your back. But it won't be easy for you in here. You're young and cute. Some of these nuts might hit on you."

Jerry's face tightened. "I'll kill them before I let them touch me."

"Yeah, kid, you look like you might. At least try anyway." Jack gave him a considering look. "But you give them that look you just gave me and they might believe you and let you alone. Me and the other guys will do what we can."

"Thanks," Jerry said.

They didn't talk much. Out in the yard, they kept together and whenever a problem boiled up, they eased back into the shadows. If somebody bumped them, they ignored it. When the guards bashed somebody in the head, they pretended not to see a thing. If they had had shovels, they would have dug foxholes and hidden in them all day.

The hours Jerry spent out of the yard inside with the doctors and his counselor were better. They wanted to know about the problems he'd had growing up. His social work counselor, Alison Atwood, was especially easy to talk to. He could tell her anything and she never flinched. He hadn't been able to talk to anybody like that since Mama Harmon in New Jersey. At night before he went to sleep, he thanked the Lord for making it through another day and for Miss Atwood.

He remembered how he'd wondered if Mama Harmon was an angel, somebody the Lord put in his path to help him. Maybe that was the way it was here too. The Lord put Miss Atwood on his case to help him get through this hall of horrors. Jerry smiled at the thought. Miss Atwood didn't look anything like he imagined an angel would look. She was tough with no saintly aura, but she was just what Jerry needed.

When he talked about how he could never please his mother no matter how hard he tried and how he often felt so alone and unloved, Miss Atwood explained that a person could be emotionally abused as well as physically abused. That could be what had happened to him even if his mother never intended to hurt him.

After he thought about what she said, Jerry told her about seeing his mother's face when he hit the man in the motel. He'd wanted to bury that memory so deep he'd never think of it, but instead the memory was like a hot coal burning inside him. He was greatly relieved when Miss Atwood said something like that wasn't uncommon after years of emotional abuse. He still didn't quite believe it could be anything approaching normal, but at least he wasn't the only person who'd done something so horrible.

No matter what he said, Miss Atwood never acted surprised, much less shocked. She didn't say it was right, just that it was understandable considering his state of mind. She understood about Jerry not even knowing that other Jerry Shepherd who killed that man in the motel. And even more important, she didn't think the rest of his life had to be a total mess up like the first part had been.

CHAPTER 19

Weeks went by. Then a month. Each day worse than the last. Finally, after the doctors picked his brain clean, they handed him his old clothes. He was going back to the Pembroke jail. He couldn't stop grinning while he got dressed. It was like getting a reprieve and it felt great. When she told him goodbye, Miss Atwood said they'd send their findings to his lawyer and the judge. Jerry didn't care what they found as long as he never had to set foot inside Central State Hospital again.

He was grateful to Miss Atwood and Dr. Mike for helping him understand things, but he could handle things himself now. Had already handled things. He was facing forward and not looking back. He didn't need counseling.

Deputy Hackett came to get him. As he headed the car away from the hospital, the deputy smiled over at Jerry. "I sure am glad to see you looking so good, kid. I have to admit I was a little worried about what might happen to you in there. They've got some real bad cases up here."

"You won't get no argument about that from me." Jerry leaned back in the seat and let out a long breath. He could feel his muscles springing loose. He'd been stretched tighter than a guitar string ever since he walked into that chamber of horrors. He should have broken a dozen times, but he hadn't. That surely meant he had learned to handle things better.

It felt like coming home being back in the Pembroke Jail. For a few days, he didn't even mind the heat or the roaches.

He hadn't written his parents at all while he was at the hospital. He didn't want to take even the slightest chance the hospital people might read something he wrote and decide he sounded crazy enough to keep him in that place. He told his mother and dad as much when he wrote to them his first day back at Pembroke.

> *July 15, 1969*
> *Wed. 5:00 p.m.*
> *Dear Mom & Dad,*
>
> *I am now back at Pembroke and I have never been so glad to get away from anywhere as I am to get away from that stinking, rotten, good for nothing place. I could add a few more, but they are not for writing.*
>
> *As for someone straightening and helping me with my personal problems, I don't need it. I have already been straightened. I know now what my problem was but it's in the past.*
>
> *I'm very sorry I didn't write to you while I was at Milledgeville. It's not because I didn't want to. I was just being on the safe side. From now on you will be getting a steady shipment of letters from me. Want to hear from you soon.*

Love, your Son

He read over the letter. He said his problems were in the past, but what did that tell his folks? Nothing. He needed to let things out, to tell people what he was feeling. Miss Atwood said that way things might not build to explode in all the wrong ways. He should have told his mother and dad how he felt a long time ago. So maybe now was a good time to start. He picked up his ballpoint pen again.

> *P.S. Just about every time I didn't do something perfect, I punished myself. I just thought about that. Maybe by going AWOL from the Army I was punishing myself. Also when I was in that motel room with Mr. Baylor all I wanted to do was get out of his room and away, but he didn't see it that way. I was scared and didn't think, cause the Army teaches you not to think when your life is in danger. When I fought Mr. Baylor, all the pressure, strain and hate that had built up in me was being released and I think I killed Mr. Baylor just to punish myself. This may not sound like me, but I was sick at the time.*
>
> *It's something to think about cause I didn't have any other reason to hurt him. Why didn't I leave instead of keeping on beating on him? I believe it was because I wanted to punish myself for everything that I had done wrong. This may sound crazy but this came across my mind and I had to tell somebody to get it off my mind.*

He folded the letter. He hoped it wouldn't upset his folks, but he thought Miss Atwood would be proud of him trying to think things out like that. She was the one who told him that a lot of the things he'd done were because he wanted to hurt himself. But he ended up hurting someone else.

More days passed. His mother came to see him and brought a box of food. They locked her in the cell with him since that was the only place they had to visit. They didn't talk about anything much, just what his dad was doing on the farm, about the new dairy operation and how hard it was to get good help. They talked about the moon shot. Jerry didn't get to see it, but he heard it on the radio. She caught him up on family news and said the people at church were praying for him.

Everybody wanted him home again and when that happened, things would be different. While she talked about him plowing come spring, Jerry could almost smell the rich dark dirt turning over behind the tractor. She urged him to keep writing down how he felt and not to worry about it bothering her. All she wanted was for him to be well and happy. And home.

A few days after his mother was there, he wrote another long letter to Mr. York to explain some of the feelings Miss Atwood helped him understand.

July 29, 1969
Dear Sir,

I'm going to try to write down the things that have happened and what my responses were. I hope for my sake this will be very helpful.

As you know during my life I had this thing of perfection to be accepted. I did this because I thought I would be rejected if I didn't. During my early part of life I was around my mother more than my father because he was working most of the time. If I had done something wrong Mom was the one who did the scolding. I just couldn't take the scoldings she gave me and I became afraid of her. I felt that when

I was scolded, Mom was rejecting me and I was not wanted. So I was determined to be perfect so Mom wouldn't get on me.

During my four years of high school I still had this perfection to be accepted and when something went wrong she would get on me. By now the pressure and strain of this was beginning to get to me and so I started fighting back. She would get on me and I would scold right back which didn't do any good at all, but made matters worse.

By not being able to do a lot of things to perfection I did a lot of punishment to myself. There were some places I would have liked to go to and things I wanted to buy and needed, so I wouldn't go to these places or buy anything just to punish myself.

The pressure and burden of this was to the limits my junior and senior year in high school. During the first part of my senior year I left home to get away from Mom. And everything was at its best, but I missed the farm. So I came back home and tried to start all over again. Instead things got worse but I still hung around.

At the end of the year I just barely passed and during the summer I started drinking to punish myself for everything that I did wrong. I didn't want to go to college. I wanted to stay on the farm, but Dad said I would be drafted into the Army. I then enlisted and took basic at Fort Knox. Everything went to perfection and no trouble at all and I was really feeling closer to my parents for once.

Well, I came down to Fort Gordon and went to a school I didn't want and I ended up making bad grades and I felt like this was going to cause trouble and the Army was going to reject me so I decided to get away from everybody and get lost. I left the army because I didn't think they would help me but instead, reject me. Every time I went AWOL and came back they would rush me right back into school when I wasn't even settled down yet. I couldn't keep my mind on school because of the things that happened. I didn't believe the Army believed anything I told them and I just couldn't face the things that I had done, so I just tried to run from it like I've been running for the past 18 years of my life. I just couldn't face reality.

I needed help of some kind but I didn't know what for at the time. It was like walking into a brick wall. So the problem of perfection to be accepted and not being able to face reality was so much of a strain, pressure, and burden that I just lost all self control of myself.

Gerald Warren Shepherd

The bugs in the jail got worse. They crawled on his face when he slept. They got in the food his mother shipped down to him. He had so many bug bites he couldn't count them all. His mother sent insect repellant, but when Jerry smeared it on his arms and legs, he broke out in a rash. So Jerry decided to get something done about the bugs.

He complained to everybody who came up to the jail—the deputy when he came to put somebody in jail, the old guy who brought his food, even visitors to the other prisoners. They all heard about how awful the bugs were. It took a month, but Sheriff Montgomery finally came up to see what he was complaining about. When the sheriff opened up the wall to the space between the cells, hundreds of roaches scattered everywhere, covering the sheriff's shoes and running up his legs. From the dance he did stomping and beating his legs, the sheriff didn't appear to like bugs a bit better than Jerry.

They sprayed awful smelling insecticide all around the place, but Jerry didn't care about the smell. At last he could sleep without roaches crawling on him. And he found out something else. He could get things done.

Nearly every day, Willie, the little man who brought meals to the prisoners, smuggled in some special treat to Jerry like an extra dessert or dinner roll. Then he'd hang around to talk or get Jerry to sing an Elvis song. Willie liked to sing along even though his voice sounded something like a rusty hinge on an old gate. Sometimes when Willie hit a particularly bad note, Jerry wanted to hold his ears.

Willie liked him. Jerry knew that, but he wasn't as sure about the sheriff until he overheard Willie talking in the next room. "Yeah, everybody likes that Shepherd boy. Ain't nobody down here can hardly believe he done what he done. I heard the sheriff talking just the other day that a boy like Jerry don't belong in jail and if it was up to him he'd turn him loose and not make him serve a minute's more time. The sheriff says Jerry ain't the kind of boy who needs to be locked up. That we got plenty of them. Some that we ain't even got locked up yet, but that Shepherd boy ain't one of them."

Jerry did everything he could to keep the sheriff thinking well of him. He even scrubbed down the walls and floor of his jail cell without being asked. He didn't know how old the jail was, but Jerry doubted if it had ever been cleaned, at least like his mother cleaned. While he'd rather be working back home on the farm, it still felt good to get his hands dirty doing something.

After that, the sheriff let him out to clean the courthouse offices on the weekends. Jerry never thought cleaning would turn out to be such a treat, but any way to get out of that cell was good. At times he didn't know how he stood being locked up, but somehow he stayed on an even keel. Even when they locked a real nutcase in the cell with him, he was able to deal with it. Maybe it was all the prayers everybody was saying for him at home. And he was praying too.

Dear Lord, thank you for this day. Bless the sheriff and deputy and Willie. Help the guy over in the next cell to quit yelling. Give Mom and Dad good crops. Thank you for my parents and help me and Mom keep trying to understand one another. Give me a special song to sing. Forgive me.

Even though he didn't pray out loud, sometimes he prayed as if the sheriff or his mother might overhear him. Jerry still wasn't sure the Lord would listen to prayers from somebody who'd messed up the way he had. He wasn't sure he had the kind of feeling a person was supposed to have inside when he was a Christian.

God expected a Christian to go to church, to pray, to read the Bible and to do right things. He knew God had given him a singing voice and he should use it for the Lord. And he wanted to. He wanted to go to church and sing. He even asked the sheriff to take him to church so he could sing a special for the people there.

The sheriff looked sorry as he turned him down. "I'd like to, Jerry. I really would, but I don't think I can. It'd cause too much commotion with the other prisoners. Everybody would be trying to get out by saying they wanted to go to church. I know you aren't saying it just to get out, but some of these others would. Tell you what. I'll ask my preacher to come see you in here."

Jerry didn't mind the preacher coming to see him. He'd be glad to sing for him, but it wasn't the same as getting up in front of a whole church full of people and singing "Amazing Grace" or "The Old Rugged Cross." He could make people cry singing those two old songs. Stuck there in the jail, he was the only one crying.

CHAPTER 20

August slid by. The middle of September, Jerry's lawyer flew down to Georgia to meet with Mr. Stedman, the district attorney. In June, the court had returned three indictments charging Jerry with murder, with robbery, and with larceny of a motor vehicle. In August, the hospital at Milledgeville had sent their findings to Judge Paul C. Rutherford who would be hearing Jerry's case. The Board of Doctors found Jerry able to distinguish right from wrong and therefore, mentally capable of being tried on all charges. They'd had no word from the Army about Jerry's discharge or any possible help from that quarter.

After the deputy ushered Mr. York into the jail cell with Jerry, the lawyer shed his coat and tie. He wiped the sweat off his forehead. "This Georgia weather is a killer. It ought to be getting cooler by now."

"It is cooler," Jerry said. "You should have been here in August."

"If it was hotter than this, no thanks." Mr. York hitched up his suit pants and sat down in the chair the deputy had put in the cell for him. "Your parents tell me they've been taking turns coming down to visit."

"Yes sir. Dad was down a couple of weeks ago. Mom sent some food."

"Your mother is a great cook. A good woman. She and your father are working very hard along with us at the firm to help you, Jerry."

Jerry watched the lawyer's face and didn't say anything. He was waiting for the chit-chat to be over so they could get to what was important—how he could get out of here.

The lawyer dabbed his forehead with his handkerchief again and fingered some papers in the briefcase on the floor beside his chair, but he didn't pull anything out.

"The district attorney has your confessions, so there's not really much we can do about that. We were in hopes the hospital report would rule you couldn't stand trial, but that didn't happen."

"I'm glad they didn't decide I was crazy." Jerry made a face.

"Well, of course, but you were under a great deal of stress and mentally unstable at the time of the crime. When you tell me about what happened now, there are murky areas. Things you can't remember well. That is an indication of your mental state at the time."

"But my mental state is better now." Jerry cringed at the thought of Milledgeville.

"And we're grateful for that, but it does mean you won't be able to avoid being tried for the charges against you."

"I understand. Will I get the death penalty?" The question was easier to ask than he'd thought it would be.

"No, certainly not," Mr. York said firmly. "But murder is a very serious charge. The state of Georgia has minimum sentences for stated crimes the same as Kentucky does."

"What does that mean?"

"It means that if you are found guilty as charged, the judge would have to sentence you to prison for at least the minimum time for that crime. He wouldn't be able to shorten the sentence due to your age or other extenuating circumstances."

"So you think I'll have to do time?"

"I'm afraid so. If you're found guilty as charged."

Jerry kept his eyes straight on Mr. York. "I did the crime. I should have to pay for it."

"That shows maturity, Jerry. And we're proud of you for being ready to take responsibility for what you've done, but this entire unfortunate situation is difficult for everyone involved. Naturally your parents want to obtain the best possible outcome for you as do I."

"That would be me going home to help Dad on the farm."

"You'd get agreement from us on that one, but the judge on your case may be harder to convince." Mr. York fingered the edges of the papers in his briefcase again but still didn't pull anything out. After a long moment of silence, he went on. "Your parents have been consulting with some doctors in Louisville to see the best way to proceed as your trial date approaches. Mr. Stedman says the judge on your case, Judge Rutherford, has a reputation for toughness."

"Have they set a date?" Jerry asked.

"The middle of October. October 16th."

♦ ♦ ♦

October 16. The day hung in Jerry's thoughts like a heavy storm cloud getting ever closer. It colored his every thought. Before Mr. York's visit, Jerry had written his folks about setting his feet on free ground again and getting a second chance. Mr. York had pushed reality at him and made him realize he could be facing years in prison and might never be free again. Maybe the death penalty would be preferable to that.

Deputy Hackett frowned when Jerry told him he'd be going before Judge Rutherford. "Oh, man, that's not good news. Any judge but him."

A prisoner in the next cell yelled, "Yeah, boy, you done got the hanging judge. He gonna throw the book at you. You'll be lucky to ever see daylight again."

Deputy Hackett made the other man shut up, but it was too late. The storm cloud hanging over Jerry's head got blacker. He poured out his heart to his parents.

Sept. 17, 1969
Dear Mom & Dad,

I can't help but worry about what's going to happen. I know my lawyer is doing his best, but I know I'll get time and I'll be lucky if I get out in five years which I doubt very much. In my case it's life or the death sentence. I know I won't get death but I'll have to face a few years or more. I hope that you and the farm will still be there but things will probably change a lot while I'm serving my time.

I was sick both physically and emotionally. I thought my life was in danger. At the time it happened I don't really believe I remembered everything that went on and what I really did do. It's just so confusing I can hardly stand it. All I know is at the time I didn't know if I was coming or going or what and at the time I just had a nervous breakdown.

It's still very hard for me to believe that this has happened to me and I get so blue and discouraged that I feel like throwing it all down the drain. I have lost some weight since Dad was here, it's just that being locked up like this

*and what has happened and that I know I'm
going to have to serve time in prison makes
you lose your hunger for food. Well, I guess I
could write a few more sad lines but I guess
this is enough for right now.*

Love, Gerald

For a week he stayed in a dark funk. All he could think
about was being put away for life. He couldn't eat. He
couldn't read. The only thing that helped was singing and
he sang through twenty or thirty songs every night. He
wrote another letter to his parents. He needed to talk to
somebody. He needed somebody to shine a light into the
darkness enveloping him.

*Sept. 21, 1969
Dear Mom & Dad,*

*I can't really think of anything to say. Right
now I'm so depressed that I feel like giving up
and ending it all and I won't be on anybody's
hands and this would be one case the court
wouldn't have to put up with. It would also
save the prison of putting up with me.*

*The closer it gets to Oct. the sicker I get cause
you can bet the court is going to try to bury me
for good. I just wish you wouldn't be there to
see it happen. The day Mr. York was here I
tried to make him think I was in great shape,
but to tell you the truth, I was nearly in tears
so I guess that I'm not a man after all. It's just
so hard for me to face up to all that's
happened. I've gone through so much
already it's very hard for me to stand on my
own two feet.*

*The really important thing that keeps me going
right now is I hope that I'm given a chance to
give you my love and loyalty and I want to give*

you both that so much that my heart aches for it. I don't have to decide to come back to the farm. "I want to." Farming is something I like and I think I could become good at. It really makes a person feel he is accomplishing something.

With your love, the farm, and my singing I can have the happiness and peace within myself.

With Love Always,
Gerald, Your Son

His appetite didn't improve much, but his spirits lifted a little when the sheriff let him and one of the other prisoners out to clean the courthouse. Work felt good. He liked being too tired to think when he lay down at night. Still in another way he wished October 16th would hurry so it would be over with. When he got a letter from his parents late in September telling him they had arranged a special private trial in front of the judge with no jury or anything, he almost believed that one more time they were going to pull off some kind of miracle and find a way to get him out of trouble. He wrote back that night.

Sept 29, 1969
Dear Mom & Dad,

Your letter came today and I was very surprised about this informal trial. There are a lot of things I would like to ask you about this special trial, but I guess I can wait till you come down. The people down here must be on my side, too, cause I don't believe you could have gotten this thing to take shape without their help and approval.

Yes, it has been very hard on me down here behind these bars, but I wanted to prove that I could stand on my own two feet and show these people what I'm really like.

I'm really looking forward to seeing you the 15th and I'll really need you the 16th cause when we see the judge you'll probably have to hold me up cause my legs will be knocking together so hard I won't be able to stand up. I just hope all things go well that day. I guess the only thing I can do till then is pray a little harder and hope, hope, hope and have faith in God so strong that it will knock anyone down.

Love,
Your Son

Jerry was trying to have that kind of faith. His parents had always had that kind of faith, the unshakable sureness of knowing God was in his heaven and watching out for them. His mother had been bombarding heaven with prayers and everybody else with letters to help him. She believed he'd come home. Jerry wanted to believe it, but secretly, down in a spot inside him where he was afraid to look, he didn't think he'd ever be free again. He didn't deserve to be free. Not after what he'd done.

CHAPTER 21

When his parents came down for the hearing, they brought the navy blue suit he wore in high school. If only he were going to a church somewhere to sing instead of going before a judge.

Jerry leaned against the wall while they waited for the minutes to inch by before the hearing. He couldn't sit down. His insides were all atremble and he thought he might throw up. His parents had on their brave faces, but his mother twisted her handkerchief into a tight spiral. His dad sat down and then popped right back up to pace back and forth while the top of his bald head turned bright pink.

They didn't say much. No need in talking about the hearing. They could talk it to death and it wouldn't make any difference. It was up to Judge Rutherford now.

And the Lord, his father reminded Jerry. "Remember, we've been praying non-stop, and the folks at church are all praying. The Lord will get us through this."

They met with Judge Rutherford in a side room at the courthouse. Mr. York stood beside Jerry as the prosecuting attorney, Mr. Stedman, presented the charges and the case against Jerry. Mr. Stedman didn't talk long. He didn't need to. Jerry's confession was in front of the judge.

Mr. York made a short appeal for mercy due to extenuating circumstances—Jerry's age and mental condition at the time. Then the judge asked what Jerry had to say for himself. Looking stern in his black robes, Judge Rutherford stared at Jerry and waited for him to confess yet again.

Jerry tried to be straightforward and honest. He'd already pleaded guilty to all three charges. Mr. York had told him to. Guilty. And he was guilty. He killed the man. He stole the man's car. He used the man's credit cards. He deserved whatever the judge gave him.

Still, when the judge handed down the sentence, it was like looking at a thermometer from inside a warm house and knowing the temperature outside was ten below but until you stepped out into the wind you couldn't quite believe it. That was how Jerry felt. He'd known it was going to happen, but at the same time he believed his lawyer, his parents, the Army, somebody would find a way to let him go home.

That hope died when Judge Rutherford pronounced his sentence. "Gerald Warren Shepherd, I sentence you to life in prison, ten years for robbery and five years for grand larceny. These sentences are to run concurrently with credit for time already served in the Pembroke jail. You will be eligible for parole in seven years." He looked almost sorry as he said it.

Seven years. 1970. '71. '72. '73. '74. '75. '76. And then he might not get parole. That was just when he could go before the Parole Board to seek parole.

After they went out of the room, Mr. York told Jerry

and his parents the sentence handed down was the minimum for the charges under Georgia law. So really none of them should be surprised. But they were.

They knew what the law said, what the punishment was, but they hadn't believed it would apply to Jerry. His mother and father kept looking at each other as if they'd just lived through a bomb exploding in their laps.

When he had to tell his parents goodbye, his mother stared at Jerry as if she might never see him again. For a minute she looked ready to scream or maybe cry, but then she pressed her lips together in a thin line and pulled in a deep breath. "This isn't the end of it, Jerry. We won't give up until you're home again. We'll never give up. The Lord has a plan for your life and it isn't in prison. He'll help us. We just have to put our faith in Him." Her face tightened in fierce lines.

"Yes ma'am." Jerry tried to look hopeful for her even if he did feel as if he'd been buried under a truckload of rocks.

Then his dad gripped Jerry's arms as though he would never turn loose. "I'm sorry, son. Maybe we shouldn't have asked for this kind of hearing. Maybe there might have been a better way."

"It's okay, Dad. I told you all along I had to pay for what I've done. I'll be okay."

His father pulled himself together. "Sure, you will, son. You just do what they say and settle down and you'll get trusty status before you know it. The trusties don't have such a hard time. At LaGrange they were almost like the hired help except they didn't get to go home at night. And there will be a chaplain. Soon as you can, you go see the chaplain. He might even need a helper. There are ways to help yourself inside. The good Lord will help you find them. He'll send a guardian angel to watch over you wherever you are. I know he will, and your mother and I will pray every morning and every night for you."

Behind his father, his mother dabbed her eyes as she whispered, "Not just in the morning and at night. Every minute. We'll pray every minute." His mother's words trailed after him as Sheriff Montgomery ushered him away.

On the ride back to Pembroke, Jerry asked the sheriff more about what he should do in prison. The sheriff said the same thing as Jerry's dad. Be a model prisoner the way he'd been at Pembroke.

"And most prisons have church services every Sunday," the sheriff said. "You'll like that. You've been wanting to go to church ever since you came down here."

"Yes sir. And I sure do appreciate how kind you and everybody have been to me."

"Fact is, Jerry, we're gonna miss your singing when you're moved out of here. We get plenty of singers but most of them are drunk as skunks. Not that that matters. They probably couldn't carry a tune in a bucket even if they weren't. Not a thing like you. You've got a fine voice. A gift. So you just keep on singing and getting your life back on track. Maybe there'll even be a chance for you to do some singing in whatever facility you end up in. If they have church, they're bound to have hymns and that kind of thing."

It was funny, but now that he knew what was going to happen, the black cloud lifted a little. It still hovered up there somewhere, but Jerry could see below it and think about the best thing to do. Prison would be different than the cell at Pembroke. They'd let him work. The sheriff told him all the inmates had jobs. That was something to look forward to. Something real to do to pass the time besides working jigsaw puzzles. And each day would bring him closer to the end of his sentence.

In a letter to his folks the day after he got back to Pembroke, Jerry vowed to do everything in his power to make the most of each day with the Lord's help.

Oct 17, 1969
Dear Mom & Dad,

I'm still at Pembroke but I may be gone by the time you receive this letter or I might still be here for another week. I don't know. As soon as I leave, I'll let you know as quick as I can so the mail will get to the right places.

When I get to prison I'm going to try to fit myself in as soon as possible and the sooner I do that the sooner I'll get to be a trusty and a trusty has a lot more freedom than the other prisoners do.

The other thing I want to do is try to become a chaplain's assistant and if I get to do that, I'll be able to study religion and the word of God and to be really able to understand better and also study religious music and with my working at this and with the chaplain's help I might turn into a good speaker and be able to preach the Word of God. When I'm dismissed from prison I'll have better knowledge of the Bible and in my spare time when I'm not farming I'll be able to go out and preach to people who need help and who want to follow God's way and to go down the path of righteousness in His Name's sake. God gave me a voice to sing with to use me to reach the heart of the people. So that's what I'm going to try to do, help those that need help and sing my heart out to reach their hearts till they understand the kind of feeling I have when I sing religious music.

You won't have to worry about me down here cause with God's help and me helping myself I'll hold up my end and when everybody gets to know me as well as Pembroke did, everything will work out just fine.

> *Just take real good care of the farm while I'm away and then before too long I'll be able to take care of the farm and you all, too. Can't beat that, can you?*
>
> *I love you both very much.*
>
> *Love, Your Son*

He wrote his last letter to his parents from Pembroke on October 24, 1969. He explained how he didn't want to limit his reading and studying only to religious material and that he intended to study other music besides just religious music.

> *Just put it this way, I want to broaden my mind on all kinds of material that I can get my hands on. I can also brush up on my English and math and expand my vocabulary and figures.*
>
> *The big thing I want to do now is just to get as busy as I can so the time will go faster until it's time for the people down here to give me a chance to be a free person again.*

He didn't let himself think about how long seven years was. He'd never been good at math. There was no sense in starting now to figure up how many months and days and hours that would be. He just had to figure how best to use them to improve his mind and voice.

He didn't understand how it could happen, but the closer the time came for him to be sent to whatever facility they assigned him to, the calmer he got. He spent hours thinking about what he would do in prison.

He would step closer to the Lord and find out what the Lord intended for him. The Lord hadn't let Jerry die when he kept trying to end it all by driving into trees. When he ran away to California, the Lord had led him all the way back to New Jersey and Mama Harmon to guide him back home. The Lord had put Miss Atwood in his path at Milledgeville so he wouldn't go completely nuts. The Lord hadn't let Judge Rutherford, the reputed hanging judge, sentence him to death for killing Mr. Baylor.

Maybe they were all angels the Lord put at the crossroads of his life. He hadn't always recognized the angels even as they'd guided him toward the right roads instead of the wrong ones. Maybe the Lord even had angels in prison. That sounded crazy, but it could be true. Jerry just had to look for them.

The Lord must have a purpose for his life the way his mother kept telling him. Maybe it was singing. Maybe it was preaching. Jerry wasn't sure. He sometimes felt as if everything he did was because that was what his parents said the Lord wanted him to do. But Jerry wanted to feel the Lord inside his heart because he had put him there and not because somebody else said he should be there. Jerry loved the Lord. He loved to sing for the Lord, but sometimes that place in the center of his heart felt so empty. It was as if he loved the Lord through everybody else's heart and not his own.

CHAPTER 22

In November, he said goodbye to Pembroke. Sheriff Montgomery and Deputy Hackett looked ready to hug him, but instead they shook his hand and wished him luck.

His next stop was Jackson, Georgia to be tested at the Diagnostic and Classification Center to determine where he'd serve out his sentence. Jerry prayed for a place where he'd be safe. He had enough sense to know prison wasn't summer camp, but at the same time, he had no real idea of what to expect. People in his family didn't go to prison. They went to church.

The center in Jackson was a new facility. Everything was white and clean, almost antiseptic, so he didn't have to worry about roaches like at Pembroke. Instead, he had to worry about bumping his head on the john when he turned over in his cot. The cubbyhole cell was that small. He couldn't sleep with his feet down by the john because the guards had to see his head when they peeked through the window in the door. He didn't complain. He just slept with his face toward the wall. He was out of the cell most of the day anyway. It was almost like being on a college campus and going to classes all day, except of course, this campus was locked up.

Jerry did whatever they told him to do. He slept when they said sleep. He got up when they said get up. He ate when they said eat. But with the truth of his future hanging over him, he felt as if he was walking down a narrow hallway that got darker and darker. He couldn't stop walking and he couldn't turn around. He had to keep going and let the black swallow him up.

He was nineteen years old. He was going to be in prison at least until he was twenty-six and maybe forever. Even if he got paroled, the best years of his life would be lost behind bars. Those were the years when a man started out on his life's work, fell in love, married and started a family, moved off on his own. He was moving off, but hardly on his own. He was a captive of the state of Georgia.

He kept praying. His parents told him that prayer could help everything. He didn't see how, but just in case they were right, every morning when he opened his eyes and had to face another day, he looked up toward the ceiling and quietly spoke a prayer.

"Since I'm not dead, thank you, Jesus. I'm locked away and the key's thrown away. So even though this is where I'm going to spend the rest of my life, I'll try to remember to say praise God."

Most days he remembered, but he wasn't able to put much enthusiasm into that praise.

He stopped writing to his folks. It was just too hard to write anything on the prison stationery with lines at the top for the inmate's name and state serial number. He'd become a number in the system, D-1902, one peg among many to be stuck in a hole somewhere and beat down to stay.

They gave him tests to see which hole he fit in. He didn't like tests. They told him he couldn't fail these tests. But sometimes he stared at the paper on the written tests until his heart started pounding and his hand got so sweaty the pencil slid sideways in his fingers.

As the days passed, he adjusted to the place. The commode next to his nose at night was way better than roaches. He did miss Willie and Deputy Hackett bragging on his singing back in Pembroke. There they were always asking him to sing for them. Here every time he started singing some voice beyond the thin wall of his cell would yell at him to shut up and go to sleep. So Jerry whisper sang himself to sleep.

On Thanksgiving Day he was really blue as he thought about the turkey and cornbread stuffing and pumpkin pies his mother would cook. He imagined her setting a plate for him even though he wasn't there. He wished he could just pop home for a couple of days.

That was all he wanted. Just a couple of days of freedom. He wanted to eat until he was as stuffed as the turkey on his mother's table and then walk out with his dad to the barn where he could smell the cows and the hay. He wanted to get up the next morning and hear the crunch of early morning frost under his feet. If it rained and brought the tobacco into case, he wanted to climb up in the barn and throw down the sticks of tobacco and help his father bulk it down to strip. He wanted his ears to ring from the loud whir of the chainsaw as they cut wood for the fireplace. He wanted to get up with the sun and do something, anything on the farm as a free man.

Inside this prison he felt totally removed from the natural world. He couldn't even keep up with the time of day since he didn't have a watch. The hours rolled into one another and stretched out too long. He knew daylight and dark, but weather didn't have any meaning to him. What difference did it make if it was hot or cold, if it was rainy or dry, if the wind was blowing or it was still?

The only storms he could feel were the ones inside him. He'd let his family down. He couldn't imagine what his mother and dad were going through at home, good Christian church folk with a convict for a son. They should disown him, say they did their best and forget about him.

But they didn't. They kept writing and telling him they loved him. They promised to never stop praying for a way to bring him home.

After Thanksgiving, one of the counselors told him he had to write his parents to explain the rules of correspondence if he wanted to keep getting mail. Prisoners couldn't get just any old letter from whoever took a notion to write him. In fact, at the Diagnostic Center he could only get letters from his parents and nobody else. Later, he might be able to add more names to his mailing list as long as everybody followed all the rules. Everything he wrote or his parents wrote him would be read and censored.

Thinking about some guard reading his letters made the words dry up in Jerry's head. Besides he couldn't think of much to write that wouldn't upset his folks. He'd done enough of that already. So he ended up writing the correspondence rules and a stiff how are you and I am okay before giving the letter to a guard.

After that first letter, somehow putting his prison number on the top of the paper to write again got easier. Things were going better anyway. They were holding him at the Diagnostic Center, and he was beginning to hope maybe they would let him serve out his time there instead of going to another prison. The Sunday after Thanksgiving, he went to church, and the chaplain let him sing "The Old Rugged Cross." Jerry put everything he had into singing the old hymn. He wanted to knock their socks off so they'd let him sing every week.

To decide where to send him, they brought in the

Milledgeville doctors. Just the sight of those doctors made him shudder. He was near panic worrying they might decide to send him back to the state hospital for more evaluation. He did his best to answer their questions the way they wanted, but the questions sounded stupid to Jerry. He was petrified he might say the wrong thing. At the end of the session, one of the doctors asked him if he remembered their names.

Jerry looked straight at him. "No sir, I did my best to forget everything about that place. I don't want to remember anything about my time there."

The doctors acted half mad about that, but they claimed they wanted him to answer truthfully. So he had. Politely. He didn't remember their names. He remembered Miss Atwood's name. She was the one who'd helped him the most.

The night after he talked to the doctors he wasn't sure what might happen. He didn't know why the prison officials had brought in the mental hospital people. Miss Atwood had helped him understand his problems while he was there, but all that was in the past. Whoever that other Jerry Shepherd was who had done that horrible thing to Mr. Baylor was gone. Gone along with the need for alcohol or pills. Gone forever.

The next day the word came down he was being sent to the Georgia State Prison in Reidsville. A maximum-security facility. Where rapists and murderers and repeat felons were sent. Where lifers were incarcerated. That's where Jerry had to spend at least the next seven years of his life if he survived that long. There were no guarantees. Bad things happened in prisons like Reidsville.

He got to Reidsville in the middle of December. At home the churches would be having Christmas pageants. Just a couple of years ago, he was a kid looking forward to singing "O Holy Night" at church and coming home to shake packages under the tree in the living room to see if he could guess what was inside. That seemed like a lifetime ago.

Now he was in a dorm with about a hundred other men waiting to be processed and assigned a spot in the prison and a work duty. He was in a holding pattern, mentally and physically. He tried not to think about going into the prison population. Better not to think about the kind of men inside there.

There had to be others like him who had done terrible crimes but were ready to reform and change. Sometimes he could keep his mind on how he hoped to take advantage of whatever learning programs they had inside, but other times he fell into a deep pit of depression and could hardly bear to think of anything at all.

He kept his letters home cheerful. He didn't write about being scared and lonely or how he cried himself to sleep when he thought about spending Christmas locked inside a prison.

Every morning, he put on the white prison uniform that had a blue stripe up the side of the pants and down the button placket of the shirt. As he buttoned up the shirt, he'd wish he could be pulling on his black leather boots and his old green coat with the tear on the elbow to go feed the cows. He didn't need a coat here. He wasn't going out anywhere.

In their letters, his parents kept asking what he wanted for Christmas. Jerry didn't want to think about Christmas. He wanted to shut his eyes and open them again in January after Christmas was over. He didn't care whether he even got a gift, but they kept asking so he finally told them a watch. It drove him crazy not knowing what time it was.

A few days before Christmas he wrote his mom and dad telling them the results of the tests he'd taken at the Diagnostic Center. He hoped just knowing he'd done well on some of the tests would be a kind of gift.

> *The Social Worker at Jackson showed me the results of my tests and I came in above average and scored high normal. The test scores showed that I had the ability to be a Chaplain's Assistant, Office or Clerical Work, the ability for the art of drawing and designs and being a teacher, actor and singer.*

It wasn't much of a gift, but it was all he had. Then since he was thinking about Christmas and how when he was a kid he'd gotten this great bike when his dad kept telling him they couldn't afford it, Jerry decided to ask for something that sounded even more impossible. But weren't preachers always telling people to pray big? So he added another paragraph to his letter.

> *The next time you see Mr. York, ask him if it would be alright if I could write a letter to the Governor of Georgia. If I can get enough people to back me up and write letters to the Governor and to the Warden of the prison, they will take notice of my case, knowing that people are interested and wanting to help me, then I can start the ball to jumping down here. Let me know what you think and what Mr. York thinks about this.*

Christmas morning Jerry woke up early. He thought about last Christmas when he'd gone home after basic training. He'd done his folks proud winning awards in basic, and that Christmas had been one of the best they ever had together. The tree was nearly up to the ceiling and his mother bought new gold bells for it. After they opened presents, he ate half dozen of his mother's sweet rolls for breakfast. One of his gifts was a black leather wallet with a twenty in it. He tried to think what had happened to the wallet. He must have left it in the barracks at Ft. Gordon.

Jerry rolled over in his bunk, pulled the cover up over

his head, and willed his body to stop breathing. His lungs betrayed him by continuing to pull in air. The get up signal was going off. The guards would be around to roust out anybody who didn't pay attention. There weren't any Santa Clauses in prison.

Jerry sat up and gave himself a talking to. Christmas had never been about Santa Claus. Christmas was the day Jesus was born. The Christ's birthday. Jerry wished he had a Bible to read the Christmas story the way his dad always did on Christmas morning, but they made him leave all his things at Pembroke. Still he'd heard it read a million times. He didn't need a Bible. He could remember it.

He stared at the wall and whispered the words, "And she brought forth her firstborn son, and wrapped him in swaddling clothes and laid him in a manger because there was no room for them in the inn. And there were in the same country shepherds abiding in the field, keeping watch over their flock by night."

Shepherds. As a kid, he never wanted to be Joseph or one of the wise men or a donkey. He always wanted to be a shepherd. Jerry Shepherd, one of the shepherds who heard the angels sing on that first Christmas Day. "And an angel of the Lord appeared unto them and the glory of the Lord shone round about them and lo, they were sore afraid."

He used to wonder exactly what it meant to be sore afraid, but now he knew. He was sore afraid of what was ahead of him. He moved his mind away from his fear and tried to come up with the next verses. It was something about not being afraid.

When he was a little shepherd in the church pageants, he had never acted afraid like the leaders told him to. Jerry had wanted to see an angel. It would be the greatest thing to sing along with the angels. Sometimes late at night on Christmas Eve, he would go outside and look up at the sky and imagine angels singing.

His voice got a little louder as he went on with the next part. "And the angel said, Fear not, for behold, I bring you good tidings of great joy, which shall be to all people, for unto you this day is born a Savior."

There was something else. Something about swaddling clothes and the manger but he couldn't remember the words well enough to say it. He skipped to the part about the multitude of angels singing. "Glory to God in the highest, and on earth peace, good will toward men."

Did he have any chance of peace in this place? Good will toward men in prison was surely a joke. These men didn't have any good will toward anybody. He didn't know whether it was the Lord's voice or his mother's voice echoing in his head. *You don't have to worry about what the other men feel. It's your good will that matters.*

"But what if I never get out? What if I'm here every Christmas for the rest of my life?"

The answer was clear in his head. *Daily the Lord will give you grace sufficient enough to meet the challenges of the day.*

"But I'm not strong enough," Jerry said. "I can't do it."

This time he knew it was his mother's voice, perhaps some memory from the past when she was pushing him to do more, to be perfect. *You can't, but the Lord can. His strength is made perfect in weakness.*

That's how Jerry felt. Weak. Not good enough. Not strong enough. Not able. Never able. As he joined the line for breakfast where they'd be sure to plop those clumpy grits on his plate yet again, he silently said a prayer. *Thank you, Lord, for being born. Forgive me for wishing I wasn't.*

Then in a very quiet whisper he sang, "Happy birthday, Jesus."

After he was through with every line of the song, he thought about singing happy birthday to himself. His real birthday, January third, when he would turn twenty was still ten days away, but this Christmas was his first as a convict. No reason to celebrate that.

CHAPTER 23

The days in quarantine dragged by. He had a watch now. His folks sent it in the package he got a few days after Christmas. The watch was great, but now he knew exactly how long it took the hour hand to make a circle. If only they'd assign him to some kind of work duty. If he had something to do, the time might pass faster.

He received some cards from the people back home even though they weren't on his mailing list The mail censors must have had a fit of Christmas spirit.

The day after he turned twenty, he got a letter from Mr. York. The lawyer told him to work hard, not become discouraged and make the most of each hour of the day. Jerry stared at the words. It was easy enough for Mr. York to write about not being discouraged. He wasn't locked up. Jerry kept reading.

> *Make the most of each day by involving your mind and take care of your health by getting as much exercise as possible.*

Jerry was all for that. He'd run all the way home if they'd just open the door. The lawyer wasn't very hopeful about getting a quick pardon from the governor.

> As you know, the Governor of the State of Georgia has the power to grant you a pardon; however, I encourage you not to build up your hopes that this can be brought about overnight. The odds are that it will never happen, and I am sure that you understood this as you made your decision to pay your penalty when you were at Pembroke. This does not mean that you should not continue to try; however, at this point, I think it would be unfair to yourself and to the authorities, which includes the Governor of the State of Georgia, to request them to take this under full advisement until you have proven yourself as a model individual at Reidsville.

At first Jerry didn't think it was a particularly encouraging letter, but the more he read it over, the more he did feel encouraged. Mr. York thought he could handle being in prison and show everybody how well he could be rehabilitated. Mr. York thought they'd give him some kind of work that would make a contribution to his fellow man. He didn't just say fellow inmates. Best of all, Mr. York promised to keep working on his case. They hadn't forgotten him. Once Jerry proved himself a model prisoner, then he could write the governor.

Finally in the middle of January, he got out of quarantine and was assigned a new number, 50687, and a spot in Dorm G-1. The West Side of the prison was mostly black inmates with one integrated dorm. The East Side was mostly white inmates also with one integrated dorm. Jerry was in the integrated dorm on the East Side. He was told it was a good assignment, the safest place for him since the hundred and twenty-five men in that dorm were mostly older inmates with good prison records.

Double bunks lined the wall. Each man had a small gray metal locker for personal belongings. Jerry didn't have much to put in his. Some letters from his folks. Paper and pencil to write his letters back. He still didn't have his Bible. His life had been stripped down to the bare essentials—whatever food they dished out on his tray when he went through the food line, water, a narrow cot to sleep on, an open shower in the middle of the dorm area, a square patch of dirt yard to stretch his legs at assigned times.

He went out and dug ditches on the work detail. Sometimes they dug them and then filled the ditch back in. Jerry didn't care. He was glad to be using his muscles again. And he wouldn't be on the ditch digging detail forever. Come spring they'd plant a garden to raise vegetables for the prison kitchen, and in six months or a year he'd be able to request a transfer to a different duty, maybe something using the aptitudes and talents they'd said he had at the Diagnostic Center.

As soon as he could, he met with the chaplain. Jerry tried to impress him by saying how he hoped to use his time in prison to study the Bible and take classes and improve his singing.

"I want to take advantage of every opportunity during my time here to improve myself and try to convince the authorities that I deserve a second chance," he ended up.

"That's admirable." Chaplain Chatham smiled at Jerry, but he looked like a man who'd heard too many promises from too many men who failed to keep them. "We'll certainly do everything on our end to help you. Are you interested in attending church services here in the prison?"

"I'm looking forward to it. I've gone to church ever since I can remember."

"Good." He looked down at some papers on his desk. "Your record says you are a member of the Baptist denomination."

"Yes sir. Where my folks live in Shelby County up in Kentucky, there's a Baptist church just across the field. When we moved there, we changed over from the Christian Church. My mother didn't much want to, but Dad and I didn't see any reason to drive a long way to church when we could see one right there beside us. But I've sung at revivals in lots of different churches. If you have a choir, I'd like to be in it."

"You sing tenor?"

"Yes sir, ever since I was in high school. Before my voice changed, I sang bass in a barbershop quartet at my junior high school."

"That's different. A boy usually goes from tenor to bass, not the other way around." The chaplain smiled again.

"I have a way of doing things backwards. You want to hear me sing?"

"That's not necessary since your aptitude tests show singing ability, but why not?" Chaplain Chatham leaned back in his chair and put his hands together.

Jerry sang the first verse of "The Old Rugged Cross."

"Nothing backwards about that." The chaplain scribbled something on a pad of paper. "I'll arrange for you to come to choir practice this week."

As long as he could sing, everything might turn out all right. The blisters on his hands turned to calluses as he kept digging ditches. He sang while he dug. Sometimes the other inmates joined in just like in some old prison movie. They sang everything from kids' songs to old hymns to pop songs.

Other times one of the men would get in Jerry's face and tell him to shut up. Jerry was ready to square off with any of the inmates, toe to toe, no matter how big they were. Jerry had flirted with death. No, more than flirted. He'd chased after death more than once, but he wasn't about to let anybody else push him over the edge. Not the tough guys who liked to flex their muscles. And not the men who sidled up beside him to tell him he was a pretty boy and they could make everything easy for him if he'd just cooperate.

Jerry should have been expecting it. His dad had warned him in a roundabout way. The guards told him to watch his step. A couple of older men in the dorm pointed out some inmates to avoid. So he should have known, but he was too young, too sheltered. The first time one of the men hit on him was like a bucket of ice water thrown in his face.

He didn't go down. He fired up. He stared the man right in the eye and told him nothing like that was ever going to happen.

"I've got friends," the inmate said. "We can take you any time we want."

"Maybe you could. If your friends are big enough. But you'd live to regret it. I promise you that," Jerry told him.

For some reason the man backed off. Jerry didn't know whether it was the crazy look in his eyes or if the Lord was holding his hand over Jerry because of his mother and dad's fervent every minute prayers.

The last of January his mother along with a church friend, Mrs. Williams, and his Aunt Adele came to visit. Since they had to come from out of state, the warden granted them permission to spend the day with Jerry. His mother brought a basket of food and Jerry ate until he couldn't swallow another bite. His father stayed home to do the milking, but he would make the trip the next time. Best of all, the captain of the guard let his mother give him his Bible, a hymnbook, his dictionary, and a shaving kit, which was completely against the rules. Everything was supposed to be mailed in. But then nobody could stand up against his mother for long, not even the Georgia State Prison guards. Especially when she was plying them with homemade brownies.

But the brownies disappeared and his mother had to go home. As the winter passed, he learned the rules of existence in Reidsville. He noted the troublemakers so he could stay away from them. He kept his mouth shut no matter what he saw. He ate whatever they put on his tray in the food line. He bought cigarettes every week even though he didn't smoke. Cigarettes were money in prison, and he wanted to get enough to trade for a radio. At least if he had a radio, he would have some connection with the outside world and he could hear music.

Music was the only thing keeping him sane. His mother sent him a book to teach him to read music the way he could read a book. He intended to be the best singer in the prison choir.

He put in his hours on the work detail. He read his Bible and studied his music books. He wrote letters home. He sang songs in his head. He tried to stay too busy to think about the days and months and years before he would be a free man again, but it was always there in the back of his mind.

The time stretched out in front of him like a row of tobacco with no end in sight. When he was in high school, they had a tobacco field with rows that must have been two miles long. While he was chopping out the tobacco, he sometimes peered ahead trying to see end of the row. When all he could see were more tobacco plants, he wanted to drop down in the middle of that field and just sit there because he was never going to get to the end of the row. Instead he'd keep chopping around each plant, one after another, until eventually he came to the last plant in the last row.

That's how prison felt. No end in sight, but he had to keep moving forward doing whatever it took to get through the next minute. Maybe someday there would be a last minute, a time when they opened the door and let him out and not just with a shovel to dig ditches while an armed guard stood watch.

That's what Everett told him. The days and the years would pass for him the way they had for Everett. Everett, who slept two bunks down, had been at Reidsville for eight years. He knew what he was talking about. Jerry reminded Everett of the little brother he hadn't seen since he got sent up. He wouldn't let his brother come see him or write to him. He wouldn't even let his mother send him a picture when his brother got married a few years ago. Everett didn't want his little brother to get the slightest whiff of prison.

The first time Everett stopped by Jerry's bunk, he gave him a long look. "I always hate to see babies like you come into the system."

Jerry's hand tightened on his pencil as he looked up from the letter he was writing to his folks. The man looked okay, but it was always best to be ready. "I haven't been a baby for a long time."

Everett slowly shook his head. "You're a just born baby in here. And you never know which way babies like you are going to go—to the bad or to the good."

"I'm not aiming to go bad. Least no worse than I already am."

"Maybe you won't, kid, but it'll take some doing for you to get through the years here with no scars. You're a pretty boy."

Jerry sat up straighter and narrowed his eyes on the older man. "You hitting on me?"

Everett gave him a sad smile. "Nope, just trying to help you. The way some old guys helped me out when I first came in. You need to get a duty away from the hard cases who'd just as soon hit you over the head with a shovel as look at you. Or catch you alone in the showers. Or out in the yard. Bad things can happen awful fast in here."

"I'm on outside duty. They said I had to wait six

months to ask for something different. That won't be till June or July."

"If you make it that long." Everett gave him another long look. "You can't ask, but that don't mean somebody else can't. I work in the shipping department. It's not a bad assignment. One of the guys over there is getting out next week. I'll see what I can do."

When Everett headed on back toward his bunk, Jerry called after him. "Why would you do that?"

"You remind me of my little brother."

"He in prison somewhere too?"

Everett whirled around to stare daggers at Jerry. "Don't ever say that again."

"Sorry." Jerry held up his hands in surrender. "I was just asking."

"Well, the answer's no. Always and forever no."

"That's good to hear."

"Yeah, it is good." The anger drained out of Everett's eyes. "He's a preacher at a big church up in Knoxville. I hear him on the radio sometimes when the signal's strong enough."

"I sometimes think about being a preacher, but I'd rather be a singer."

Everett's lips twitched up in a little smile. "Yeah, I heard you in the choir last Sunday. You not only look pretty, you sound like a girl."

Jerry clinched his fists and sprang off his bunk to face off against Everett. Some of the other guys in the dorm looked over at them expecting a fight.

Everett stepped very close to Jerry and kept his voice low. "First lesson, kid. Learn who's a friend and who's not. I'm a friend telling you the truth. You're pretty and you sound like a girl." The man poked his finger in Jerry's chest. "Worse than that you're stupid, but I like you anyhow. God knows why. So back off and live."

Jerry relaxed his hands. "Okay, sorry. I am stupid."

"Nearly every kid your age is. But most of them don't know it, so you're one step closer to smartening up. Another thing. Don't be so ready to fight. You ain't mean enough to fight in here. You better hope you never get that mean."

"Are you that mean?"

"No, but I'm that smart." Everett's thin lips turned up at the corners before he walked away.

CHAPTER 24

Jerry sang in the prison church choir two Sundays. Then the choir director quit and the chaplain called Jerry into his office and gave him the director job. Jerry was in hog heaven. He had to keep digging ditches during the week, but on weekends he got to sing. He aimed to make the choir the best ever, and he had the voices to do it if he could get them to reach down and pull out their best efforts.

The first practice on Friday went great. The tenors sang higher. The basses sang lower. All of them put feeling in their voices.

After the practice, Chaplain Chatham threw his arm around Jerry's shoulders. "Great job, Gerald. That's the best I've ever heard any choir here sing."

Some of the choir members came by to talk to Jerry before they reported back to their duties. "Hey, man, I like the way you give it all you've got," said one of the basses who'd hit notes so far down the scale Jerry didn't even know they were there.

A big guy named Rawlins with a jagged scar across his cheek stepped up beside them. "Yeah, Shepherd, we like the way you bounce around and listen at the same time. We're going to blow them away on Sunday."

"For sure you're going to be opening some eyes and ears Sunday. You've got a great voice." Rawlins had surprised Jerry by singing a solo part with a voice straight out of heaven.

Jerry practically floated back to the dorm. He was doing something good. Men ten times tougher than he could ever imagine being had paid attention to him and they had sounded good. He'd even seen the shine of tears in some of the men's eyes while they sang "Amazing Grace."

You couldn't direct emotion like that, but at the same time, Jerry had to tamp down his emotions in order to make sure each note was on key and in harmony before they sang at church. If the Lord wanted to use the music in some special spiritual way, that was up to him. Jerry just wanted it to sound good.

And on Sunday it did. They had two services with about a thousand men at each one. Jerry had led a lot of revivals, but he'd never sung to so many people at one time. Best of all, the inmates seemed to like it even if they were a captive audience. He was a captive performer. His parents had written to ask if they could come to church with him when they came down to visit, but no visitors were allowed at the prison church services. So he could only share with them how the choir was going in his letters.

He kept writing lots of letters. He even wrote to Judge Rutherford. His mother said it might help and she didn't see how it could hurt since Judge Rutherford told Jerry's mother how interested he was in Jerry's case. His mother must have been right because the judge answered Jerry's letter. He told Jerry to take advantage of every opportunity to improve himself while he was in the prison system until he had the chance to be paroled. Jerry turned his mind away from how many years that would be. He had to take things one day at a time.

Everett put in Jerry's name for the job in the shipping department. Jerry got the job. A few days after he started working on the line packing the prison uniforms Reidsville made in boxes to ship to other prisons, Everett pulled him aside.

"You know how to type, Shep?" he asked.

"No, but I guess I could learn." Jerry shrugged. "Why?"

"Well, it's like this. The Parole Board finally decided I've paid my debt to society and they're letting me out in a couple of weeks."

"That's great, Everett." Jerry made himself smile. He was happy for Everett, but he hated the thought of losing his friend so soon.

"Yeah, it is. And don't worry. You'll make out fine without me. You know the ropes now. Just keep your temper under control and don't be so ready to fly off the handle. Stay calm and live."

"That's what my dad tells me. I'm trying. I haven't socked anybody yet."

"And make sure you don't. You don't want to get written up and sent to the hole. Better to keep your record spotless." Everett frowned and shook his head a little. "But I didn't mean to give you no sermon. I just wanted to know about you typing. I've got a typing book and you can practice on my typewriter some in the afternoons. You learn fast. I know you can do it, so I'm putting you in for my job."

"Shipping clerk?"

"It ain't all that hard. As long as you watch the numbers."

"Numbers?" Jerry's stomach sank. "Numbers aren't my strong suit."

"It don't take a math genius, Shep. You keep a record of what's shipped out and where. What needs to be shipped out. That kind of stuff. And you'll be back here in the warehouse away from the hard cases. I'll get you in. All you got to do is learn to type."

"I'll learn to type." He'd practice till his fingers were sore.

"Good. Come on back to my desk now and you can practice on some shipping slips."

Everett sat beside him while Jerry hunted and pecked the keys. It took him three times as long as Everett but he got it done.

"See I told you it wasn't so hard," Everett said.

Jerry sat back and looked at the man. He had no idea how old Everett was. His face had the worn prison look of a man who had spent a lot of his life locked up. "What are you going to do when you get out?"

"First thing, I'm gonna take a big lungful of free air. Then if that don't make me cough too much, I'm gonna go to some restaurant and order all the peach pie with ice cream on it that I can eat. After that I'll go see my family."

"You have a wife and kids?"

"Nope. Not yet, but who knows? Maybe that's what I'll do after I get full of peach pie and ice cream." Everett smiled. "But my mother will be glad to see me."

"What about your brother? You going to go to his church and hear him preach?"

"I don't know." Everett looked over at Jerry. "What do you think, Shep? It hasn't been so long since you went to church on the outside. You think those good Christians would want an ex-con sitting in their pews? I wouldn't want to cause my brother no trouble."

"The people back at my old church pray for me all the time. I think they'd be glad to see me sitting in the pews there again. And I'll bet your brother would be glad to see you in his church. Besides, the Bible says we're all sinners, doesn't it?"

"Some more so than others."

"Not in the Lord's eyes. At least that's what my father always said."

"We aren't talking about the Lord here. We're talking about the good folks at my brother's church." Everett sounded doubtful.

"You won't be wearing your prison uniform when you get out." Jerry pulled out his button placket to show the blue stripe. "Won't nobody know you're an ex-con if you don't tell them."

"Maybe not. But I've heard some that got out and came back claim that free world people can smell you or something. That they always know. But one thing you can count on. When I get out of here, I ain't never coming back. If they throw up bets in the dorm the day after I leave on how long before I'm back, you bet on never."

Everett had a few days to train Jerry on the job before he walked out of the prison a free man. The first week after Everett left, Jerry had a run in with the prison boss over shipping. He didn't want to let Jerry off on Fridays to work with the choir. The shipping clerk job was a five day a week job and that was that. It didn't matter if Jerry worked extra the other days to keep the work caught up. It didn't matter that all the uniforms were getting shipped out on time and the orders written up without the first mistake. Nothing mattered except what the boss man said mattered.

Jerry had his worst week in prison up till then. He wasn't giving up choir director. He couldn't give up choir director. Music was his life. And it could be the Lord wanted him to do the choir. That's what he told himself anyway even if he didn't exactly open up the conversation with the Lord. Some things didn't need prayer. God knew already. The choir was like that. Jerry wanted to stay with the choir. He wrote his parents that he'd go back to digging ditches with work detail 22 before he'd give up leading the choir.

And it wasn't just the choir and the job conflict. Everything was going wrong. Everett was gone. He was out breathing free air and eating peach pie with ice cream. Jerry was glad about that, but he didn't have anybody to tell him to stay calm and clean.

Other guys talked to him, told him not to get jumpy, told him not to be expecting everybody to be sweet and kind. After all if they were all sweet and kind, they wouldn't be locked up behind barbed wire fences with guards on every corner. Bad things happened in prison. He had to make sure the bad, the really bad things didn't happen to him.

Things like happened to Bobby Joe. He wasn't much older than Jerry. Had only been there a week when they found him in the showers half dead. Things like happened to Jimmy who was always ready to play Jerry one on one on the basketball court out in the yard. The other guys told Jerry that Jimmy must have stepped on the wrong people's toes. Tuesday night Jimmy was in line four men up from Jerry for supper. The next thing Jerry knew, Jimmy was on the floor with a pool of red spreading out around him toward Jerry's feet.

Somebody pulled Jerry away. He didn't know who. He heard somebody talking in his ear, telling him not to look too close at anything. That some things were better not seen and they weren't talking just about the blood.

The guards locked down the prison. Nobody got to eat. Not that Jerry felt like eating. He stared at the ceiling above the bunk and listened to Oscar snoring below him. Oscar was a scrappy looking black man around forty. He was in on a life sentence for killing some white guy in a fight. Everett had told Jerry Oscar was innocent, that he'd gotten a raw deal, but Oscar didn't talk about it. He didn't talk much about anything. He mostly slept all the time, but tonight before he'd pulled the blanket up over his head, he said, "You'll get used to it, boy."

Jerry didn't see how anybody could get used to somebody getting knifed right in front of him. He kept his eyes wide open in the dim light. The dorm was never completely dark. The guards wanted to see the men in their bunks. The supper line hadn't been the least bit dark, but that hadn't made any difference. Jimmy still got a knife in the gut. Jerry was locked up in here with a bunch of animals.

It was funny when he thought about how he'd wanted to die all those years when he was a teenager. He drove into trees. Drank himself into a stupor. Swallowed handfuls of pills. But now, with death stomping all around him, he wanted to live. To do something with his life even if that life was spent behind bars.

He wondered if Jimmy had wanted to live. He didn't know much about him except that he had a great jump shot. He'd been in for a while. Would have been up for parole in a year or two. Now he was dead. Paroled to heaven. Or maybe not. Jerry tried to remember if he'd ever seen Jimmy in church. He wished he could remember seeing him there, but he couldn't. All he could see was the desperate fear on the man's face as he crumpled to the floor while his blood drained out.

Jerry wondered if somebody stuck a knife in him, he'd be paroled to heaven. He'd joined church. People said that was his ticket to heaven, but sometimes he wasn't sure. Preachers said you should be sure. That you weren't supposed to wonder about that. Not if you were right with God.

But how did you get right with God? He'd done what the preachers and his parents told him to do. He walked the aisle. He prayed. He sang hymns. He was willing to go back to digging ditches rather than quit directing the choir.

Then why did he still have questions?

For one, if he'd been right with God, he would have never done all the things he'd done. Not even if he was sick the way Miss Atwood said. He wished he were out in the field with his father planting something. Anything. He didn't care what. He just wanted to hear his father's voice. He wanted to hear his father telling him he could survive prison. No, not could. Would. He wanted to survive. He wanted to live.

In the morning, he'd write his folks. They surely didn't know how bad things were or they would find some way to get him out. And even if they couldn't get him out, then at least they'd know he wasn't just having some walk in the woods here. They'd know he was in a jungle with a bunch of wild animals who could jump out of the bushes and kill him any time they wanted to.

He started writing the letter in his head.

> *My lawyer says sit back and wait and you say take it easy and everything will be all right. Well, you know good and well that everything isn't all right, and I can't sit back and wait for time to pass. I'm under pressure. I can't plan ahead because I don't know what's going to happen from one day to the next. It's like a jungle. I'm alive one day and I may be dead the next. Just like Jimmy.*

Of course his folks didn't know Jimmy. They didn't know anybody here.

He mentally scratched out Jimmy's name. The censors wouldn't let it go out anyway. It might make the prison look bad if the free world knew people were dying in here.

He shut his eyes to try to sleep, but then the body sinking down into the pool of blood wasn't Jimmy's. It was his. Jerry popped his eyes back open wide. He began trying to lay out the typewriter keys on the ceiling above his head. He was trying to remember if the y was on the top line

under the numbers or on the bottom line when he finally
fell asleep.

He wrote the letter to his parents the next morning
before he went to breakfast. The cafeteria lines were just
the same as always with the men shuffling along fussing
about the food. Jimmy's blood had been scrubbed up off
the floor.

CHAPTER 25

Chaplain Chatham worked things out with Jerry's prison boss so Jerry could keep his job as shipping clerk and still direct the choir. A bit of a reprieve but not a complete one. The boss piled on extra work, but Jerry worked hard to keep things caught up.

He refused to let the boss man win. Every time Jerry felt like shoving the papers down the man's throat, he remembered how Everett had gone out on a limb pushing Jerry for his job. And while the boss couldn't do anything to Everett now since he was out there somewhere breathing free air and eating peach pie, Jerry still wanted to prove Everett was right about him.

To do that he had to stay out of trouble. He was trying. He really was, but the boss was ready to write Jerry up for any little mistake. He acted like he wanted to send Jerry to the hole.

Each new day got a little harder to bear than the last.

Jerry wrote home. His mother wrote back to tell him to stay calm, but she didn't understand. She wasn't inside this jungle with people shoving him toward some big hole with stakes in the bottom to skewer him. She didn't see Jimmy's blood spreading out at her feet every time she closed her eyes. She meant well, but he was glad his father was the one coming to visit in March. His father could tell him how to make it in a place where people kept beating him down. He couldn't trust anybody in this place. Nobody.

At night faceless monsters tormented him in nightmares and spiders crawled on him. Even worse, in his dreams, he'd be writing down orders and the numbers wouldn't add up. Finally one night he jerked awake after a particularly bad dream to see Oscar's face right in front of him. Jerry swung at him, but Oscar caught his wrist and held it in a vice grip.

"You gonna have to get hold of yourself, boy. You is messing with old Oscar's sleeping time," Oscar growled.

Jerry pulled in a shaky breath. "I can't help what I'm dreaming."

"You gonna have to learn to. This fighting bears and yelling all night right above my head is gotta stop one way or another. You understand what I'm saying, boy?" Oscar loosened his fingers on Jerry's wrist, but he didn't let go.

"You tell me how to stop it and I will." What did the man expect? Jerry didn't want to have nightmares.

"You think too much, boy." Oscar gave Jerry's arm a little shake.

"I can't quit thinking." Jerry wanted to yank his arm out of Oscar's hand, but the look in the man's eyes stopped him.

"Maybe not, but you can quit always thinking ahead or behind. What you got to learn to do is think right now. Think I'm eating now. Think I'm working now. Think I'm breathing now. Think I'm sleeping now. Don't let none of that other stuff come in while you're thinking them things.

Especially on the sleeping one."

"I can't...."

Oscar tightened his grip on Jerry's wrist and didn't let him finish. "I ain't hearing no can't. Think I'm sleeping now. Better yet think old Oscar's sleeping now. Think I ain't bothering old Oscar who don't like mad dogs fighting in the bunk over his head."

"I'll try."

"That's good to hear." Oscar turned loose of Jerry's wrist. "Cause you a nice enough boy, but fact is, I done been accused of snuffing out one white boy. I could do it again. They can't add no time on to a life sentence. They might put me in the hole, but leastways it'd be quiet down there and a man could sleep."

"Everett said you didn't do it."

Oscar smiled, but it wasn't a nice smile. "Then maybe the State of Georgia owes me one." He ducked back down to his own bunk. Two seconds later, he was snoring.

Oscar knew how to sleep. Most of the men in the dorm knew how to sleep. Snores echoed all over. Maybe Jerry could learn their way of sleeping. Just shut his eyes and think sleep. Forget about the boss man. Stop thinking about falling in a pool of his blood or worrying about a gang catching him alone in the showers. Just think this moment.

That's all the Bible said a person had anyway. The minute right now. Wasn't there something in there, something Jesus had said, about not worrying about tomorrow because there was plenty enough to worry about today? And nobody even knew if they'd have a tomorrow. A person's heart could explode inside his chest. A tornado could come along and blow the whole prison to kingdom come. Oscar could put a pillow over Jerry's face. Jerry didn't think the old man could take him, but he was pretty strong. Jerry rubbed his wrist.

The kids' song "Jesus Loves Me" popped into Jerry's

head. He hadn't sung that song since he'd helped with the music in Bible School years ago. *Jesus loves me this I know for the Bible tells me so. Little ones to him are weak. They are weak but he is strong.*

That was Jerry. Weak. But the song said Jesus was strong. Maybe he should ask the Lord to help him sleep without nightmares. That had to be easier than bringing Lazarus out of the tomb, and he'd done that.

What was it everybody was always saying? When all else fails, pray. Jerry wondered why people didn't pray before all else failed. He wished he had done more praying and less failing. Then he might not be in this place. He repeated the Lord's Prayer over and over, moving his lips silently. He didn't want Oscar back in his face.

At last the time for his father to visit got there. His father knew how things were inside from when he worked at the LaGrange prison. So when his father said to hold on and things would be okay, Jerry believed him. Maybe the boss man would get off his back. Jerry could find ways to stay too busy to think about the years stretching out in front of him. He could survive.

He was surprised when his mother wrote that she planned to visit Miss Atwood at the Milledgeville Hospital. His mother said she realized now she was part of Jerry's problems and while she couldn't do anything about the past, she didn't want to hold back his progress in the future. While there was no shame in making a mistake, it was shameful to not try to correct wrong actions. She wished she could go back in time and do whatever she needed to do differently to keep Jerry out of prison, but she couldn't. But she could listen to Miss Atwood and find out how to be the right kind of mother. After her visit with Miss Atwood, she would come to Reidsville for a visit and bring all his favorite foods.

The days passed. The boss man quit hounding Jerry when he finally opened his eyes to see how hard Jerry worked. Another inmate was assigned to help Jerry. Things got so much better in the warehouse after T.C. started working there that Jerry almost decided the man might be one of those angels Jerry had wondered if he'd find in prison.

The thought made Jerry smile. The big, ugly, rawboned man looked more like a linebacker than an angel. T.C. was in for bank robbery. Never killed anybody. Never even shot at anybody. The judge went easy on him the first time he got caught since T.C. played football at the local high school. He got light time, but after he was paroled, he went straight back to doping and hitting banks again to pay for the stuff.

"Folks always did say I was a slow learner." T.C. laughed. "But I've learned this time. If I ever get out again, I ain't never going in another bank. They tell me convenient stores have more cash anyhow."

One day T.C. came in from the dock area where they loaded the trucks carrying this pitiful excuse for a kitten in the palm of his hand. "Did you ever see such a sight? It don't have but two legs and no tail."

Jerry always liked the cats they had back on the farm. He'd rub them all the way down their back so fast their fur would crackle.

Jerry looked from the kitten to T.C. "But how does the poor thing get around?"

"Wait. You got to see this." T.C. put the kitten down. The little animal picked itself up off the floor, balanced on its back legs and jumped like a rabbit over to Jerry.

"That's the funniest thing I ever saw. It must be half rabbit." The kitten began purring the minute Jerry touched its head.

The week before, a letter from his dad saying he had a new pup had made Jerry extra homesick. He wanted to be at the farm watching the pup to figure out if it was a Chief or a King, a Jerome or a Hugo. He wanted to feel the pup licking his fingers and get mad when the dog chewed up his shoes. A two-legged, tailless cat might not compare to a German shepherd pup, but it was surviving when odds said it shouldn't.

"You think we could keep it here in the warehouse?" T.C. asked. "I could sneak it a little food now and again. And it might catch a mouse."

"I wouldn't bet on that. But then I wouldn't have bet on it being able to walk either."

"Or hop," T.C. said.

"Let's call it Cabbit. Part cat, part rabbit."

The cat helped Jerry settle into the prison routine. He still sometimes felt like a goat kid turned loose in a jungle of hungry beasts, but when he came into the warehouse and Cabbit hopped toward him, it was proof anything was possible. He could survive. The choir members might get more dedicated. He could hit those extra high notes on the new song he was learning. The Governor might give him a pardon. Anything was possible.

The choir did the best they had ever done the next Sunday morning. In the exercise yard that afternoon, men told him how much they liked the music and how he should be on the radio. Maybe he would be if he weren't stuck in prison.

And then the letter came.

CHAPTER 26

When Warden Stamper called Jerry in and handed him the fat brown envelope, he said he had discussed with Chaplain Chatham whether to give it to him at all. Jerry couldn't imagine what they were worried about. He'd never even heard of Joletta Ballard and had no idea why a woman he didn't even know would write him such a long letter

But Warden Stamper looked uneasy as he handed over the envelope and told Jerry he could decide whether he wanted to get more letters from her or let her visit. Visit? Jerry didn't even know who she was. If they were going to let anybody visit, he had some better candidates. Maybe Amanda Sue, the girl from back home.

Jerry didn't pull the letter out of the envelope until he was on his bunk after supper. A good thing because the first two words nearly stopped his heart.

Dear Son. What did that mean? Why was this woman calling him son? Jerry stared at those two words until they seemed to lift off the paper and float in front of him. He closed his eyes but he couldn't pretend he hadn't read them now. He had to know. He opened his eyes to look at the next line on the page. An icy hand squeezed his heart as he began to read again.

You may not remember me. Your father never wanted you to know who I was, but I am your mother. Your natural mother. The woman your father has told you is your mother all these years is your stepmother, not your real mother. I gave birth to you on January 3, 1950, and I almost died doing it. I'm not telling you this to make you think more of me, but just as a fact. I had a difficult pregnancy. Your father, he never gave me the first bit of notice when I would tell him what a hard time I was having carrying you. His mother had a whole pile of kids and he thought it was easy as baking a cake or something. He even told me she did bake a cake or canned beans or something the day she gave birth to him. But I wasn't his mother, and I came close to dying when you were born. He didn't know what was going on half the time anyway because he was always off working while I was stuck home alone. I mean I was just a kid. A 19 year old can't handle things like that alone. I had a sister that wanted to help me but she was all the way down in Tennessee and your daddy got mad whenever I went down there.

So there wasn't anybody close by to take care of me and it's not easy having a first baby. Especially when the daddy don't care about nothing but making more money taking on another run for Greyhound. You'd have thought that Greyhound bus was his wife. But I did have you. I walked right through all the

dangers of childbirth to have you. You were
my first. And even though we haven't seen
each other for a heap of years since you were
four years old, I'm still your mama and a mama
always has a special place in her heart for her
first baby, especially her firstborn son. There
wasn't no way I could ever forget you even if
your daddy did everything he could to make
you forget me. Along with that woman they
taught you to call mama when she never was
your mama. I am your mama. I remember the
day you were born. There was a little snow
and it was cold, but we made it to the hospital
okay. Then when you were born, you were so
tiny and precious. I haven't ever stopped
loving you even though I didn't come visit you.
It was just too hard seeing you there with
another woman acting like your mama when I
was your real mama.

Jerry quit reading. He kept his eyes on the papers in his hand, but he quit reading. The handwriting was big and loopy with frilly capital letters at the beginnings of the sentences and circles instead of dots over the i's. The strokes of ink looked flamboyant. Nothing like his mother's no nonsense script. His mother. Which mother? Both of them said they were his mother. Just like in that Bible story about two mothers claiming the same baby before King Solomon.

This had to be some kind of crazy joke. How could he have a mother named Joletta? He'd never heard of anybody named Joletta. He shut his eyes to see if his head would stop spinning, but that made it worse. His whole world was spinning like somebody had picked up his life and was shaking it around like one of those hand held games where the little balls roll into the holes except his life was opening up new holes he didn't even know were there.

A mother he couldn't remember. A mother he didn't even know he had. His mother wasn't his mother.

Little bits of memories edged into his mind. Some lady at church telling him how fortunate he was to have a woman like Hazel as his mother. Like that was a choice he'd made. His mother—Hazel—telling him how his father had sacrificed to give his son a good home. His son. Not our son. His feeling that if he didn't do everything right nobody would love him. The feeling he didn't belong to anybody, that he was just a visitor in his parents' house.

Jerry licked his lips and focused his eyes on the words in the letter. The woman, this woman who said she was his mother, went on and on about how much she loved him, about how she'd just been so young when she and his father had married. She wrote a whole page about how she wanted to see him, had wanted to see him for such a long time but didn't know how to go about it. But now with Jerry in prison, it seemed a good time since maybe she and her husband could help him.

She had remarried. Actually for the second time. The man she was married to now worked on golf courses getting the greens just right. Very successfully. They had money. They could hire new lawyers to get Jerry out of prison.

She wrote another page or two about her sister and her brother-in-law. She was sure Jerry would remember them since they had doted on Jerry from the day he was born until Jerry's father quit letting Jerry visit them after he married Hazel. She wrote how it was all Hazel's doing. That Hazel didn't want Jerry to have anything to do with his mother's family. She didn't have anything good to say about Hazel. Jerry read the words, but they didn't really sink in. He couldn't get angry. Not at this woman who said she was his mother. Not at his mom and dad who should have told him. Not at anything. At least not yet. He had to figure out what it meant before he got mad.

Jerry read it all, every word on every page and then he read it over again. He thought if he'd known what her voice sounded like he would have almost been able to hear her shouting in his ear. The words looked like they were shouting. But he didn't know. He had no idea what her voice sounded like. His own mother's voice.

She ended up begging to come see him. She said he was an adult now and didn't have to let his daddy decide everything for him. He needed to get re-acquainted with his mother. She loved him. She had another son from a different marriage and she loved him, but the love a mother had for her firstborn child was special.

She wrote more about this other son, Charles. She called him Charlie. Jerry skimmed over the words. He didn't care about how good this half brother was doing. This woman who claimed she was Jerry's mother had mothered the half brother. She hadn't just pushed that son off her lap and forgotten about him for years.

Jerry folded the sheets together and put them back in the envelope. Then he stuffed the whole thing under his mattress as quietly as possible since Oscar was snoring below him. Jerry didn't expect to do much sleeping. He needed a telephone to call his father and demand to know what was going on. He needed a jet plane to take him home to confront his mother—the woman he'd always thought was his mother—and ask why she'd pretended to be his mother all these years. He needed this Joletta to take a lie detector test to see if anything she had written was true.

How could a mother just walk away from her son and then out of the blue write a letter saying *Hi, it's me, your mama*? What kind of mother was that? Perhaps the kind of mother he had. And she wanted to see him. She wanted to help him. As if his folks hadn't already done everything possible. She was going to fly in here from nowhere and save the day like Superwoman or somebody.

Did he even want to see her? He felt all jumbled up inside. She hadn't ever wanted to see him before. She could have if she'd wanted to. His folks hadn't kept him in a locked room. She could have found him. Why had she found him now? What did she want?

He shifted on his bunk. Old Oscar's snores kept going. Jerry shoved his pillow up into a little ball and lay down. What was it Oscar had told him? That he did too much thinking behind and ahead. But how could he keep from thinking about a mother who'd popped up out of nowhere?

A million questions spun around in his head, but he couldn't come up with any answers. His parents would know the answers. His mother was coming next week. Well, at least the woman he'd always thought was his mother. She had a way of fixing things.

While she had never been able to exactly "fix" him the way she'd wanted to when he was a kid, she fixed other things. The church needed something, she did it. A job needed doing on the farm, she took care of it. For years, she worked for Greyhound taking care of things there too, before she married his father. His father said the whole company was sad when she quit. She bought their first farm while Jerry's dad was away on a Greyhound run, and then just told him they owned a farm when he called home. She took care of everything.

Jerry would show her the letter when she came. She wouldn't like this Joletta saying she was Jerry's mother, but she'd know what to do. She always knew what to do. He wasn't sure how she'd fix it, but she would.

He punched his pillow a few more times and shut his eyes. He ran a stream of words across his mind like a plane pulling a sign over a football stadium. *I'm not thinking about anything but sleeping. I'm sleeping now. I'm sleeping now.* Old Oscar gave good advice.

The next day he told the warden he wanted to talk to his folks about the letter before he decided about the woman coming to visit him. The warden thought that was wise. Jerry didn't say he was going to let his mother, his stepmother, Hazel, whoever she was, handle it for him. Then he threw himself into his work and didn't even look at the envelope holding Joletta's letter again until he pulled it out of his locker to take with him to the visiting room the day his mother came.

CHAPTER 27

The envelope lay between them on the table in the visitors' room like a coiled snake. His mother looked at it once when he put it there and said what it was. That had been awkward.

He practiced in his head what to say while walking to the visitors' room. *This is a letter from my mother.* He couldn't very well say that, because this woman he was going to see was his mother, the only mother he'd ever known. *This is a letter from Joletta.* He couldn't say that because it made it sound like he was on a first name basis with this Joletta while the truth was he wouldn't know her if he bumped into her on the street.

This is a letter from my birth mother. That was what he finally decided on, but it sounded strange when it came out of his mouth. His mother stared at him as though the floor had dropped out from under her and she had absolutely nothing to grab to keep from falling.

Her eyes burned into the envelope. Then she tightened her lips and pulled in a deep breath. "Why don't we talk about it later?" She pushed a smile across her face and started lifting plastic bowls and tinfoil wrapped packages out of her basket. "First, how about some food? I brought some of those fudge brownies you like. I had to be careful what I brought this time since I went to see Miss Atwood yesterday and everything had to sit in the car. I kept the cooler full of ice, but I wanted to be sure I didn't bring you anything that might give you food poisoning. Here's a can of Vienna sausages. I know you like them. And I found a Kentucky Fried Chicken restaurant on the way down here this morning. I knocked on the door and got them to open up early so I could bring you some chicken."

She tried to act relaxed and easy, but her voice sounded tight and her hands trembled as she unwrapped the brownies. He'd almost forgotten about her going to see Miss Atwood. He grabbed on that as something to talk about other than the letter.

"How was Miss Atwood?"

"Doing well." His mother's smile looked a little easier. "She had nice things to say about you and told me to tell you hello and that she hopes things are going well for you. I told her that, of course, everything isn't exactly great, but that you were directing the choir and hoping to get on as a chaplain's assistant soon. How is that coming?"

"I'm still hoping." Jerry dug a chicken leg out of the box his mother sat in front of him and took a bite. He chewed a while before he went on. "But I don't know if it's going to happen. Seems like something always goes wrong."

"Maybe not this time. Your dad and I have been praying extra hard for you these last few weeks because of how upset you sounded in your letters."

"Things happen in here that upset you."

"We know. That has us worried. Reverend Jacobson

says not to worry, just pray, but it's hard not to worry." She popped the top off a bowl of baked beans and stuck a plastic spoon in it for him. "I didn't think beans could ruin, and I kept them in the cooler. I tasted them this morning and they tasted fine."

"Yes, ma'am." Jerry dug into the beans. "They're better than fine. Way better than prison food."

She sat down to watch him eat. That was the one way they'd always been able to connect. She loved to cook for him, and he loved to eat. Carelessly, almost as if by accident, she dropped one of the dishtowels from the food basket on top of the envelope to get it out of sight. They had time. Because his parents lived out of state, the prison officials allowed them to stay all day instead of just a couple of hours.

They chatted about the farm and how much milk the cows were giving. She said his father named the new pup Hugo the way Jerry had suggested.

"You can't leave a shoe anywhere on the porch or it's gone. Chewed up and gone. Your father learned that the hard way. Lost one of his barn boots. You'd think he'd never had a pup before." His mother smiled. "But I don't guess either one of us has ever had a pet like your Cabbit. I can't imagine how that cat gets around."

"I wish you could see him, Mom. It's the funniest thing." Jerry stood up and gave a little hop to demonstrate.

They both laughed and when he sat back down, his mother put her hand over his. "You always were a funny thing." Her smile disappeared. "I'm sorry for all the things I did wrong when you were little. I don't know what I was thinking, but I really was trying to be a good mother. I didn't want you to grow up wild. I wanted to raise you right."

"I know, Mom."

"And your father and I didn't aim to keep any secrets from you about Joletta." Her tongue tripped a little over the name. She cleared her throat and went on. "You were four years old the last time you saw her. We thought you would remember her, but Miss Atwood says that it's unlikely you'd remember much about anything before you were five or six. Especially since you were getting moved around a lot and probably felt abandoned and lost some of the time. She says you might remember a face or some special thing that happened from those years. Of course, if you did remember a face it might be Carla's instead of Joletta's."

"Carla?" Jerry remembered the name from the letter on the table. "Oh, Joletta's sister."

"Right. Your daddy says she kept you more than Joletta did when you were a baby. Your daddy says she wanted you for her own. I guess I shouldn't find fault in her for that. I did too."

"I've been trying to remember, but I can't."

"I guess you were too young. And you stayed some with Mama and Papa Shepherd too, before Dewey and I married. We never told anybody in the family not to talk about it. We just never did talk about it ourselves. We did try to explain some of it to you that last time you came home from the army."

"I don't remember much about that weekend."

"I know." She squeezed his hand. "You were so tired and sick I don't think anything we said got through to you. But as for when you were little, I guess we didn't talk about it then because we didn't want you to feel sad about Joletta never coming to see you or calling or anything. She could have. We wouldn't have stopped her. We couldn't have stopped her. Your daddy got custody of you when they got divorced, but she had visitation rights."

"Maybe you should read the letter." Jerry pointed at it. "I can't tell you everything she said. She wrote a lot."

His mother looked at the tea towel covering the letter as if somebody had thrown up on the table and she was going to have to clean up the vomit. Her face turned stone hard. "All right. Do you want anything else to eat?"

"Yes ma'am, I do, but I couldn't stuff in one more bite right now. Just cover it up and I'll eat some more before you leave. Wouldn't want it to go to waste."

They wouldn't let him take any of the food back to his dorm. They always searched him when he left the visitors' room to be sure he didn't smuggle something into the prison, and as much as he loved brownies he couldn't chance a black mark on his record. He still planned on making it to trusty status.

His mother covered up the dishes and gingerly picked up the tea towel as though the envelope under it might have hatched little snakes that had crawled up into the towel. She shook the towel a little before she spread it over the brownies. "You might want to snack on these while we talk."

"I really want you to read it, Mom."

"If you think I should." She sighed and picked up the envelope. "My word. How many pages is it?"

"Thirty some."

"Good heavens. I wouldn't have thought Joletta could have written thirty pages about anything. She must have been trying to make up for lost time."

Jerry watched his mother's face as she read the letter. Color rose in her cheeks and she pressed her lips together so tightly Jerry thought they'd be bruised. Once or twice she looked angry, but she didn't say anything as she read through Joletta's words. Then, still without a word, she carefully straightened all the sheets, folded them, and slid them back into the envelope.

Jerry waited for her to explode, for her to tell him none of it was true, that Joletta wasn't his real mother the way she'd claimed, but she surprised him. She blew out a breath and said, "Well, that was interesting."

"But is it true?"

"It's true she's your birth mother. As for the rest of it, I think your father needs to answer that question. I never knew Joletta. I met her that one time she came to see you when you were four, but I didn't know her. I do know some of the things your dad told me about her when we first got married." She pressed her lips together again as if to keep from repeating any of those things. After a minute, she went on. "You know I wouldn't agree to marry your daddy until he gave me his word I could be your mother. I wanted to raise you. Even if I didn't always do it right, I wanted to. You're a wonderful boy with a good heart and I've known right from the very first time I saw you with Dewey that the Lord has a purpose for your life."

"In prison?"

"Maybe here too, but for sure when you get out. And you will get out. We, your father and I, are doing everything in our power to keep your case in front of the people that matter. We were so happy to hear Judge Rutherford wrote you. We can't be sure what good might come from that in the future, but it has to mean he hasn't forgotten your case. And since he's the one who sentenced you, it might make a real impression on the Parole Board if he recommended an early parole."

"Do you think he might do that?" Jerry asked.

"I don't know." His mother reached across the table and put her hand on his arm. "But I do know that I'll never give up till you're out of here. I'll do anything. Go anywhere. I'd write the President himself if I thought he would help. I'll be like that woman Jesus talked about in the Bible who kept pestering the judge till he granted her petition. And I know the Lord is hearing our prayers. He'll make a way out of no way and help you straighten all this out." His mother gestured toward the envelope. "Don't worry overly about it until your father writes you. He'll tell you the truth. He's always told you the truth. You believe that, don't you?"

"Yes ma'am."

"Good." She smiled. "So why don't we talk some more about the farm? Or you can tell me which songs you're going to sing next Sunday. And you say the men here in prison are flocking to church to hear all of you sing?"

Neither of them spoke Joletta's name again. She was there hovering in the background, but Jerry couldn't ask any more about her. He couldn't ask what she looked like. He couldn't ask if he was like her. He couldn't ask if it was something he did that made his birth mother abandon him. He couldn't ask if any mother had ever loved him.

But a couple of days after her visit, his mother answered that question in a letter she wrote in the parking lot before she left the prison.

> *Dearest Son and you are my son, the son of my heart if not my womb.*
>
> *I've always been better at saying what I feel on paper rather than in person. That's not good. I should have told you I loved you a million times when you were a little boy. I should have told you I loved you even more times when you were a teenager trying to hurt yourself with alcohol and by driving too fast. I should have said a zillion times how proud I was of you instead of always finding fault.*
>
> *I was and I am proud of you. I've never done anything in my life to compare to the honor of being able to raise you as my son. I love you, Jerry. Forgive me for not saying that more often. You are a wonderful person and I'm proud you are my son.*

Jerry put his mother's letter on top of Joletta's letter in his locker. Somehow that helped as he waited to hear from his father. Meanwhile he would remember old Oscar's advice and think on what he wanted to do right now. He wanted his trumpet. A little trumpet music would add some pizzazz to the church services. So he pulled out some paper and wrote to Warden Stamper to ask if he could have his trumpet sent to him. Then he wrote his mom and dad and signed the letter your loving son.

He didn't mention Joletta. He wasn't Joletta's loving son. He didn't even know Joletta. At this point he wasn't sure he ever would. But he did include her in his prayers that night. It wouldn't hurt to ask the Lord to bless her. The Lord had plenty of blessings to go around.

CHAPTER 28

A long week passed before his father's letter came in the mail. The letter was typed single-spaced. Jerry's mother must have typed it for his dad so the letter would fall into the prison's two-page limit for inmate's letters. Joletta's letter had exceeded that by a bunch, but they'd passed that letter on to Jerry.

His father started out by saying he wished he didn't have to write the letter at all, but he wanted Jerry to have the facts. After that Jerry's dad didn't pull any punches. Whether he wanted to write it or not, he had plenty to say about Joletta and none of it good.

His dad met Joletta on one of the buses he was driving. She told him she was eighteen, but she looked twenty-one. He didn't know she was only seventeen when they got married. His dad was twenty-four and had been home from the war for two years. Thirteen months later, Jerry came along, but Joletta wasn't ready to be a mother, something she had admitted in her own letter to Jerry.

As Jerry read his father's letter, he could almost see the grim set of his mouth and the hard look in his eyes. His father was strong, rock solid in what he believed was right and wrong. He didn't have much use for anyone who made excuses for failing to do the right thing in life. Jerry had seen that look himself often enough, but at least behind it he always knew his father loved him even when he was angry at him for messing up. If his father ever loved Joletta, those feelings had died a long time ago.

You were born Jan. 3, 1950 at Good Samaritan Hospital in Lexington, Ky. She had no problems and did not nearly die when you were born. She had the best medical help available. She did not want the responsibility of a baby and left you with her sister (against my strict order that you were to be kept home where you belonged), but I'd come home from my Greyhound run and you'd be at Carla's house 180 miles from home. You were gone so much you didn't know where home was nor who she was. I have seen you sit in her lap and cry for your mother.

Jerry looked up from his father's words to stare at the wall with his stomach in knots. Even if Jerry couldn't remember his mother, he didn't want to read bad things about her. Better that a missing mother had fallen in a river and drowned or nobly given him up to be raised by his father and Hazel because she thought they could provide for him better. Jerry didn't want to know his mother was a loose woman who hadn't honored her wedding vows and hadn't wanted to be a mother.

But that was what his father wrote. He accused Joletta of leaving Jerry with her sister so she could have more time for her boyfriends. He claimed he caught her with another man once when he came in early from a run. Even with all that going on, his father said he tried to make the marriage work.

> *She was given every chance to straighten up and make a home for you and me. She promised dozens of times, but never did it. She continued to have one affair after another and was dating four (4) different men in Jackson when I divorced her Nov. 3, 1952.*

Jerry could see his mother's fingers on the typewriter keyboard emphasizing the number four to make absolutely certain Jerry got the full impact of what Joletta had done. He was surprised the word wasn't underlined. Jerry shut his eyes. He didn't want to think about his mother typing the letter. Jerry forced open his eyes to start reading again.

> *After the divorce she cried and threatened and tried to make me take her back. The day after this outburst she went up north and married a Perkins. It was at Jackson where she left you several nights by yourself to cry all night while I was on a bus run. I didn't find this out until after the divorce.*

Had she really done that? Just put him in his crib and gone off and left him? His father said so. His father didn't lie. All the noise in the dorm faded away as he concentrated on the typewritten words in front of him. It was as if he had been transported somewhere away from here to a strange place he thought he'd never been before, but then when he looked around, he wasn't so sure. Something about it all felt familiar.

He was two and a half years old when his parents divorced. For the next year he was shifted about between his dad, his dad's parents, and the Dugans, Joletta's sister and her husband. His father claimed he had to let them keep Jerry because they kept threatening to go to court and find a way to take Jerry away from him for good. His father was afraid a judge might side with them since those weren't good times for a father to win custody of a child in court. He didn't want to chance another hearing and another judge. He wanted his son with him.

The only reason you were ever at the Dugans or anywhere else except with me was because Greyhound doesn't allow drivers to raise children on buses, and I had to make a living for us.

Then the accusations against Joletta got even worse.

You were about 6 months old when she and her current boyfriend tried to kill me with my own car for my Navy and Greyhound Insurance. In Jackson, she tried to have me shot.

Maybe that was where the other Jerry Shepherd had come from. The Jerry Shepherd who had done that awful thing in the Richmond Hills motel. Maybe it hadn't been a Jerry Shepherd he didn't know after all, but his natural mother coming out in him. Jerry wasn't sure if he wished his father had written more about that or if he was glad he didn't. He simply stated it as fact without the first line of proof or explanation of how he escaped death. Instead his father wrote about Joletta trying to force him to give Jerry to the Dugans after he married Hazel. His father said Joletta never once asked for Jerry for herself.

Jerry wanted to quit reading. Why hadn't his mother wanted him? At least Hazel wanted him. At least Hazel claimed to love him even if Jerry didn't always feel that love.

But in her letter, Joletta also claimed to love him. She'd gone on and on about how cute and smart he'd been when she last saw him when he was four and how it nearly killed her to leave him there with Hazel. His father's description of the visit was nothing like Joletta's.

> *In the fall of 1954, Joletta came by one night and stayed about fifteen minutes. She didn't tell you who she was and you didn't know her. She never showed up, called or wrote again until last May.*

That must have been after Jerry had been arrested. Joletta must have seen his name in the newspaper, but what about him being arrested had made her want to contact him after so many years of not caring? His father hadn't forbidden her to come. He even copied two paragraphs verbatim out of the divorce decree in the letter to prove it.

> *Dewey W. Shepherd is hereby granted the permanent custody and control of the infant child of plaintiff and defendant, namely Gerald Warren Shepherd, with the privilege of the defendant seeing said child at all reasonable times so as not to interfere with his health and education.*

Well, she hadn't done that. She hadn't interfered with anything while he was growing up since he didn't even know she existed. His father should have told him who she was when he was four. His father should have told him about her when he was six and when he was sixteen. It might have helped Jerry understand why he never felt as if he belonged anywhere. But his father didn't believe talking about Joletta would have made a difference. And he wanted to make sure Jerry knew he was nothing like his birth mother.

> *Son, these kind of character traits are not traits people are born with. They pick them up*

because they want to. You are certainly not like her. You are a decent, self-respecting, fine young man, and I and your Mom are very, very proud of you. I would give anything if I didn't have to write this letter, but we know you have the intelligence and ability to handle it.

Don't let this worry you, Son. It is all in the past and they can't hurt you now. I love you and so does your "real" Mom.

Jerry shut his eyes after he read his father's signature. He didn't need to read the letter again. It was burned onto his brain. Why couldn't his father have simply said Joletta left and went too far away to visit? Why did he have to prove she was such a bad mother? Was it so his "real" mom, Hazel, would seem like a better mother?

If only he'd just written the bare facts. Joletta gave birth to him. Joletta was too young to be a mother. He divorced Joletta. He couldn't take Jerry with him on his Greyhound runs. After a while he married Hazel and they tried to make a good home for Jerry. Maybe Joletta didn't come see him because she didn't want to confuse him. Maybe she moved to California or Maine. Maybe she lost their address.

She had contacted him here in prison—not exactly when a long lost mother might most want to show up to claim kinship. Why admit she had a convict for a son? Then again maybe she wanted to show up to prove she could have raised him better or at least her sister could have. Jerry tried to delve deep into his mind to pull out an image of either Carla or Joletta, but nothing was there.

What was it his father wrote? *Don't let this worry you, Son.* Good advice that sort of went along with Old Oscar's advice to not think about things he couldn't change. He'd sleep on it. Next week he might read Joletta's letter again and then his father's letter to figure out what was what. Then again, maybe he would never read either of the letters again. But could be he'd write Joletta and tell her she could come visit him. At least then he'd know what she looked like. A man should know what his mother looked like.

Maybe he'd even tell his folks that. He wouldn't keep secrets the way they had. How could it hurt to meet Joletta? That wouldn't change his Mom and Dad being his parents. Joletta couldn't get custody of him now. He was an adult. An adult in prison.

Of course she'd promised to help him get out. Everybody was always promising to help him get out, but he was still here. Locked up. He wasn't going anywhere for a long time. What could it hurt to see if Joletta had any tricks up her sleeve?

His whole past had blown up in his face. He wasn't who he thought he was, but he was getting used to the idea. His father thought he could handle finding out about his birth mother and he had. He could handle meeting her too.

He was curious about her. So what if people said curiosity killed the cat? Jerry hadn't seen the first cat actually killed by poking its paw into a black hole or climbing on top of a stack of hay bales to see what might be there. The hay might topple, but the cat could spring to safety. That's how Jerry would be. Ready to spring to safety no matter what might jump out at him next.

He hadn't expected a new mother to jump out at him, but now that one had, he wanted to see her. That wasn't a betrayal of his parents. If anybody had betrayed anybody, they had betrayed him by not making sure he knew the truth.

Jerry punched his pillow and tried to get comfortable. It might only be April but the dorm was already too warm. He didn't want to think about how hot it would get in August stuck in here with a hundred and twenty other men trying to breathe in the heat. Some of the men already had fans running.

At home on the farm, Jerry kept a box fan in the

window right beside his bed to draw in the cool night air. That damp air had felt like night licking his face as it blew past him to rustle the calendar on the wall by his door. He remembered lying in bed whispering prayers and imagining the fan blowing them right up to heaven.

His prayers now seemed to get stuck in a little cloud right over his bunk. For sure, there was no wind to carry them up and out through the prison roof.

He whispered, "Dear Lord, bless my mother and father and Amanda Sue. Bless Chaplain Chatham and help me do the right things to get the job as chaplain assistant. Give our choir strong voices Sunday. Help me, Lord, to live in here, one minute at a time so I won't go crazy with worry over everything. Bless Joletta and help me know what to say to her if I ever do meet her."

He lay there a few minutes before he added, "And help me not disturb Old Oscar's sleep. Amen." Then he blew softly into the air above his head. Maybe that would move the prayers on toward heaven.

He grinned at how silly he was being. God heard his prayers no matter where he prayed them. Every preacher Jerry ever heard preach on prayer said that. They might disagree on how a person should pray or what a person should pray, but they always said the Lord heard the prayers no matter what. There was even something in the Bible about the Holy Spirit praying for you when you were in too much misery to come up with the right words to pray on your own. Jerry had been miserable plenty of times, but he hadn't ever felt the Holy Spirit praying for him. A person ought to be able to feel that.

Sometimes after he sang a song in church, people would tell him he was full of the spirit, but all he'd ever felt full of was the song. Ever since he could remember, his mother had been telling him the Lord had something special in mind for him, but Jerry had no idea what. Nothing he'd thought about doing had ever seemed like

God's plan for him. Instead it had felt like Jerry's plan or a plan his mother or father had for him or something a preacher somewhere along the way thought he should do.

One sure thing, all their plans must have gone bust. It couldn't be the Lord's plan for him to end up in prison even if he was singing here and leading the choir. The Lord hated sin and Jerry had sinned big time. How could God have a purpose for somebody who had done what Jerry had done? Maybe the best Jerry could hope for was putting on a show to entertain the other inmates. If that was it, then he'd knock himself out and sing every chance he got. It didn't have to be church singing. He'd sing anything.

Singing was keeping the prison from winning and turning Jerry into a man who belonged here. He didn't belong here. He was going to get out. Someday. Someway. Somehow.

CHAPTER 29

Jerry told Warden Stamper he would see Joletta if she came to visit. Then he wrote Joletta, but the words didn't flow out on the paper the way they did when he wrote his folks. He wasn't sure what to say to a mother he hadn't even known existed a month ago. He also wrote his mom and dad to assure them he wouldn't let Joletta upset him. He didn't know whether that was true or not.

Then he sort of forgot about it. He was getting like Old Oscar told him he needed to be to make it in prison. Out in the free world, life kept happening the way it always had. People had babies. People died. Girlfriends got married to somebody else. People sold farms and bought new ones. Fields were plowed and crops were planted. Kids started school. Kids graduated. Dogs died. It rained and it snowed. The sun came up in the morning, and the moon slid across the sky at night.

Life went on, but without the men stuck in prison.

Here behind bars was a whole different world. Jerry had been inside long enough to feel the power of the place and how it was swallowing him. Some days he could hardly hang on to the hope of ever being a free man again. But then he'd wake the next morning and hope would be flickering within him once more. He watched other men getting their chance at the Parole Board. Some came back beaten down and defeated, swearing to not even try for parole again, but others returned with a release date floating in the air a few weeks away.

Even when that happened, even when they walked out the front gates as free men, the prison kept an invisible elastic band connected to them and often as not yanked them back inside. Any time one of the men was paroled or released the dorm started a betting pool on how long they'd stay free. The free world was hard, and some men ended up back in the prison world.

Jerry was determined not to let prison absorb him, but then he'd notice more loose hairs in his comb and worry he was going bald like his father. His heart would sink at the thought of getting old in prison. Nobody liked a bald singer.

He tried to explain prison to his folks since his mother was always on him to write whatever might make him feel better.

> You want to know what prison's like. Let me tell you. Prison is a place where the first prisoner you see looks like an All-American boy, and then you find out different. Prison is a place where hope springs eternal, where each Parole Board appearance means a chance to get out, even if the odds are hopelessly against the prisoner. It's where the flame in every man burns low. For some it goes out. But for most, it flickers weakly, sometimes flashes brightly, but never seems to burn as bright as it once did.

Prison is a place where you learn to hate through clenched teeth, where you want to beat and choke and kick and scratch but you don't know who you want to do these things to. It's a place where you feel sorry for yourself, then you get disgusted with yourself, then you get mad for feeling disgusted, then you try to mentally change the subject. Prison is a place, but the wrong kind of place.

I have seen what prison can do to a man, but it is not going to do me that way. I'm going to stand up against it till my last dying breath. I'm not going to let it get hold of me like it does others. I won't give up, but I will fight till I get my freedom. Prison is a place, but not a place for me and it knows it won't be able to hold me.

The weeks passed. It got so hot he would have paid triple price in cigarettes for a fan, but nobody would sell. Finally his folks shipped one down to him. At least with air blowing against him he had the illusion of cooling off when he went to sleep. Then the Georgia mosquitoes sneaked into the dorm and added to their misery. Even Old Oscar had to slap at them when they started sucking out his blood. Pretty soon the whole dorm smelled like bug repellant, and the mosquitoes kept up a constant whine in his ears as they searched for a spot of skin he forgot to spray.

He got up early and worked hard every day. T.C. got transferred to another prison, so he lost his helper, but he managed to get the work done. He liked being busy. He wanted to be so busy that the only thing that could sneak into his head was a snatch of whatever song the choir was singing the next Sunday.

He didn't make it as chaplain's assistant. He didn't dwell on it long. He just sat down at the typewriter with

Cabbit in his lap and thought up a new goal with the two-legged cat there to prove nothing was impossible. He set his sights on the jazz band.

Every Sunday afternoon, the prison put on entertainment programs. Southern Gospel groups and country western groups came into the prison to do their bit for mankind. Jerry didn't know much about either of those kinds of music, had never listened to country western and hadn't even known there was such a thing as Southern Gospel—trios and quartets that harmonized. The songs were religious but the kind that made a man tap his feet and clap his hands. Jerry liked it. Inmate groups shared the stage with the pros and radio disc jockeys came in to run the shows.

Jerry wanted to be on the stage with the other performers and have a chance to get to know the disc jockeys. He wanted to find out how to get started in the music business so that when he finally did get out of prison he'd know how to launch his singing career. Jerry set his sights on the jazz band since he didn't know the first thing about country western music. At least he'd heard some of the stuff the jazz band sang. All he had to do was convince Mr. Brodson, the prison official who ran the extra-curricular activities that he could sing better than anybody else in prison.

Jerry prayed Mr. Brodson would come to the church services and hear his choir, but he put feet on his prayer by writing Mr. Brodson to let him know how much he wanted to be part of the band. Didn't the Lord help those who helped themselves? He didn't know where it said that in the Bible. Maybe it didn't, but his mother and father said it plenty.

His singing plans kept him from worrying too much about the soap opera going on in the letters coming in from his folks and Joletta. His folks didn't think he should see Joletta. Then when Joletta broke the first date to visit Jerry, his parents claimed that proved he couldn't depend on anything she said.

After a while, he dreaded opening his parents' letters full of accusations against Joletta. He asked his folks to stop dredging up the past, but his mother couldn't let it alone. She kept harping on how Joletta was no good. Maybe Joletta did have problems when she deserted Jerry, but people could change. Here he was, doing his best to change.

Jerry still hadn't made the band when Joletta finally showed up on a hot day the end of June. Jerry's heart pounded up in his ears, his hands were sweating, and his mouth was dry as paper the way it was sometimes before he started singing in front of a crowd. Once he was into the song, he always forgot about being scared. Maybe after the first hellos his nervousness at facing his birth mother would fade away too.

That is, if he could figure out how to say hello. He couldn't call her mother and certainly not Mrs. Ballard, her married name now. Joletta. He'd just have to call her Joletta although that felt awkward on his tongue when he tried it out on the way to the visitors' room where she and her husband waited. He wished he could peek in at them before going inside. He should have asked her to send a picture.

He expected to feel a sense of recognition when he first set eyes on Joletta. After all, she was his mother, and he had seen her. He just couldn't remember seeing her. But there was nothing. No recognition at all. The man and woman watching him come into the room were strangers.

This woman with the bouffant black hair looked like she might be somebody's sister or maybe one of the country music singers that came in from the free world to entertain on Sunday afternoons, but certainly nobody's mother. Everything about her was small except the big hair. Her hazel eyes darted to Jerry's face and away while the tips of her red painted fingernails chattered against the tabletop. The man beside her looked much older than her with thinning hair and a paunch hanging over his belt. But he had the broad shoulders of a working man. He put his hand on top of Joletta's to stop her fingers bouncing.

Of course Joletta was only thirty-eight. Years younger than his mother who was older even than his dad. Jerry stopped a few feet from the table and said, "Hello."

Joletta glanced up at her husband standing behind her now with a hand on her shoulder as if to give her his strength. Then she pushed a big smile across her face even as tears slid down her cheeks.

She wiped at the mascara running from the tears and smeared black on her cheeks before she reached a hand toward him. "Hello, sweetie. Come on over and sit down."

When Jerry hesitated, she added, "I promise not to bite."

CHAPTER 30

He didn't know her. No echo came up from deep inside him at the sound of her voice. Still, even though he felt more than a little awkward, he could surely come up with some kind of chitchat to fill the visiting time.

So he sat down across from her. "Thanks for coming. In here, a visitor is a big deal."

"I'll bet." Joletta glanced up at the man behind her again. "This is my husband, Bob. I wrote you about him, remember."

"Sure." Jerry stood up to shake the man's hand. "Good to meet you, Mr. Ballard."

"Call me Bob." Joletta's husband gripped Jerry's hand. Then he squeezed Joletta's shoulder one more time before he sat down beside her.

"Bob." Jerry sat back down too. He looked at Joletta. "Are you a singer?"

"A singer?" Joletta looked puzzled. "What makes you think that? Because you sing?"

"Just curious."

"It's the hair, Jolie." Bob looked at Jerry. "She looks like Loretta Lynn, don't she? Except Jolie's lots prettier."

They all laughed and that seemed to break the ice. Joletta reached over and put her hands on Jerry's. He had to make himself not jerk away. He wasn't going to run out of the room just because she touched him, but she could have waited a few minutes before she latched onto him and tried to make him acknowledge her as his mother.

Her hands tightened on his as she started talking. "First off, I want to say how sorry I am that I didn't come around more when you were little. But it seemed for the best to let you alone. I knew your daddy and that woman he married would take care of you. They were church people who'd raise you right. Probably better than I ever could. My sister, Carla, you remember her, don't you?"

"I've been trying to," Jerry said.

"Well, anyhow, she was into church. Still is. And me and Bob go some now, don't we, honey?" She glanced at her husband again. "As long as Bob doesn't have to work. You know he does the grass on those big golf courses and if something needs doing, the folks that run those places don't like to wait till Monday. Especially if they're having a tournament."

Joletta paused like she expected him to say something, so he said, "Sounds like interesting work."

"Yeah, I think you'd like it. Bob says you can work with him when you get out. When we get you out."

"That's right, son," Bob said.

Jerry bit his tongue to keep from telling the man not to call him son, that he wasn't his father even if Joletta was his mother. If Jerry had learned nothing else in prison, he'd learned to keep his mouth shut or at least think first before he talked. "I would like to get out."

"You shouldn't have ever been put here in the first place," Joletta said. "Any fool can see that you're not a murderer."

"I did kill a man." Jerry couldn't deny that as much as he wished he could.

"But there were extenuating circumstances. There had to be. Like I said, anybody could look at you and tell you wouldn't hurt a fly under normal circumstances. They should have let you have a trial where that kind of thing could have been brought up." Joletta squeezed his hands.

As if he suddenly had an itch he couldn't ignore, Jerry eased his hands out from under hers to scratch his nose. Then he put his hands down in his lap under the table. "My folks are working with our lawyer to get me out."

"Sure they are, but we might be able to do some things they can't." Joletta clasped her hands together. "We've got a little money. Bob's business is good, and the truth of the matter is that money can make a difference. We'll hire you the best lawyer we can find down here. The lawyer you had was probably okay. I'm sure he was, but everybody I've talked to says you have to get somebody who knows the judges and the people on the Parole Board."

"He'd still have to go through my lawyer, Mr. York. He's the one who knows about my case and everything."

"No problem. All we want is the best for you, honey, and all of us–even your daddy and Hazel–know that being here in this place isn't good for you. You don't need to be in here with a bunch of hardened criminals."

"I'm managing," Jerry said.

Tears welled up in Joletta's eyes again. "You've always had to manage, haven't you, sweetie? You can't imagine how bad I've felt all these years, just going off and leaving you the way I did. I was just too young to be a mother when you came along. I told your daddy that. He was so serious, ready to settle down and do the grownup stuff, but I wanted to have some fun. I guess we should've never married. We weren't a thing alike, but your daddy was so cute sitting up there in that bus driver's seat and he took a shine to me. I'd never had a man like him looking at me. I mean he'd been in the war and there was something different about him. So we probably shouldn't have got married, but people are always doing things they shouldn't.'"

"I can't argue with that." Jerry smiled and then wondered if maybe he shouldn't have.

"But I'd give a lot to know you aren't harboring any ill feelings about the way I didn't take as good of care of you when you were a baby as maybe I should have."

"I can't really remember any of that." Jerry pushed out of his mind the things his father said about Joletta.

"I know, sweetie. You were just a little bitty thing, but now that you're all grown up and everything, you might be able to understand." Joletta glanced down at her watch. "We've got quite a bit more time. Let me tell you about what went on the way I saw it. I know I wrote a lot of it to you in that letter I sent you, but sometimes it's easier to explain things in person. Or harder. But I want to try."

So Jerry listened as she went through a lot of the same stuff she'd written in her letter. Some of it sounded rehearsed. Some of it didn't. She kept going over and over how young she was and how she and Jerry's dad just didn't see things the same way. She didn't say the first thing about having boyfriends or trying to kill his father to collect his insurance money. He considered asking her about that, but he just let her talk. Maybe his dad was wrong about her. Maybe she had loved Jerry the way she said.

She claimed he was a sickly baby who cried a lot. Her sister, older and more settled, could calm Jerry down better. And then with him down at Carla's, Joletta would get lonesome at the house by herself while his father was driving that infernal bus. Sometimes she believed he was next to married to the bus.

"He had to make a living," Jerry slipped in when Joletta paused to take a breath.

"I know that now, but I was too young to know anything then. Sort of like you were when you got into trouble. Too young to know better."

"I wasn't too young to know better." Jerry frowned a little. "I've known the Ten Commandments since I was seven. Thou shalt not steal. Thou shalt not kill."

"Yeah, I know them too." Joletta kept her eyes on his face. "Honor your mother and father. I might not have been much of a mother to you before, but I want to make that up to you now so you'll think I might deserve just a smidgen of honor."

"You aren't my mother." Jerry didn't intend to sound mean or anything, but she had to realize she couldn't just show up after sixteen years and pretend she'd never left. He tried to soften it a little. "At least not the mother I've always known. Hazel's that mother. But I appreciate you giving birth to me, Joletta." Her name wasn't as hard to say as he'd thought it might be. It just rolled right off his tongue without the least bit of trouble. "And like you say, it was probably for the best that Dad married Hazel. She's been a good wife to Dad and wanted to be a good mother to me."

Joletta's smile faded for a moment before it came back brighter than ever. "I made mistakes, Jerry. Lots of them. And believe me, I'm sorry for them, especially the ones that have to do with you. All I'm asking is that you let me try to make it up to you by helping you get out of prison."

Jerry liked the sound of that even if he didn't think she could do it. When he thought about his case in the stark light of reality, he wasn't sure he'd ever get out of prison. He had to serve seven years before he could even get a hearing with the Parole Board and other inmates told him that hardly anybody got out on their first hearing unless whatever they were in for was some nickel and dime stuff.

The State of Georgia was tough on making men serve out their terms and Jerry's term was life. He'd served a little over one year counting the time at Pembroke and sometimes when he thought about it that seemed like a lifetime. He couldn't imagine six more years in prison and then maybe six more after that on and on until one day he just didn't get out of the bunk when the guards started banging on the cells.

So he was ready to grab at anything that gave him hope of getting out of this place. His parents were doing what they could, but he was still here. Maybe the lawyer Joletta could hire with her husband's money might know a way out nobody had thought of yet. It was worth a try.

Back in his cell, Joletta's words kept echoing in his head. He told her what she wanted to hear, that he forgave her. She was just a kid back then. She made mistakes. She was sorry. Coming to tell him that took courage. While he wasn't sure he could ever say he loved her, he might develop some kind of affection for her.

He hadn't had much luck with women in his life. Before he'd ended up in prison, he'd never been able to please his mother. She always wanted him to be better than he was. Even teachers had a way of either expecting too much from him or simply disappearing from his life. He loved his first grade teacher. The school system made her quit at Christmas because she was pregnant.

Then there was Mrs. Gravitt in fifth grade. He liked going to school and having her smile and tell him he did a good job on his assignments. But one morning he went to school and the principal was standing beside another woman sitting in Mrs. Gravitt's chair. Mrs. Gravitt had died the night before. A heart attack, the principal said.

Jerry wanted to quit school. The new teacher didn't smile at Jerry. She covered his papers with lots of red marks. That made his mother yell at him too.

And now Joletta had found him, promised she'd be

there for him. Jerry didn't know whether to believe her or not. Either way, his folks weren't going to be happy he'd seen her. He worked a couple of hours on the letter telling them about Joletta's visit. He called her visit rewarding and wrote how he felt better about the whole situation of suddenly discovering this mother he didn't know about. Surely they'd understand that he wanted his natural mother to love him even if she had deserted him. He wrote that he and Joletta were friends and he hoped and prayed they could share those friendly feelings. Then he wrote a whole paragraph about how Joletta could never take the place of the only mother he'd known.

> *Of course I have made it plain to my natural mother as I will to you, Mom. She or no other woman can begin to take your place or be worthy of the love I have for you. The love I have for you is the love a son has for his blessed mother. My love for my natural mother is a grateful love for giving birth to me. Whether you can understand this or not, I do not know. But please always know this, Mom. You are, always were and always will be my mother. And I thank God for you.*

He hoped he hadn't poured it on too thick. Hazel was his mother and he did thank God for her in spite of their hard times. He turned his thoughts to his father. His father didn't have any use for Joletta. That was more than plain in the letters he'd written about Joletta. Still he needed his dad on his side. Jerry desperately wanted to believe Joletta could help him, but she could only do that if his parents and his lawyer cooperated with her and whatever lawyer she found. He chewed on his pencil a while before he started writing again.

> *I know, Dad, that you may not feel as I do, and your feelings in a way are justified. But it is in*

> *the past, Dad, where I'd like to see it stay. So*
> *I ask you, son to parents, to let the past be*
> *and accept the help and friendship they are*
> *so willing to give. As you know, I need all the*
> *help and support I can get. Please don't fight*
> *against Joletta, but work as a team for me.*
>
> *Your loving son, Jerry*

Jerry said a prayer and sent the letter the next day. He tried to imagine his mother and dad reading it and nodding their heads with little smiles as if they understood, but he couldn't hold on to that image. They were too against Joletta. They weren't going to be swayed by Jerry's sweet words.

Sometimes Jerry wished people had knobs like a radio so you could just tune them into a happy station with nothing but good music. That's what he decided to do to himself after he sent the letter. Tune out all the static and find a good station of hope. Besides, he had enough to worry about here on the inside without piling on more. He'd worry about staying out of trouble. He'd worry about not waking up Old Oscar. He'd worry about getting in the band. Three things. That was enough.

What he forgot to worry about a few days later was his footing as he loaded one of the trucks to ship uniforms to one of the road camps. One minute he was up on the loading dock. The next minute he was on the ground several feet below with his foot in a funny twist.

"My ankle's just twisted," he told the boss when he came to check on him, but he couldn't put any weight on it. They had to carry him up to the hospital floor.

CHAPTER 31

His ankle was broken. Just when everything had been going so well. Mr. Brodson had come to church, heard him sing, and even talked to Jerry about the bands. He wasn't in yet, but he was so sure he would be soon, he'd written his mother he was practically in the band in hopes she'd stop harping about Joletta.

His job in the shipping department kept him hopping, but he was getting everything done and done right. The boss man hardly ever got on his case anymore, and a new inmate had just started working in there with Jerry. Keevin had taken to Cabbit the same as T.C. had. Jerry wouldn't have to worry about the cat while he was laid up. Besides the cat was a survivor. Like Jerry.

Cabbit would make it as long as he stayed away from the trucks. Jerry was the same way. He needed to avoid the big trucks that could smash him here in the prison. He sure hadn't noticed many angels ready to help him out, but then maybe angels came in all shapes and sizes. Old Oscar might even be some kind of helping angel to set him straight on how to survive inside. Maybe angels were there around Jerry if he only opened his eyes and paid attention.

They wanted to bring in some doctors from Augusta to make sure the fracture was properly set before they'd let him out of the hospital. The days dragged by with nothing to do but lie there. Jerry begged to go back to work, but the prison doctor laughed and shook his head.

"Take it easy, Gerald. Most of the guys would be happy for a week or two to lie around and do nothing. Fact is, even if these bone specialists say the set is fine and we don't need to do anything else to your ankle, you'll be on crutches a while. You won't be able to go back to your shipping room job until you get the cast off."

So Jerry stayed in bed and fidgeted. He did leg lifts to keep his muscles from melting away. He read old sports magazines and sang until he was hoarse. He prayed for everybody he could think of, but still the time crawled by. He hated not having anything to do. He couldn't even write his folks to tell them about his ankle since he didn't have any paper or stamps. Being laid up in the hospital without his folks knowing it made him wonder how long it would be before anybody told them he was dead if he were to cross the wrong people inside these walls and somebody stuck a knife in his gut.

He was still in the hospital when Mr. Brodson asked him to be in the country western band. All the extra time praying must have paid off even if all his prayers had been for an opening in the rock and roll band. But a band was a band. He was ready to sing any kind of music if it meant he got to be up on the stage.

So once he got out of the prison hospital, singing became his job. He was still in prison. The beasts in the jungle might yet devour him, but from eight o'clock in the morning until four o'clock in the afternoon he didn't worry about anything except hitting the right notes and planning the band's act for the next week. Sometimes he sang the solo part. Other times he backed up the other singers. Usually that was Jesse who not only sang great but also wrote lonesome prison songs as good as anything playing on the radio. At least that's what the disc jockey, Lyle Keller, told them.

"You boys are good. If I could somehow get you all out of prison at the same time, I'd take you on the road and we'd make something happen," he'd tell them every week.

Lyle was so skinny his fancy clothes looked like they were draped on a wire mannequin. Dark-rimmed glasses dominated his narrow face until those glasses and his big nose were all anybody noticed. But what he looked like didn't matter behind a radio mike. His smooth voice and fast wit had big audiences tuning into his country music show that aired out of Nashville. Some weeks he taped their country band and played it on a local program in Augusta, but he had them half believing that someday they'd make the Nashville show.

In September they put on a show for a special meeting of the prison's Alcoholics Anonymous organization with between two and three hundred free world guests. A few months earlier Jerry had gone to his first AA meeting after Chaplain Chatham pushed him to join the group. The first thing Jerry had to do was own up to the truth that he was addicted to alcohol and that when he got out, he could never take another drink or he'd find himself in the same sorry, hopeless state he'd been in before he was sent to prison.

At the AA meetings, the men were encouraged to look to some higher power to help them through bad times. The literature didn't actually say the Lord. Each individual had to decide on his own higher power. And while Jerry still didn't know what the Lord wanted from him or even if the Lord could want anything from somebody who'd messed up the way he had, he did know, without a doubt, there was no higher power than God.

Jerry had never quit praying. He hadn't quit reading the Bible and singing church songs. He was grateful his folks and not just his parents but his whole family were praying for him. Yet, in spite of all that, his heart felt strangely empty. He kept trying to shove some convictions in there, but somehow nothing he came up with ever felt like his own convictions. He was leaning on everybody else's beliefs.

Now as he learned more about AA and thought more about the Lord as his higher power, the door of his heart began to edge open a tiny bit. Could it be the Lord did have a purpose for his life? Even if he never got out of prison, he might do some good things inside and be an example to others. Maybe someday he could point out the right direction to someone like one of those angels that kept stepping into his own path.

The show for the AA meeting went great. After Jerry sang "Danny Boy," the crowd cheered him back on stage to sing "I'm So Lonesome I Could Cry." The only way Jerry could have been happier was if it had all been happening out in the free world instead of inside prison walls.

With every show the band's fame grew. People said the free world bands the prison officials brought in weren't a bit better than their own Rebel Band. That kind of praise kept them working to come up with new programs to make the men laugh and cheer.

Jerry sang his heart out at every show where free world people could hear him. Mr. Brodson said if enough people got to talking about Jerry maybe that would help him get an early parole. Jerry told his folks once he would sing his way out of prison. Now it looked like that might actually happen.

For sure, the lawyers Joletta and her husband hired hadn't pulled any rabbits out of any hats. They came up with the same answer Mr. York and his parents had come up with. Stay out of trouble, keep a good record in prison, and wait for the Parole Board to review his case. In five plus years. Jerry liked the idea of singing his way out better.

So he put his heart and soul into his songs. He polished his gospel songs and pushed his voice to the upper limits in the tenor range. The band sang all sorts of songs, but when they sang gospel music, Jerry was always the star. Mr. Brodson even brought in a free world piano player, Perry Patterson, for Jerry since Perry had a way of banging out gospel music that fit Jerry's style.

With everybody telling Jerry he was great—the free world groups, Mr. Brodson, Perry, the people from Pembroke who came down every week just to hear him sing–he knew he could make it in the singing business if he could only get out of prison.

He'd sing so great they'd have to let him out. Jerry could almost feel it happening. He could imagine walking out the prison gates a free man and straight into some Nashville studio to become the next radio star.

The days passed, turned into weeks, then months. December came again. Every morning when he woke up with the bars holding him inside, he thought of something new he missed about Christmas outside. The shopping. The anticipation. The carols at church. The great food. Seeing family he hadn't seen since the last Christmas. Singing "O Holy Night" at a dozen different churches. The decorations. The smell of cookies and pies baking. Everything. His folks sent him boxes of food, but no matter how well the candy and cookies traveled, it wasn't like gathering around the table with family and saying grace before enjoying a holiday feast.

Not that he didn't enjoy the care packages that let him

gorge on sweet things. Plus it made him popular in the dorm and with the guards because he always got plenty to share. Sometimes one of the guards would stop him to ask when he expected a new package from home.

No amount of cookies in a box could make up for missing Christmas at home, but he couldn't change things. He was stuck there. He'd done the crime, and he had to pay the price. He knew that, but his heart still yearned for home.

Jesse got out. He was a short-timer anyway, and he got the good news from the Parole Board right before Jerry turned twenty-one on the third day of January.

Twenty-one. Back when he was fifteen, he and his buddy at Oldham High, Billy, had talked about turning twenty-one when they would legally be of age. Finally adults. They'd wondered where they'd be and what they'd be doing. Never in a million years would Jerry have ever thought he'd spend his twenty-first birthday behind bars.

The day after his birthday he got a letter from Amanda Sue. She wrote that even though she thought the world and all of him, she'd started going out with this guy at church. Jerry told himself he didn't care. He told himself he could barely remember what Amanda Sue even looked like unless he pulled out the picture she'd sent him. He had plenty of girls wanting his attention at their shows or at the big AA gatherings with all the free world people. Even so, his spirits took a nosedive.

So did the fortunes of the Rebel Band. With Jesse gone, it just wasn't the same. Jerry was happy for Jesse, glad he was free to go out and make his name in the music world, but he wanted to be out there with him. He'd done everything they'd asked. He'd sung his heart out. He'd prayed. He'd read his Bible. He'd gotten past the shock of finding out about his birth mother, Joletta. He'd forgiven his mother and father for keeping him in the dark about that. He'd made peace with them, and they'd quit talking about Joletta. He'd kept an iron grip on his temper in this prison jungle even when people did their best to push him over the edge. But he was still in prison. He couldn't sing his way out.

He took off the blinders of hope and looked squarely at another year in prison. No miracle was going to happen just because he wanted it to. The governor wouldn't suddenly pardon him. He was going to be in prison for a long time.

Jerry lost his enthusiasm for the choir. They were just singing words. None of it meant anything. The chaplain started pushing him to do things that he couldn't do, that the men in the choir couldn't do, so he quit. His parents weren't happy with him, but that was far from a first. They didn't know how it was inside. They couldn't. Nobody could who hadn't been there, who hadn't crept through the jungle searching frantically for a way out only to have more jungle vines growing up to choke him.

But then he bumped right into another angel, Millard Cleveland, assistant warden at Reidsville. Mr. Cleveland reached out and grabbed Jerry before he took that first step down the wrong road in prison. He pushed Jerry to get involved in two new prison programs, R-inc and Guides for Better Living.

"R-inc or Reclaim, Inc. was started by some inmates who wanted to stop the revolving prison door," Mr. Cleveland explained to Jerry. "Their intent is to help men change. Men like you, Gerald, who want to break the cycle and get off the treadmill of going to prison over and over."

Mr. Cleveland sounded like a revival preacher trying to get people saved. He even sort of looked like one of the preachers Jerry had known when he was a kid. He was about six feet tall and wide, not fat but stocky and strong. His suits always looked too tight in the arms and half the time he yanked his tie loose at his collar. He had a fire in his eyes as if he really thought he could make a difference.

"If I ever get out, I'll never come back," Jerry assured him.

"That's what everybody thinks, and believes on the day they leave here, but things happen. Things you can't do anything about. A man has to be strong."

"Yes sir, I'm working on that."

"I know you are, and I know you've got good parents supporting you while you're here, but some things nobody can do for you. Things you have to do for yourself. This course can help you succeed not only when you get out, but inside here too. I've kept tabs on you the last few months. How you've gone to the AA meetings and how well you've done with the band, but sometimes you're too ready to throw it all in when anything goes against you."

Jerry winced at his words. "You're talking about the choir, aren't you? It all got too stale. And I was always losing my best singers."

"I'm not talking only about that." Mr. Cleveland kept his gaze straight on him. "You have to stay focused, Gerald. Keep moving forward and not slip back because of things you can't control."

"Yes sir."

"Keep your eyes on the mountain."

"I want to, sir. I try to, but sometimes it's like I'm walking and walking and I look up and God has moved the mountain back a few miles until I'm even farther away than I was when I started." Jerry blinked in hopes the man wouldn't notice tears pushing at his eyes.

"The Lord doesn't work that way, Gerald. That mountain's closer no matter how it looks to you." Mr. Cleveland leaned forward in his chair and pinned Jerry with his stare. "You just keep moving your feet and you'll make progress. Keep growing so that when you are set free, whenever that is, you'll be ready to face the challenges of life on the outside."

CHAPTER 32

So he stepped back on the high road in prison. Bad things happened all around him. One kid about the same age as Jerry tore his blanket into strips, braided them together, and hung himself one night while everybody was sleeping. The boy had only been there two weeks and hadn't said the first word about anything or anybody tormenting him. He picked dying over learning to survive inside.

That could have been Jerry. He'd courted suicide often enough, but the Lord had protected him even from himself. What Jerry had never been able to figure out—still didn't know—was why. Was it his parents' unshakeable love and prayers for him? Or his mother's absolute certainty that his life was important to the Lord even when Jerry felt he wasn't worth two cents? Maybe it was simply because his mother couldn't stand to be wrong. Jerry had no problem imagining her storming heaven's gates and demanding the Lord give Jerry another chance. That she not only knew Jerry could do better, she'd see to it that he did.

Whatever the reason, the Lord kept giving Jerry more chances. Even in prison he had chances to improve and learn. The Guides course kept him so busy he hardly had time to write to his folks, but he could feel a difference in his life already. The focus on keeping a positive mental attitude sank down into Jerry's brain and took root there. He could eliminate negative thoughts that kept him down. He'd done bad things, but he could be–no, he was–a worthwhile person.

Even if he never got out of prison, he could do good things and help others not make the mistakes he had made. He could step closer to his parents. And if he did get out, he had abilities and energy to find his way and obtain the true riches of life. He vowed to learn everything he could to be ready if he did get to be part of the free world again.

The band took an upswing along with Jerry's spirits. Mr. Brodson found a new singer who fit in with their band, and The Rebels were on the rise again. It wasn't Jesse with his original songs, but they found plenty of other songs to sing. Mr. Cleveland began taking a special interest in the band. As their free world crowds grew, they got donations of new equipment and offers for radio time.

Out in the yard, grumbling started about how the black jazz band wasn't getting equal time on stage. The disc jockeys weren't taping their performances to air on the radio. Mr. Brodson tried to smooth it over. The prison was in the south. Country music was all the rage. The jazz band was getting as much stage time as the Rebel Band.

Besides, it was impossible to keep everything perfectly equal. As Mr. Brodson said, all singers weren't equal and right now the Rebel Band was made up of singers and musicians who meshed and didn't mind looking silly to make a show go over. They'd even dressed up in diapers to look like Cupid on Valentine's Day and shot paper arrows out into the crowd. When the song "Elvira" started playing on the radio, Jerry slapped on a wig and a dress to keep the audience laughing. The jazz band made fun of those kinds of crazy stunts.

Mr. Cleveland and Mr. Brodson took the Rebel Band on the road the end of April to another prison to put on a show. Being outside the prison walls felt great even if they were just driving to a different prison. Mr. Brodson promised them more trips. But in prison, promises were sometimes upended.

The end of May, Jerry's mother had her turn to come visit while his dad stayed home to milk the cows. They laughed and talked while Jerry gorged on the food she brought. Somehow they'd found a way to shut the door on the bad times they'd had when Jerry was a kid. His mother no longer talked about things he could do better. Instead she talked about what they'd do when he came home as if that might be next month or maybe tomorrow. She caught him up on the news about the people at church and the family. She talked about the cows and how the hay was ready to cut. If she noticed him getting the least bit upset, she changed the subject. The mother he'd had when he was six and sixteen disappeared when he went to jail. In her place was this new, more loving and sympathetic model.

On his side, he kept the conversation upbeat. He didn't want to upset her by talking about how a guy in his dorm got beat up because he dealt himself a winning hand in a poker game. He never mentioned the checkpoint guard who enjoyed making Jerry feel lower than a bug smashed on a rock by strip searching him in front of everybody. And of course he didn't say anything about Joletta's letters or visits.

So instead of telling her things that were eating right through him, he talked about the band and sang songs from their last shows or asked her advice about a crazy skit they were working up. He talked a lot about the Guides to Better Living course, because self-motivation, positive attitude type things were high on his mother's list. She thought anybody could think and pray things better.

She listened intently to his every word, then bragged on him. "I'm so proud of you, Jerry. Not many young men your age could handle what you've had to handle. And you're not only handling it, you're growing stronger in every way. Your dad and I are both so proud of you." She laid her hand on his cheek and smiled at him. Tears popped into her eyes but didn't overflow. "I'd do anything to get you out of here. Anything. You know that, don't you?"

"I know, Mom, but if it's not to be, then I just have to make the best of it till I can go before the Parole Board five years from now."

"No, five years is too long." With a shake of her head, her tears disappeared, burned away by her sheer determination. "We'll get them to review your case before that. I've been in touch with Judge Rutherford again. I won't let him or the Parole Board forget about you."

"It would be great if they'd look at my case and decide I was ready for release, but even if they don't, I'm doing okay in here. Did I tell you I've been picked as corresponding secretary for our Tatnall AA Group?"

"Yes, I know you'll be great at it." His mother smiled. "You've always been good at writing. Your letters home mean so much to us."

"I know I should write more, Mom, but things get busy here sometimes."

"It's okay. We understand. You've always been a hard worker." His mother patted his cheek.

"On the farm maybe. This kind of work is different, but I love it. I get to correspond with people all over the country. Just the other day, I got a letter from this couple out in Wisconsin. The man used to be an alcoholic, but he's been dry now for twenty years and he runs this great big farm out there."

"Wisconsin." His mother sounded as though Jerry had said he knew somebody from Mars. "They have a lot of dairy farms out there, don't they? You'll have friends all over before long."

"Nobody can have too many friends." He reached over and touched the hand she'd let fall back to the table while he was talking. "So even if we don't find a way for me to get out right away, I'll be okay. Guides is teaching me to keep the right mental attitude so I don't let every little thing push me down into a deep black hole the way it did before. I still have to live with what I did, but I don't have to let it paint everything in my life black. I need to go forward, so when I do finally get back out into the free world, I can be successful in whatever I do with the rest of my life."

"You'll do great things, Jerry. I've always known that. But I can't help worrying about you and wanting you home now."

"You'd better believe I'd like to walk out of here with you today, Mom, but things aren't that easy. I can't always expect everything to go smooth. I just have to make sure I can handle it when it doesn't."

"I pray every day, every hour, that the Lord will keep you under his wings, Jerry." Her eyes on him were intense. "And never, never underestimate the power of a mother's prayers."

He didn't. But he didn't think about it all that much either. His folks prayed for him. He prayed for them to make a neat little prayer circle. He did it automatically the way he got up in the morning and stripped down to take a shower. Part of his routine.

Time passed. He didn't exactly feel the Lord's wings hovering over him, but at the same time he was staying alive in the jungle. With their band gathering strength, more and more people were patting him on the back telling him how great he could sing. He graduated from the Guides for Better Living and became an instructor for the program. That along with the secretary work for the AA group and his band practices kept him so busy he barely had time to eat. And he was happier than he could ever remember being.

That seemed a strange way to feel since he was locked up in prison with more long years of confinement stretching out in front of him. But it was as if he'd taken life by the horns and was guiding it the way he wanted to go instead of just letting it pitch him around willy-nilly wherever. He tried to explain it to his parents in a letter.

Guess what??? I feel Healthy! I feel Happy! I feel Terrific! People here cannot understand why I'm full of happiness. Well, they just don't know what it is, but I do!! We can find happiness in what we are, not in what we have. I used to confuse happiness with pleasure. Pleasure is an agreeable sensation or emotion, while happiness is the basic quality of life. Right??? One of the reasons it is sometimes hard for people to have happiness is that they chase it too aggressively. I believe happiness comes when we least expect it. I might say to myself, I'm going to be happy, but it does not respond to this kind of treatment.

Happiness lies within. In a way happiness can be a habit. If we want to form the habit of happiness, we must develop certain things like: hopefulness, patience, love, good cheer, and a forgiving spirit. To be happy, make others happy! Right on!!! To have a good habit, have a happy habit!

Your Loving Son, Jerry

Two weeks after he wrote that letter, life tossed its

horns high and almost threw Jerry off. That Sunday their band could hardly wait to start performing. One whole section was filled with free world people while inmates filled the rest of the seats until the place was packed. The jazz band didn't play. Several of them were down with the flu and didn't even come out for the entertainment.

An up and coming free world country band took the stage first, but the crowd was restive while they played. The energy in the place was pulsing against the walls as the free world band cleared the stage and Mr. Brodson introduced the Rebel Band. When Jerry and the other guys ran on stage, cheers rocked the place.

They put on a great show and kept the crowd on their feet, clapping and singing along. The electricity in the air was so potent Jerry almost expected to see crackles of lightning flashing over the audience. His skin tingled as he sang the encore the crowd demanded.

After Mr. Brodson made them end the show and they had their few minutes of socializing with the free world band while they helped them pack up their equipment, Rusty, the drummer, grabbed Jerry's arm. He clicked his sticks in rhythm against his leg. Rusty was always clicking something. If he didn't have sticks, he tapped his fingers, toes, spoons, whatever he could find.

"Hey, come on, Shep. Let's head out to the yard and let the men tell us how great we are some more. I know you can't ever get enough of that."

"Man, it was something today, wasn't it? It was like an electric charge shooting through the air. You sure B.J.'s guitar didn't have some kind of short in it?" Jerry's ears hadn't stopped ringing from the noise of the band and the cheers.

"Don't blame me, Shep." B.J. ran his hands through his mop of blonde hair to smooth it down before one of guards ordered him to find a comb or worse, a barber. B.J. kept his hair as long as the prison officials would let him so he could whip his head back and forth to flop his hair against his face while he was playing. "It was all them high notes you bounced off the ceiling that came back down and fried their ears."

"I don't think we're going to be able to top this one, guys," Walt said. "I wish Jesse had been here to hear this."

"Jesse's out with a new audience now," Jerry said.

"Yeah, where we all want to be." Rusty tapped his sticks fast on the stage floor to make running footsteps.

"Don't be trying to put no damper on our spirits, Rusty. We may be locked up, but we can still sing and play," B.J. said. "So come on, we can clean up this place in the morning. Mr. Brodson won't care. Let's go do some celebrating."

Jerry started down the hall toward the yard with the other guys, but as he passed by the corridor that led to the AA office he remembered seeing Arthur, the head of their AA group that morning at church. He'd promised Arthur to type up some letters to other groups that afternoon. Jerry stopped. "I'd better not go out. I'm way behind with the AA stuff and all."

"Oh come on, Shep. You can do it tomorrow. Don't always be so responsible," Rusty said. "We're convicts, remember? Bad guys. The only thing we're responsible for is trouble."

"Can't argue with that." Jerry shrugged. "But I promised to get a bunch of letters out this week and I'm not exactly Speedy Gonzalez when it comes to typing. I better work on them. You guys go ahead. You can tell me all about it tomorrow."

"Yeah, I don't blame you." B.J. looked back over his shoulder as they went on up the corridor. "I wouldn't want to go out amongst all those crazy for women men either if I sang like a girl."

"Stick a sock in it," Jerry called after him with a grin.

That was the last time he ever saw any of the guys.

CHAPTER 33

Jerry was typing away when one of the guards yelled out in the hallway.

"You in there, Gerald?" Stevie sounded out of breath as if he'd been chasing somebody.

"I'm here," Jerry called back. "Something wrong?"

"Man, am I ever glad to hear your voice." Stevie came down the hall where he could see Jerry, but not all the way into the room. "I got to be quick. Bad things are going down. They put out a hit on your Rebel Band."

"A hit? On us? Who would do that?"

"Can't say. I done said more than I should, but I know you won't be telling and getting me in trouble. And best you know what's going on to stay alive." Stevie pulled a handkerchief out of his pocket and wiped his forehead. He was on the heavy side, but as strong as ten men. Nobody would mess with Stevie even if he didn't carry a gun and a billy bat.

Jerry stood up and stepped toward Stevie.

Stevie held up his hand to stop him. "Stay put. I'm locking you down in there. Nobody will be able to get to you in here so just sit tight till things settle down."

Jerry froze. "The guys okay?"

Stevie pressed his lips together in a grim line and shook his head. "The goons that jumped them not only had baseball bats but eight inch prison honed specials. Your guys didn't have a chance. Fists against knives don't even up too good."

Jerry had to swallow twice before he could ask, "They dead?"

"I wasn't out in the yard, so I can't say. All I'm knowing for sure is it was bad. Real bad. The whole place is on lock down, but since your name was on the hit list, you're better off here than in the dorm. Look, I can't talk no more. I gotta go bash heads to keep the place from blowing up. Besides, come tomorrow, you'll know more about what happened than I will anyhow. If you're still breathing." He grinned a little. "Don't look so worried. We aim to keep you breathing."

The doors crashed shut behind Stevie and the locks clicked into place. Jerry took a deep breath that felt inordinately good. He stared at the door another long minute before he sat back down in front of his typewriter and stared at the letter to the secretary of an AA group up in Indiana. He read over his words telling about how they'd added a new member to their group last week. That member had been Walt. And now Walt might be gone. Not just out of prison or transferred to another prison, but gone.

He might be gone too if the Lord hadn't sent an angel to keep him out of the yard by nudging him down the corridor to the AA office. Then again, maybe Arthur was the angel that morning in church when he made Jerry promise to get the letters out. Or could be his mother was the angel with her constant prayers for him. Earth angels watching over him.

"Thank you, Lord, for keeping me inside. For keeping me safe," Jerry whispered. Then he felt guilty thanking God for being alive when the others maybe weren't. Walt, B.J., Rusty, Jake, Pewee, Shorty. They could all be dead. Jerry felt weird as if he should be with them. He could almost feel the blades ripping into his body and the bats bashing out his brain. The muffled sound of alarm signals and running feet came through the locked doors, but in the AA office the silence banged against his ears. Just a few hours ago cheers had been echoing through his head. They'd thought everybody loved them. They were going to get out and go right to the top of the charts. Now they might not be going anywhere except to meet their maker.

Could be he was there too. Maybe he just thought an angel had pushed him toward the AA office and instead he was in a waiting room for heaven. Jerry shook his head. That was idiotic. He was at his desk in the AA office with his heart hammering in his chest, his blood swooshing around his body and his lungs taking in air. His fingers could feel the typewriter keys. Jerry typed the word the. The little ball on the electric typewriter spun around and clattered up against the paper. A good, ordinary noise. He stared at the stack of unanswered letters.

No need sitting there with his fingers trembling. Whatever had happened was done. He couldn't change it. Better to shut his eyes and pull up that positive mental attitude he continually harped on in his Guides classes. He was safe in here at least until they unlocked the door and who knew how long before they remembered him in here? Could be hours. He might as well finish answering the letters. Then whatever happened after they let him go back to the dorm, he'd at least be caught up on his AA work.

Besides, the guys might not be dead. Stevie hadn't

known anything for sure. He had just heard things. Rumors could flash like wildfire through the prison when something went down. Sometimes the fire flared up bigger from the wind in the mouths repeating the story until what had really happened and what was being told weren't much alike. The guards in the yard wouldn't just stand around and let bad stuff go down without breaking some heads to stop it. They would have been happy to break heads. The guys were probably getting stitched up in the hospital.

So Jerry locked out the fear and read over the half finished letter in his typewriter. He erased the first letter of the word he'd typed a few minutes earlier to capitalize it for the beginning of his next sentence. Then he typed up the details of their last AA meeting and their plans for the summer meeting with one of the free world groups.

Now and again, Rusty's face would pop into his mind or he'd think about how B.J. was always laughing about something stupid. Jerry shut those thoughts out. Better to concentrate on not hitting a wrong key. Typos were a pain to fix since he had to stick a piece of paper between the top page and the carbon copy to erase the mess up. Then he had to pull the paper back and erase the error on the carbon copy.

By the time a guard came get him, the letters were in their envelopes ready to go out. It was late. There would be no supper. When Jerry asked what happened, the guard told him to shut up and keep walking.

The prison was extra quiet as if the inmates' mouths had been locked down along with the doors. When the guard opened up the door to put him back in the dorm, every eye fastened on Jerry. Even the men who pretended not to be looking were watching him as he crossed the floor to his bunk.

Old Oscar wasn't in his bunk below Jerry's. Instead a big white guy with dirty blonde hair grinned at Jerry. He kept his voice low. "You must have a lucky star shining on you, boy."

"Where's Old Oscar?" Jerry asked.

"They done moved him over to the west side. He'd sure enough be dead if he was still over here. Ain't a one of us in here would let one of them live after what they done to the band."

"Old Oscar didn't do nothing, did he?"

"He did enough. He was born black." The man narrowed his eyes on Jerry. "It's them against us. If you didn't know that before, you better be knowing it now. That is, if you want to keep breathing. There's some that ain't and some more that ain't gonna be once we get to them. We've got long memories."

"Pipe down in there," a guard yelled from out in the corridor. "This ain't social hour. Be good little boys and go to sleep, and we might let you have breakfast in the morning."

"I'd like to put his name on a list," the big white guy muttered.

"We'd just get somebody worse."

"Maybe, but he'd be gone." The guy growled the words.

Jerry climbed up in his bunk and turned on his lamp. Moths and all their friends would be flying around his head in no time flat, but he needed the light. He kept his voice barely above a whisper and talked toward the ceiling. "My name's Jerry."

"I know who you are." The other man's voice came through the cot up to him. "You sing in the Rebels, or you used to sing in the Rebel Band. There ain't no Rebel Band anymore. You might be the only one standing now."

"No way." Jerry's heart clinched.

"They went down. A gang jumped them over around the basketball courts."

Jerry turned off his light. He didn't want any more of the man's words to crawl up the wall to his ears. He wanted

Old Oscar to be down there snoring and daring Jerry to do anything to wake him up. He wanted to go back to this morning and live the day over, only this time the whole bunch of them would stay in the theater and work on a new show.

That might have kept it from happening on this day, but that didn't mean it wouldn't have happened tomorrow or the next day. Then he might have been in the middle of it. Not that he was safe because he hadn't been out in the yard when it went down. The beasts in the jungle wouldn't forget him. He'd have to watch his back every minute of every day.

Maybe they'd transfer him out of here. He'd actually been approved for a transfer to another prison months ago, but what with the band going so well and him so involved in AA and teaching the Guides for Living courses, they'd filed the idea away. Why move him when everything was going good here at Reidsville? He was almost up to trusty status, his major goal when he first came into the prison. And rumors were floating around that Mr. Cleveland might get a job at a new facility being built as a model prison down in Montgomery. He could get Jerry transferred there when it opened. But would it open soon enough to help him now?

The man below him quit talking and started snoring. Jerry stared up at the ceiling, thankful he could still pull in air to fill his lungs.

The next morning an old inmate named Harry filled Jerry in as they ate breakfast. Harry had been at Reidsville for over ten years. Jerry didn't know exactly what the old man had done to get locked up. He couldn't imagine Harry killing anybody, but then when he thought about it, he couldn't imagine killing anybody himself and he had.

Harry was short and skinny with a bald head that made Jerry think of his dad. His faded blue eyes looked tired of seeing as they stared out of his weathered face. Being on the ditch digging detail in the hot Georgia sun for long years had dried up and cracked his skin like an old piece of leather. Now because of the way his fingers were twisted with arthritis, Harry worked in the barbershops sweeping up hair clippings. It was rumored the old Cajun sometimes put a snippet or two of the hair in his pocket and played at voodoo. Jerry didn't believe it. He liked Harry, and while the wrinkled old man didn't talk much, when he did say something, every word was true.

"Were you out there where it happened, Harry?"

"I was." Harry gave him a look. "Lucky you weren't."

"Are they all dead?"

"Maybe not all of them. It was crazy like those pictures you see on television of them fish down in South America or wherever. Them kind that strip the flesh off a man in nothing flat."

"You mean piranhas?" Jerry shuddered.

"Yeah, whatever they're called. That's how it was for those boys. The poor suckers didn't have a chance. Must have been two dozen of them, maybe more, and only five or six of your boys."

"Where were the guards?"

"Same as always. Not where they needed to be." Harry slurped his coffee. He wallowed the drink around in his mouth before he swallowed. "They came running and did some shooting and bashing, but it was already too late for a couple of the boys."

"Which ones?"

"Can't say. I backed off at the first flash of a knife. I ain't got no fight with nobody. But I think I saw them carrying B.J. out to the hospital. With all the blood, I couldn't be sure, but it was a big guy and B.J.'s the biggest of you boys. One thing sure, whoever it was looked more dead than alive, but I reckon he must have still been breathing or they'd have pulled the sheet up over him before they carried him in. Then again maybe the guards just wanted us to think he was breathing."

"Why would they do that?"

"So the white boys would back off and give them a chance to herd them that did it inside before the whole place exploded. It wasn't far from it. I'm surprised it didn't."

"Why'd they do it?" Jerry asked.

"Rumor going around says the Jazz Band got sick of you guys getting all the candy and decided to put you out of the singing business. Permanently."

"Not Adrien and Joel surely. Or Burton." Jerry couldn't imagine any of Jazz Band wanting them dead. They had shared practice times for months.

"I ain't saying names. I'm just telling you what's going around, but if I was you, I wouldn't go anywhere near the west side of this place for a long, long time. In fact, it could be you should go beg them that pull the strings to let you go somewheres else." Harry looked at him over his coffee cup. "You ain't never gonna be safe in here again."

"We weren't doing any harm. Just having fun singing."

"Not no more. They seen to that."

CHAPTER 34

With the blacks all on the West Side and the whites all on the East Side, things began to settle back into a routine. Jerry got up, went to eat, did his jobs without ever seeing a black face. Both bands were disbanded. All entertainment programs were canceled indefinitely. Mr. Brodson transferred to another prison. Jerry quit even singing when he took a shower. It seemed wrong somehow to sing when all the others were gone.

He never found out for certain what happened to them, but the rumor mill had Rusty and Walt dead and B.J. and Shorty the next thing to it. The rest of the boys had been shipped out to other prisons. Every day when he got up, Jerry expected to hear they were moving him out. But the days passed and he was still there.

That's what he told his folks each time he wrote them. *I'm still here.* It was a silly thing to write since he was locked up and had no choice about going anywhere, but at least it told them he was alive and breathing. Of course they didn't know how close he'd come to not breathing. He wrote them about the place being in an uproar because of trouble between the blacks and whites, but he kept the reasons why on the vague side. He did tell his dad enough of the story when he came down to visit in June to explain why the band had been shut down.

Jerry was careful not to tell too much and start up the worry machine on the home front. Better not to let his folks know about the shivers that ran up and down his back when he walked to his job at the AA office or how he kept expecting somebody to jump out of the shadows and take him down.

He was glad it was his dad's turn to visit while his mother stayed home to do the milking. His father never seemed to want to know about anything bad going on at the prison. Jerry never had to explain things in living color detail to his dad the way he did to his mother. She always asked him a million questions. In contrast, sometimes when his dad visited, they ran out of anything to say once they'd covered how much milk the cows were giving and how the crops were growing and what was going on at church. That never happened with his mother. His dad said that was because women didn't appreciate how a little silence every once in a while let a man gather his thoughts.

A week after his father was there, Miss Atwood came to see Jerry. She'd heard about what had gone down in the prison and wanted to help. She looked the same—short, sturdy, in control, with her brown hair chopped off just below her ears. She kept pushing her glasses up on her nose while she talked the same as she had when she'd counseled him at that chamber of horrors, the State Hospital.

"I've changed positions," she told him. "I'm a counselor at the Richmond County Correctional Institution in Augusta now. It's a road camp. Nothing like here. And if I can get you transferred there, I think you'll be in a better place. You've done well here at Reidsville, but it's time for a change. Especially now with all the tension here. It could still boil over at any time, and you'd be safer out of here if that happens."

"Yes, ma'am." Jerry had no argument with that. He was tired of listening for footsteps behind him in this jungle.

"I've kept up with what you've been doing here, and your mother has been writing me too. In spite of the trouble the two of you had in the past, she cares deeply for you. I don't believe there's anything she wouldn't try if she thought it would get you out of here."

"I know. She says you don't know what might work until you try it. But so far, the Parole Board just keeps telling her I have to wait until my regular parole date comes up. April 1976."

"Right. That must seem like forever to you." Miss Atwood gave him a sympathetic smile.

"Almost four years from now. And the men in here say that hardly anybody gets paroled at their first hearing." Jerry felt depressed even talking about it. He didn't usually think about the date so far in the future.

His Guides to Better Living course and his AA literature said a person shouldn't dwell on things he couldn't change. Instead, he should take positive action like writing a letter to someone who might help him or researching what the Parole Board needed to consider an early release. It was better to plan how to make something different happen than to sit around worrying about what was happening.

When he told Miss Atwood that, she looked at him as though she were a teacher and he was her prize student. "It's good to hear how you can think things out now. You're really doing well, and I don't want to see your progress falling back. So if you agree, we'll work on getting you transferred to Augusta. Trust me. It will be better for you there."

Two weeks later, a guard caught him before he went to breakfast and told him to pack his things. He was moving out. He didn't have much to pack. His fan, some music books, a few letters and pictures from the folks at home, his underwear, his ink pens and radio. Maybe reception would be better in the new prison. His trumpet was locked in the band room, so he lost that.

He couldn't tell anybody goodbye. There wasn't time. He scribbled out a couple of lines to Harry.

> *I'm being transferred out. Not free, but maybe someday. Stay as tough as ever. J.*

He really didn't care about telling anybody else goodbye except the guys he worked with in the AA office, and he could write to them after he got to Augusta. The only other man he wanted to tell goodbye was on the West Side. He would have liked to tell Old Oscar he was leaving and that he appreciated him not killing him when Jerry disturbed his sleep. He even thought about telling Oscar that he'd once wondered if Oscar might be an angel the Lord had dropped down in Jerry's path. Old Oscar would laugh at that for sure. At least as much as Old Oscar ever laughed which was just a sort of heavy heave of breath.

♦ ♦ ♦

At Richmond County, the buildings looked more like a school than a prison. Nothing like Reidsville. They drove through a gate in a fence, a regular wrought iron fence without any barbed wire or spikes at the top. Even the air inside felt different.

Maybe that was because he went in as a trusty from day one, or maybe it was because he could breathe in and out without wondering if he'd better enjoy the privilege of filling his lungs with air while he could. He saw plenty of black faces in his dorm and everywhere he went since races weren't segregated at Richmond, but he didn't feel the first hint of tension between the blacks and whites.

They were all the same—men serving out their terms. Jerry had been lifted up out of the jungle of Reidsville and taken to one of those modern zoos that didn't believe in cages. The inmates at Richmond did their assigned jobs and came back in at night to be fed and locked in. Nobody was out to devour anybody else. Nobody had to wander around in the hopeless fog of life with no chance at parole like some of the Reidsville inmates. Here everybody had hopes of getting out. Even Jerry. Maybe not soon, but someday.

Jerry was assigned to the chapel as assistant music director and chaplain counselor. Miss Atwood made sure the people at Richmond knew about Jerry's musical talents. The chaplain, Elton Foster, was a great lead singer, and luckily enough the two other chaplain assistants sang bass and baritone. Or as Chaplain Foster said, luck had nothing to do with it. Jerry joining them with his tenor voice to complete their quartet was the Lord's providence.

Jerry was back in the singing business big time, and he loved it. He had great voices in the choir, most of them coming out of black faces. But these faces were smiling at him, laughing with him, paying attention when he told them how to make the choir sound better and better. Jerry got what his mother called holy goose bumps every time the choir sang.

Chaplain Foster heard the call to preach when he was a teenager, but years passed before he discovered his true calling of working with men who needed to transform every aspect of their lives to become the men the Lord wanted them to be.

"Every man has a calling," he told Jerry. His dark blue eyes were intense and the lines on his face deep and serious. His black hair fuzzed up at the ends and sprang away from his head with no respect for a comb. Chaplain Foster never worried about how he looked. He said the Lord looked on the inside, and he had too much work to do on that part to worry about how the outside looked. "It's our duty to seek out and find that calling, to see what the Lord has in mind for us. We're not to think about what we want to do and see if we can fit it into the Lord's plans. We just need to jump right into the circle of God's purpose for us."

"My mother's always saying something the same about how the Lord has a purpose for me, but what if I never figure out what that purpose is?" Jerry asked.

Chaplain Foster's eyes got even more intense on Jerry when he answered. "It's a blessing to have Christian parents, but a man can't hold onto their shirttails forever. You can't find out what the Lord wants from you by way of your mother, Gerald. You have to go directly to the Lord. Go right up to the throne and ask what cross he wants you to carry because all men, all people, have their own cross. We can't pick up somebody else's or the one that looks best to us. The Lord picks it for us. But, praise the Lord, if it's heavy, he's right there beside us, helping us carry it on down the road of life. That's what our drama tries to get people to see."

Chaplain Foster liked showing people the messages the Lord laid on his heart instead of just telling them about it. With all inmate actors, he took one of those messages to the churches on the outside through a drama called *The Challenge of the Cross*. Chaplain Foster said if he could reach people for Christ using men who were paying their debt to society then he was surely changing all their lives for the better.

Going out the prison gates and into free world churches felt great. They wore their prison stripes, but nobody at the churches seemed to mind. In the drama some of the inmates would sit out among the congregation. The inmate playing the role of the evangelist would throw out a challenge for someone to come up and take a cross from the container at the front. One of the inmates would jump up out of the pews and say, "I accept the challenge." He'd go forward and pick a cross, usually a small one.

The evangelist would stop him. "No, brother, that's not the cross the Lord has chosen for you to carry. You can't just come up here and pick up some easy cross you think you can get by carrying. The Lord is talking to you here. You can't be listening to what you want. You pay attention to what he's telling you. He'll show you which cross to pick up." He'd pick up one of the bigger crosses and hold it out toward the man.

"But that one looks too heavy," the man would say. "I can't carry that."

"And who made your back?" the evangelist would say. "The Lord, that's who. If he doesn't know what you can carry, who does?"

Everywhere they went, the powerful message of the drama inspired people to make decisions for Christ. Jerry and the others in the quartet stood in the background and sang songs about the cross. They had no music other than their voices. Singing a cappella seemed to give the words of old hymns like "The Old Rugged Cross," "Near the Cross," and "Wherever He Leads, I'll Go" extra power. It was like old times when he was a teenager singing in churches where people out in the pews dabbed their eyes when the message of the songs touched them.

As he listened to the actors arguing about which cross to take and then the church people coming forward with glowing faces to rededicate their lives, Jerry felt a tug or two on his own heartstrings. He sometimes felt that kind of glow while he was singing, but when the song was over, the glow seeped right out of him and left an empty place in his heart.

He told himself his heart wasn't really empty. He was doing plenty for the Lord. His whole life revolved around singing for the Lord. His songs made people feel spiritual. He could see it on their faces when he sang. And he said his prayers. He prayed for his family. He prayed for the other men in prison. He thanked God for keeping him alive and helping him have a positive mental attitude. He read the Bible when he had time and wasn't too tired at night after all his other duties.

That surely was purpose enough. Maybe he wasn't supposed to feel anything more. He might be imagining that others had something he didn't have. After all, hadn't the Lord been setting down angels in the crossroads of his life? Pete and Mama Harmon, Miss Atwood, Mr. Cleveland, even Old Oscar. While Jerry hadn't always gone down the right roads, he'd recognized the Lord's hand in his life. Why was he always expecting something more?

He talked to Chaplain Foster about it. He told him how he walked the aisle to accept Christ when he was twelve. "Everybody kept telling me it was time to go forward, and I felt like I should. They knew more about what Jesus wanted and all than I did."

"Jesus just wanted your heart, Gerald. Did you give him your heart?"

"I think so. I meant to."

Chaplain Foster smiled at him. "If you truly did, you'll know it. And if you didn't, there will come a day or night when the time will be right." The chaplain put his hand on his shoulder. "I'm praying for you. The Lord will show you which cross he has for you to carry. And when he does, you'll know it. My prayer is that you'll be ready to pick it up."

CHAPTER 35

O n a sizzling hot day in August, they took *The Challenge of the Cross* to a church youth camp about forty miles from the prison. As they unloaded their sound equipment and set up the props for the drama, heat rose up off the ground in waves.

When some of the men wished for an air-conditioned church, Chaplain Foster told them to stop grumbling. "Did any of you ever read the first thing about an air-conditioned church in the Bible?"

"I'm guessing there weren't no Georgia summers either." Sam, a big black man with a deep bass voice, wiped the sweat off his face.

Chaplain Foster laughed. "There's plenty of hot desert country in the Holy Land."

"Desert heat ain't the same as Georgia heat," Sam said. "Desert heat is just hot, dry baking type heat, but Georgia heat makes a body feel like a dishrag that's done been dipped in boiling water on top of a woodstove and then wrung out and left to steam on the back of the stove."

"Man, would you hush up?" Jerry told him. "Don't talk about hot stoves. Talk about ice boxes or snow."

"Can't talk about snow. I ain't never seen no snow."

"You're kidding," Jerry stared at Sam.

"Nope. Not the first flake. You ain't in the north no more. You in the south now."

"Well, let me tell you about it." Jerry looked up and held out his hands as if he could wish down some snowflakes to catch. "Snow can come down soft and fluffy and pile up deep as your knees in no time flat, or it can come down hard and mean with the wind whipping it in your face and drifting it up over the fence posts. You can do a back flop in a nice smooth patch of the white stuff and wave your arms to make a sweet snow angel. Trouble is all that arm waving pushes plenty of snow right down your collar. Believe me, snow down your collar cools you right down."

"Well, I ain't got no snow down my collar and I ain't a bit cooler." Sam flapped his shirttail to make a breeze.

"Jerry isn't either on the outside, but his brain's done froze," Dave spoke up with a grin.

Dave, the baritone in their quartet, and Jerry had hit it off from the first day. Dave had a wife and kids on the outside, but he let alcohol and drugs mess him up. He was off the stuff now and had Jesus in his heart, but he still had to pay for what he'd done. That meant he couldn't be home with his kids, and what kind of daddy could he be only seeing his kids on prison visiting days?

A few months after Dave got sent up, his oldest boy was diagnosed with leukemia. It tore Dave's heart out every time little Davey had to get a treatment because he wanted to be there to hold his son when things got bad for the boy. Dave wanted to do whatever he could to keep others from making the same mistakes he'd made.

Now Dave's smile faded as he looked around at the men. "Shouldn't none of us be complaining about a little hot weather. The Lord gave us this opportunity to tell kids about Jesus. A little sweat won't hurt us."

"Oh, quit preaching and find a power outlet." Jerry pitched him an extension cord.

"I've already found my power outlet." Dave pointed up at the sky.

"The best source of power." Chaplain Foster looked up at the clouds and frowned. "But I'm not liking the looks of those clouds. I hope the storms slide around us."

As the young people filed in to fill the wooden chairs under the big shelter, thunder played an accompaniment in the distance and lightning ran jagged streaks along the horizon.

Heat gathered with them under the flat roof of the shelter and sweat was soaking through their shirts before they finished singing one verse of "The Old Rugged Cross" for a sound check. Moths and hard shell bugs clicked against the floodlights on the shelter.

Chaplain Foster led them in prayer before they started. "Here we are, Lord. Use us. Lend us your power as you open hearts to receive your word. If it be your will, hold off the storm and help us present the message you want these people to hear. In your precious holy name we pray. Amen."

As they began the play, dozens of fresh young faces watched while the air fairly crackled with electricity. The lightning licked at them from the edges of the campground, but some unseen force seemed to hold the storm back and keep the shelter a safe harbor in the midst of the storm.

The men pushed their voices to the limit to be heard over the thunder, but nobody missed a note or flubbed their lines in the drama. They forgot the sweat rolling down their faces and their shirts sticking to their backs. They forgot the lightning flashing around them. They forgot the bugs dive-bombing their heads. They forgot everything but the message the Lord was channeling through them out to these young people.

And the kids were right there with them. They didn't giggle or whisper to one another. Every eye was fastened on the actors and singers.

Even before they started singing, "Take up thy cross and follow me," Jerry knew something special was happening. At the first word of the invitation song, kids leaped out of their seats. Practically every person in the crowd came forward to make decisions for Christ. The men stopped singing and got down on their knees to pray with the young people.

Tears mixed with sweat as they knelt in groups. Jerry put his hands on the young boy's shoulders next to him and someone else put his hands on Jerry's shoulders. All at once the spirit slammed into Jerry and the door to his heart was knocked wide open. He felt Jesus, not just in his heart, but in every inch of his soul and being. At last, he understood what everybody had been telling him. He did know. This was what the Lord wanted from him. Not merely lip service and prayers thrown out into the dark of the night. Not just his songs, but his heart and soul, his whole being.

With joy, Jerry surrendered it all to the Lord as he accepted Jesus as his Savior, his Lord, and his God. He finally believed the Lord loved him in spite of the bad things he'd done. Not just with his head because people told him so, but with his heart. As sure as he could feel the damp concrete under his knees, he knew that the rest of his life he would be a witness to the love and forgiveness of the Lord.

A prayer rose from his heart. "Dear Lord, I'm yours. Use me to demonstrate thy love and mercy. Help me grow in the spirit as I dedicate my life to thee forever and ever. Amen."

A rush of raindrops spattered down on the shelter's roof and then the storm turned and passed them by, leaving behind a cooling wind to sweep through the shelter. Chaplain Foster moved from group to group, encouraging the young people to go back to their home churches and share their decisions with their pastors.

When at last every young person had been prayed over and Jerry rose up off his knees, he was a different person. He'd come into the shelter, a man unsure of his path or what was in his heart, but now the Lord filled his heart.

Chaplain Foster put his hand on Jerry's shoulder. He'd been crying and his voice was hoarse. "I've never seen a night like this."

"Me either," Jerry said.

Chaplain Foster gave Jerry a closer look as if Jerry's very voice sounded as different as he felt. Then the chaplain smiled and gripped his shoulder harder. "Didn't I tell you you'd know?"

"Praise be the Lord." Jerry almost sang the words.

"Why don't you lead us in a couple of verses of 'Amazing Grace' to close out the night."

Jerry started out and those in the shelter joined in. As the voices rang out clear and true, shivers ran up and down Jerry's back. The words of the song were true. How sweet the sound. Angels must have come down to sing along with them.

CHAPTER 36

B ack at the prison, Jerry looked the same in the mirror when he shaved in the mornings, but he wasn't the same. Everything was different. Even the Scripture he read over the intercom in the morning to get the day started seemed different. Before he'd read the Bible dutifully because people told him he should, but now he wasn't just reading words. He was reading a message written for him, and he wanted to know what that message meant. So he enrolled in a Bible study correspondence course.

Things were different on Sundays too when he went out with the quartet to sing and give his testimony in churches. It was no longer simply a performance or a way to escape the reality of prison for a few hours. Now when he talked about what the Lord had done for him, how the Lord had protected him and watched out for him even when he was straying—no, more than straying—running

251

down the wrong paths away from God, his words had conviction. He personally knew the Savior he was talking about, and he wanted everybody else to know him too.

At the churches, Jerry sometimes saw himself in the teenage boys in the pews. He recognized the desire for God warring against the temptations they faced out in the world away from their families and churches. From the way some of them turned their eyes away from him when he talked about how alcohol and drugs had stolen his youth, he figured they had already started down some wrong paths. After all, he'd sat in a lot of church pews on Sunday mornings after he'd drunk himself unconscious on Friday or Saturday nights.

Jerry wanted to go grab those young people and make them really see the prison stripes he wore. He wanted them to see what alcohol and drugs had done to him and might do to them. If only he could be the angel in their crossroads to stop them from going down wrong roads the way he had.

But he couldn't force them to listen. He could only tell what Jesus had done for him and could do for them. Some did listen and came forward with tears in their eyes and a new life in their hearts. Others stayed stuck to their pews, but sought out Jerry or one of the other quartet members after the service.

Sometimes a boy would look at Jerry and say, "Man, I might do a little partying now and then, but I could never do what you've done. I could never kill somebody."

"I pray you're right," Jerry would tell him. "That's what I would have said when I was your age. I didn't care about my own life, but I never dreamed I might take another man's life. But when you start down the road with the devil, things can happen you can't even imagine."

The boy would shake his head. "I wouldn't never have no truck with the devil."

Jerry would look straight in his eyes. "Who do you

think is putting that beer in your hands or slipping you that pill and telling you how good you'll feel if you swallow it? Who do think is laughing the next morning when you wake up sick as a dog or when you get in trouble at school?"

Some listened. Others didn't. As Chaplain Foster reminded the men the Lord was in charge of the harvest. The Bible said to sow the seed, broadcast it far and wide, and pray that it would find good ground to take root and grow.

Chaplain Foster was tireless in seeking places for them to take their stories and the drama. Somehow he got them in Bell Auditorium in Atlanta in front of fifteen hundred people to put on the drama. When they gave the invitation, more than a hundred people came forward. Everywhere they went, people made decisions for Christ. Jerry felt as if the Lord had turned a spotlight on over his head that let people see what a difference the Lord could make in one man's life if he moved away from the darkness of sin into the light of life.

In August his folks hired somebody to do the milking and came down together to see the quartet sing. It was the best visit ever. He was in prison, but his parents were proud of him. His mother even told him in person that she loved him. She'd written it in her letters, but he couldn't remember actually hearing her say those three words to him. Even more amazing, he said "I love you" right back without the words tripping over his tongue and getting stuck on his lips.

They were a family. Maybe not the usual Mom and Pop family since Joletta was still lurking in the background even if he hadn't heard from her since she and her husband moved to California months ago, but more of a family than they'd ever been. He told his parents that in his next letter home.

Words cannot express the feeling I had being

with you Sunday. This move here has got us all on cloud nine. And Sunday night, it's still hard to believe the change. It would never have been like that at Reidsville. I know Sunday night we were brought closer together as one family. I love you both very much and thank God that I've got two wonderful parents like you!

Who would have ever thought he'd have to go to prison to feel as if he belonged with his parents? That strange lost feeling he had as a kid had vanished. He knew who he was now. He knew his parents loved him. Best of all, he knew Jesus loved him.

The quartet went to South Carolina to sing at Chaplain Foster's home church and then Warden Talbout's church. They recorded a television program. Jerry did his Bible study lessons and got A pluses. He even asked his mother to send him some math books, so he could tackle that roadblock in his mind.

He could do math. He checked into taking some college correspondence courses. With the help of Jesus, he could do anything, including win a silver medal in ping-pong at the prison Olympics. He might never get out of prison, but at least he was serving the Lord and keeping his mind and body strong and positive.

Then things changed at the prison. Warden Talbout had a heart attack. They quit letting Jerry have counseling sessions with Miss Atwood. She sent him a message not to worry, but two weeks later she was gone, her position eliminated. Chaplain Foster explained the prison had lost funding for the social programs. Warden Talbout had another more serious heart attack, and Mr. Marley, the assistant warden, took over. Mr. Marley decided they had too many chaplain assistants. Since Jerry could type, Mr. Marley moved him to the newspaper office.

Jerry didn't mind the newspaper work, and Mr. Marley

let him keep working in the chaplain's office after six in the evenings and on weekends. Mr. Marley didn't stop the quartet from going out to sing, and the church choir was as strong as ever in spite of some of the best singers being released. New singers came in to take their places. They started work on a new drama to present the Christmas story in scenes while someone narrated the Bible story.

Jerry worked to hang onto a positive attitude. As Chaplain Foster told him, sometimes a person just had to bloom wherever he was planted even if that meant he had to squeeze out between the rocks of all the restrictions of prison to reach toward the sun.

Dave's son died a few days before Christmas. A guard accompanied Dave home for the funeral. He came back on Christmas Eve, and so Jerry spent his fourth Christmas in prison comforting his friend. They sat in the chapel, read Bible verses to one another and cried.

"Why didn't the Lord take me instead of Davey?" Dave asked. "He was just five years old with his whole life ahead of him. He was such a good little boy. Marlene said he was smiling at her right to the end and telling her about the angels he was going to play with up in heaven. And me, what was I doing while my boy was dying? I was stuck here, not doing anybody any good."

"That's not true," Jerry countered. "You've been a blessing to me and you've brought people to Christ with your singing."

Dave's head drooped over. Tears dripped off his face and made wet splotches on the wooden floor. "But I wanted to be my son's father at home, not a man who had to have a prison guard with him to attend his son's funeral. Why did we ever let the devil get such a hold on us that we ended up here?"

"I don't know. But I guess that's why the Lord wants us to keep telling our story so we can keep others away from places like this."

Dave gave Jerry an anguished look. "But do you think anybody listens? Did you listen when you were a kid?"

"Not to my folks. Not to the preacher," Jerry admitted. "But I might have listened to somebody like me. I might have. And if even one kid listens, that's something good."

"Right now I can't think about other kids. Only Davey." Dave wiped his eyes.

"I know. The Lord understands. He's right here beside us crying too."

"Do you really believe that?"

"I really do."

"Read Psalm 23 again, Jerry."

"The Lord is my shepherd; I shall not want." Jerry read through the Psalm once and then again. Somehow they got through the day.

Three days later, a guard called Jerry out of the newspaper office. "Pack your bags, Shepherd. You're being transferred out of here."

CHAPTER 37

The move took Jerry totally by surprise, but when he heard Millard Cleveland was an assistant warden at the institution where they were sending him, he was happy to go. At Reidsville, Mr. Cleveland had taken a personal interest in Jerry, and now he was dipping him out of the pool at Richmond just as the water had begun to stagnate there.

"It's the Lord's doing, Jerry," Chaplain Foster said. "The good Lord's been right beside you all the way and now he's moving you to a place where you'll have even more opportunities to shine like a beacon to lead others to him."

He clapped Jerry on the back and wished him luck before leaving Jerry alone with Dave to say their goodbyes.

"Don't forget me, buddy." Dave hugged Jerry as he fought back tears.

"Never, brother. You can't forget somebody when you're praying for them every day."

"Do you think I could hide in your duffel bag and you could carry me on down there with you?"

"I would if I could, but the guards don't allow no passengers."

"I know. It's not like we can pick and choose which five-star hotel they put us up in." Dave's lips trembled as he tried to smile.

"That's true enough. And somebody has to keep up the good work here with Chaplain Foster. I'll pray for the Lord to send you a tenor."

"Now are you saying you're going to pray some nut who sings like a girl will do something he ought not to do to make the State of Georgia lock him up in here with us so we can keep our quartet going? You think that's something you ought to pray?" Dave's smile got wider, more like Jerry was used to seeing.

"Not when you put it that way." Jerry laughed. "How about I pray that some nut case already locked up will see the light and start singing like a girl for the Lord, and that's the one that will get transferred down here to help you guys sound halfway decent?"

Jerry hated leaving Dave, but Chaplain Foster said if a man had to be behind bars, then the new state of the art facility in Montgomery County, Georgia was the place to be. The staff had been hand-picked and maybe the inmate population as well to make sure the prison was successful in its mission of not simply punishing the inmates but giving men who'd made mistakes a second chance. Besides, as Dave said, it wasn't as if Jerry had a choice of where he was locked up. He had to go where the authorities sent him.

The first thing Jerry noticed about the Montgomery County Correctional Institution when they brought him past the front gates into the huge rotunda was the new smell. The place looked more like a convention center than a prison. Jerry's and the guard's footsteps echoed in the huge open area as they passed by entrances to the cafeteria, a barbershop, and the chapel on the way to the dorm where Jerry would sleep. Light exploded down from the windows at the top of the rotunda. Jerry glanced over his shoulder, but he didn't catch any shadows in the corridors. Were there really none of the shadows he'd hated at Reidsville or did he simply not see shadows in the same way now that he was walking fully in the light of the Lord?

The dorm reminded him of Reidsville with the same double bunks and storage cabinet size lockers, but that's where the comparison ended. This place was so clean it sparkled. Even better, it was air-conditioned. Sweat soaked, mosquito swatting summer nights were in the past.

Jerry was assigned the job of server in the officers' dining area. He carried food to the tables and kept the coffee flowing. The first day there, he met the chaplain, Ben Kelley, who was continually wagging his cup up in the air for a refill. Chaplain Kelley had a full head of silver hair, but his eyes were young and alive. He told Jerry people in his family all turned gray way before their time but he preferred turning gray to his hair turning loose.

Jerry laughed a little. "Men in my family have that problem. Their hair turns loose. My uncle was bald by the time he was twenty-five." Jerry put his hand on top of his head as if he could make the roots of his hair hold tight.

Chaplain Kelley smiled. "Don't worry, son. It hasn't fallen out yet, but if it does, you can buy one of those fuzzy rugs to smack on top of your head."

"You can buy dye too."

"True, but the gray makes me look wiser than I am." Chaplain Kelley gave Jerry a considering look. "Mr. Cleveland tells me you're a great singer. We want you in the choir on Sunday."

"Sure thing."

As Jerry hustled on to the next table to refill more coffee cups, he had the feeling Chaplain Kelley might be one of those angels the Lord kept dropping into Jerry's path. Jerry certainly didn't plan to ever take the wrong fork at a crossroads again, but everybody needed guidance to make sure they stepped out on the right roads. With both Mr. Cleveland and Chaplain Kelley pointing the way, Jerry surely wouldn't take a wrong turn.

He hardly noticed his twenty-third birthday passing on January 3, 1973. It was his fourth prison birthday and his first birthday as a truly committed Christian. He remembered standing before Judge Rutherford when he was sentenced and hearing the years count off in his head before he'd be eligible for parole. At the time, he couldn't even imagine that many years passing, and now he was more than halfway through. He still didn't like to think about being incarcerated years longer, but whatever happened, he knew he could survive it. No, not just survive. He could flourish and bloom wherever he was. Inside prison or out in the world.

Here at this new institution designed as a showcase of prisoner rehabilitation, Jerry felt like a blank notebook just waiting for his pages to be filled up with work for the Lord.

Mr. Cleveland began filling his pages before the week was out. He organized a Guides for Better Living class for Jerry to teach in the evenings. He pointed Jerry toward the AA Group, and at the first meeting, the group elected Jerry secretary the same as he'd been at Reidsville. Mr. Cleveland took him and a couple of the other inmates out to tell their stories at high schools, junior highs, and colleges in a program called Operation Get Smart. They took turns at the podiums telling their stories and how with the wrong steps the students could end up in trouble themselves.

Some of the kids listened. A lot of them didn't, but Jerry didn't get discouraged. If even one kid heard what they said and moved down the right road in life instead of taking the wrong turn, then they'd done something good.

But Mr. Cleveland didn't just get Jerry busy in the prison activities. He tried to set up a meeting with Judge Rutherford for Jerry in hopes the judge might recommend an early release date to the Parole Board. The judge didn't agree to a meeting, but he did ask Jerry to write him a letter detailing everything Jerry had done in prison.

Jerry spent hours on the letter, filling page after page with not only what he'd done in prison but also what he'd learned about himself. He didn't want to leave out anything that might make the right impression on the judge.

> It was at Reidsville in Chaplain Chatham's therapy group that I started finding myself. One of my problems was self-acceptance. I would have no satisfaction in life until I gave up the shams and pretenses and was willing to be myself. This was when I found out I had another problem. I was using alcohol to drown all my mistakes, failures, and fears of being humiliated. So I started to solve this problem by joining the AA Group in the institution.

When Jerry read over what he'd written, he could hardly believe that once he'd thought so little of his life that he'd tried to throw it away so many times. It had taken prison for Jerry to decide he was a person with worth, someone the Lord could love and use. That's what he wanted the judge to know. He kept writing about what he'd done, being secretary for the AA group at Reidsville, teaching the Guides for Better Living classes, singing in the choir and band, putting on the dramas at Richmond. He wrote about how he'd sung and given his testimony at churches and how much he appreciated the opportunity to witness to young people through the Operation Get Smart program there at Montgomery. The more he wrote, the more he saw the hand of the Lord in his life. All of these things couldn't have simply fallen into place without divine intervention.

He chewed on the end of his pencil and thought a while before he wrote the final paragraphs in the letter.

> *To me, the four years I've spent in prison have not been wasted. In fact, they have been the best years of my life. My parents and I are closer together than we have ever been. I have also become closer to God and able to understand His way for my life. I now have a better outlook on facing everyday life, and more encouraging ways of facing problems. To rid my mind of cobwebs, think clearly, and explore my subconscious for new ideas. To set my sights on a goal and attain it, through persistent thinking and positive action. All this could not have been possible if I had not at first wanted to help myself, and then gotten help from people like yourself who are concerned and wanted to lend their helping hand. And most important was the help of God, because I put all my faith and trust in Him to help me climb up the steps these past four years.*
>
> *My "self" right now is what has always been, and all that it can ever be. I did not create it. I cannot change it. I can, however, realize it, and make the most of it. I know now there is no use straining to be somebody. I am somebody, not because I've made a million dollars or can sing high notes, but because God created me in his own image.*
>
> *Whenever I am able to leave prison, I will be a better, wiser, stronger man and not a mixed up nineteen-year-old kid. I hope from this letter, you have gotten to know me as I am now and not what I was. I know now that I have the ability to "take it" no matter how rough the going may be. Why? Because I*

*believe and I have faith. I will always be
striving to do my best.*

*Respectfully Yours,
Gerald Warren Shepherd*

He reread the letter a dozen times and let Mr.
Cleveland check it over as well. He wrote his parents and
told them the letter was nineteen pages of the truth, the
whole truth and nothing but the truth.

Two weeks after he mailed his letter, Judge Rutherford
sent him a copy of the letter he'd sent to the State Board
of Paroles and Pardons. The judge said he did not usually
make recommendations, but that he felt Jerry had been
rehabilitated and was ready to face life. He recommended
that Jerry be released on parole as soon as the rules
permitted.

Jerry wanted to frame the letter. It was that good. He
wanted to hang it on a wall somewhere, preferably at his
house in Kentucky. Even Mr. Cleveland said he'd never
seen a letter from a judge quite like it and that Jerry couldn't
have asked for a better letter. Jerry could almost hear the
prison doors unlocking. He could almost feel his feet
walking in the fields back home on the farm. The Parole
Board would have to take notice of such a good letter from
a judge.

They didn't, or maybe they did. Maybe the rules didn't
permit them to consider Jerry for early release. That's what
Mr. Cleveland told him after a couple of weeks. What
they'd really needed the judge to do was give Jerry a time
cut on his sentence. Then the Parole Board could have
taken action. But he hadn't done that. He'd written a great
letter, an encouraging letter, but nothing was going to
change. Jerry was still going to have to serve out his time
until he could go before the Parole Board in 1976. Three
more years.

Jerry was disappointed, but he was too busy to dwell

on it. He had AA meetings to attend and letters to write. He had Guides classes to teach. He had songs to practice for the choir. He had speeches to give for Operation Get Smart. He had his Bible study courses and college classes to enroll in. He had coffee cups to fill.

CHAPTER 38

The person Jerry most liked pouring coffee for was Chaplain Kelley. They kept a running conversation going and never had any problem picking right up where they'd left off whenever Jerry had a few minutes break in his serving duties.

"I heard about that drama you and some of the other inmates put on over at Richmond. You think you could do that here?" Chaplain Kelley asked him one day.

"I don't see why not. You'd have to recruit the men to act the parts and for the quartet."

"I don't think we would necessarily need a quartet. You can do the singing." Chaplain Kelley took a sip of coffee. "And you could pick the actors. You know more about what kind of men the drama needs than I do."

"Can I pick anybody? I mean if they fit the part. They wouldn't have to be Christians already?" The idea was intriguing.

"You got somebody in mind?"

"A couple." Just two days before, Jerry had talked to a new inmate and thought how much his life mirrored one of the parts in the drama. Then there was Big Jake, a tall man with vivid blue eyes. One of his hands made two of Jerry's and would be perfect for pounding a pulpit to get a congregation's attention. His grandfather had been an old time fire and brimstone preacher, and Big Jake had spent every Sunday of his growing up years hearing the gospel shouted out. Big Jake said it never did take with him, and he guessed that was why he ended up in the slammer.

"If you can get them to agree to do it, I'll get it cleared with the warden for them to come to practice." Chaplain Kelley peered at him over his coffee cup. "How soon do you think we can get the show on the road? I'll need to line up some churches."

That was the way it was with Chaplain Kelley. He expected things to get done. He didn't make excuses for himself or let those around him make excuses. A man was responsible for what he'd done and responsible for what he could do. Chaplain Kelley thought Jerry could do a lot.

"The Lord's loaded you down with talents." Chaplain Kelley told Jerry in one of their early conversations. "You wore blinders for a while and tried to run your own race without paying attention to the course the Lord was urging you to run. You kept trying to knock him out of the way, but that's the great thing about our Lord, he doesn't give up on us. He knows our hearts and he just keeps right on running there beside us nudging us back toward the right track and sometimes he picks us up and carries us through the roughest times."

"That's what he must have done for me at Reidsville. That's the only way I could have stayed alive in there."

"And your rough times might not be over." Chaplain Kelley made sure Jerry understood that. "Can't any of us

266

know the future. But the Bible promises Jesus is the same yesterday, today, and forever. He's always there, helping us. That's how Stephen could ask forgiveness for the men who stoned him. That's how the old first century preacher Polycarp could help gather the wood to lay around the stake where they burned him to death. That's how your friend, Dave, back at Richmond can bear the loss of his little boy. With the help of Jesus. And that's how you can do whatever you're called to do now that you've quit running away from that calling."

Jerry took the chaplain's words to heart as he settled into the routine at Montgomery. Up every other day at three a.m. to serve in the dining room. In the chapel or teaching Guides or doing AA correspondence on the other days and at night when Mr. Cleveland wasn't taking him out to present his testimony. He felt so good running the course the Lord laid out for him that sometimes his feet seemed to barely skim the ground.

In the middle of February, his feet could have slipped out from under him. A weird cold front dipped down from the north deep into Georgia to dump several inches of snow on them. A lot of the inmates and prison workers had never seen a snowflake much less a blanket of the white stuff on the ground covering up the harshness of the prison fences and concrete barriers. Out in the exercise yard, the inmates built snowmen, pummeled one another with snowballs, and tried to catch snowflakes on their tongues. Jerry thought about Sam back in Richmond who had never seen snow. He smiled thinking about the big man flopping down on the ground to make an extra large snow angel. He hoped he got snow down his collar.

When the snow hung around into the next day, the state of Georgia practically shut down. The guards on night duty were afraid to drive home, and the guards on day duty called in, afraid to drive to work.

A short sturdy guard named Marvin found Jerry in the

dining room. "Hey, Shepherd, you're from up north, aren't you?"

"If you call Kentucky north."

"It snows in Kentucky. It's north," Marvin said. "Look, I know this is going to sound crazy, but Warden Powers says you and a couple of other inmates from up north have to go out and bring the day guards in."

"Are you joking?" Jerry stopped sorting silverware. "You're sending us out to get our own guards?"

"Yeah, that's a rip, ain't it? You do know how to drive in the snow, don't you?"

"Well, yeah. If I can remember how to drive at all. It's been a while."

"It's like riding a bike. You don't forget how." He handed Jerry some papers. "Go get the guards listed up on top there first and then Warden Powers. Directions are there along with a map."

Jerry took off his serving apron and reached for the keys Marvin held out. He'd forgotten the good feel of a set of keys in his hand.

Marvin must have noticed his smile. "Now don't you go forgetting the way back. We'd catch you and you'd have to start all over getting to where you are now."

"I'm not that dumb," Jerry told him.

But it was a thought. A thought that lay there and tickled his brain as he drove out of the prison. Hearing the tires against the road felt almost too good. He wanted to mash down on the gas and see if he could do donuts on the slick roads. He wanted to go crazy and drive to Atlanta or Florida. It might be years before he got to drive anything again, but even while all those reckless thoughts flashed through his mind, his foot was steady on the gas pedal as he kept the wheels turning slow and easy in the snow.

The roads were nearly empty except for the cars abandoned in the snowy ditches. The highway didn't seem all that slick to Jerry, but then he knew not to slam on his brakes at the first slip. Jerry's heart gave a little lurch when a police car with flashing lights came up behind him, but the policeman just waved as he went by as if Jerry were a fellow officer.

Jerry drove slow while hunting the right road signs, but he finally pulled up in front of the first house where he was supposed to pick up a guard. He tooted the horn.

Petey came to the door and did a double take when he saw Jerry behind the wheel. He backed out of sight and then peeked outside again. Jerry tooted the horn again, and Petey leaned out the door. "Hold onto your horses. I gotta get my coat."

A few minutes later he was climbing in the car. "Man, I can't believe this. I thought I was gonna get the day off, but no, they send a convict out to pick me up."

"What can I say?" Jerry grinned at him. "We missed you back at the Georgia State Hotel."

Finding the other guards' houses with Petey directing him was easier than reading the map. Jerry had never been good at reading maps. When he'd been on the run, he hadn't worried about maps. He just took a road until it ran out, then took another one. But then all the roads had run out, and he'd ended up behind bars.

Now he needed to use maps to stay on the right road no matter how enticing the open road looked. Warden Powers trusted him. Chaplain Kelley depended on him to keep his coffee cup full and make him laugh with his stories about life back on the farm. He had even been talking about getting Jerry assigned as his assistant since his desk was piled high with unanswered correspondence and overdue paperwork. Just the week before he asked if Jerry could type and take shorthand, and then claimed one out of two wasn't bad. He said he could always talk slow when he was dictating a letter, that he needed time to think about what he wanted to say anyhow and just how fast could Jerry scribble?

As it turned out, fast enough. In April, Jerry was assigned to the chaplain's office. Now he and Chaplain Kelley spent all day working together, and Jerry felt as though he'd found a second father. He didn't know why he'd been so blessed. His own father was a strong man confident in his belief in the Lord and his purpose in life to serve and be faithful. His eyes gleamed with the joy of living.

Chaplain Ben was the same way. He not only truly believed that with the help of the Lord any man could succeed in life, he had a way of making the inmates he counseled believe it as well. They could stay off the drugs. They could go back out into the world and be good citizens. They could hold down jobs and support families. They could be forgiven for the bad things they'd done. They could feel the love of God. They could believe anything was possible.

Between Chaplain Ben and Mr. Cleveland, Jerry was often on the road to share his testimony. Jerry didn't always plan out what he was going to say. Rather he opened himself up to be that beacon Chaplain Foster back at Richmond had encouraged him to be. He prayed that everything he said or sang might let others see what the Lord had done for him. In nearly every church, young people came forward to surrender their lives to the Lord.

Summer came and at last he got enough actors rounded up for *The Challenge of the Cross*. Some of the men only agreed to take part in order to get out of their work duties and to have the opportunity to be outside the prison walls for a few hours whenever they presented the drama.

When Jerry recruited them, they were like Big Jake.

"Now I don't have to believe all this stuff, do I?" That's what Big Jake said when Jerry asked him to be the evangelist in the drama. "My folks shoved enough religion down my throat to choke a horse, and it never did me the first bit of good."

"Nope," Jerry told him. "I'm picking you because you look right for the part. I'll leave the rest of whatever the Lord wants from you up to him. I just want you to play the part."

"I reckon I can do that. I've seen plenty of pulpit pounders in my day, but none of them ever said a thing I thought made sense," Big Jake said.

"What about Chaplain Kelley?"

"He's a good man, and he can spout off some good Bible verses, but it's yet to make me any better."

"You come on out to practice next Sunday afternoon. I've got a feeling you're going to make the best evangelist this drama's ever had."

Jerry didn't try to convert the men he picked for the drama. He'd let the drama do that. After all, he knew what had happened to him on that stormy night at the youth camp.

The first night out, Big Jake ended up in tears as he finished his part of the drama. He looked around at Jerry singing "Take Up Thy Cross and Follow Me" at the end of the service and nodded a little before he raised his hands and shouted "Praise the Lord."

The people in the church thought it was part of the drama, but Jerry knew the Lord had written a new ending to their drama that night. Or maybe a new beginning for Big Jake. Two of the other actors also ended up on their knees with new commitment in their hearts.

By the middle of August they had taken the drama out to six churches and one hundred and sixty-seven people had come forward to make decisions. Chaplain Ben said sometimes the best thing a man could do was simply get out of the Lord's way and let him work.

The Lord kept opening up churches for them to present the drama. One Sunday night, Jerry looked out into the congregation and saw Judge Rutherford's eyes fastened on him. At the end of the service, he got his mother's holy goose bumps when the judge came forward to accept the challenge of the cross. Jerry could hardly believe he was part of something that could move and inspire the judge who had sentenced him to prison.

Chaplain Ben was right. The Lord could use anybody as long as that person was willing to lay his life down at the Lord's feet.

CHAPTER 39

A few weeks later, Jerry was pounding out letters on Chaplain Ben's old typewriter when four state troopers burst through the doors of the office followed by a blond man about Jerry's size and a slim, dark haired woman. Jerry's fingers sprang out and hit a few wrong keys before he stood up to meet the onslaught of policemen. He didn't know the couple being escorted into the prison, but they had to be important to need so many guards.

The man showed a lot of teeth in a big smile as he came toward Jerry with his hand out. "Hello, I'm Governor Jimmy Carter, and this is my wife, Rosalynn."

Jerry's knees turned to gelatin, but somehow he managed to stay upright. This man had the power to pardon Jerry. Jerry's mother had already appealed to him for Jerry's early release and been turned down. Now the governor of the State of Georgia had Jerry's hand clasped in his.

"We're making the rounds of all the state's correctional institutions, and we've been told this one is a model first class institution. So we came to see for ourselves." The governor had a soft southern drawl. "Sit down and tell us how things are going here. We don't want any practiced speeches. We want to hear it straight. That's right, isn't it, Rosalynn?"

"Yes, Jimmy." Jerry hustled to pull a chair forward for her. "But first, please tell us your name."

"Jerry, I mean Gerald Shepherd."

Without paying any attention to the troopers taking up positions around him, the governor sat down in a chair beside his wife. "Well, Gerald, tell us about the institution here. How is it helping the men who are here?"

So Jerry went through the programs and activities available to the inmates and how so many of the men were going back out into the world, finding jobs, and not returning through the prison system's revolving doors.

"Good to hear. We want our institutions here in Georgia to rehabilitate men so they can become good citizens once they've paid their debt to society," Governor Carter said. "But I want to hear about this Operation Get Smart program you mentioned. Do you go to schools and churches?"

Jerry forgot about being nervous as the words flowed out the same as they did when he gave his testimony. It wasn't Jerry. It was the Lord working through him. "Yes sir. A few of us inmates go out to schools to present our witness to the students. We go to churches too and put on a drama called *The Challenge of the Cross*."

Governor Carter nodded when he mentioned the drama. "I've heard about that. This *Challenge of the Cross*. It must be powerful."

"Literally every time we do it, people come forward to make decisions for the Lord," Jerry said. "And the story doesn't only change the lives of those watching. It changed my life. I always tried to serve the Lord in church activities and things, but I was doing it on my own strength because that was what everybody told me I should do. Then one night after we performed at a youth camp, I opened up my heart and let the Lord take over. After that night, everything about me changed."

"For the better, I'm sure," Governor Carter said.

"Yes sir. The drama has a way of reaching a person wherever they are and showing them where they should be and how they can get there. I've been a front row witness to the changes it's made in the lives of the men taking part in the drama. That's been quite a few different men since a lot of them were short-timers, not in for very long. They do a few performances and then they get released from prison. So I'm always recruiting new men for the parts."

"And how do you do that?" Mrs. Carter leaned forward as if she didn't want to miss a word.

"First I pray, and then I watch out for somebody who maybe has something near the same life story as one of the characters in the drama. That way it's not so much acting a part as doing a part they've already lived. So far, it's worked really well. Once the men get involved in the drama they start wanting to learn more about the Christian life. You can almost see them growing stronger in the faith with every performance."

"I'd like to see it." Mrs. Carter kept her eyes on his face as she sat back in her chair.

So that's how they got invited to the church Governor Carter attended in Atlanta, Georgia. When Chaplain Kelley pulled up in front of the big church and stopped, the men inside the vehicle stared out at the impressive building in front of them.

After a couple of minutes, Big Jake said, "I've never known you to lead us wrong, Chaplain Kelley, but are you real sure we're at the right church?"

Chaplain Ben peered out the window at the church sign. "Northside Drive Baptist Church of Atlanta, Georgia. This is it."

"Where the governor goes to church? They're wanting us in there?" Big Jake said.

"You did tell them that some of us are a shade on the dark side? I'm not sure those doors will open up to let me walk through," Jerome, one of the black actors, spoke up from the front seat beside the chaplain. "I doubt there's ever been a man with my particular skin tones inside there unless it was for cleaning the johns on Monday morning."

"There's a first time for everything." Jerry opened his door. "They asked us and here we are. Ready or not."

"Who are you talking about being ready or not?" Big Jake shook his head. "Them or us?"

"Them, of course," Jerry got out and looked back at the others. "We're always ready, right, guys?"

"If you say so," the men echoed weakly as they climbed out of the van to follow Jerry and Chaplain Kelley up the church steps.

But once they set up their props and began presenting the drama, as always the Lord took over and they forgot the vaulted ceiling and the pews filled with well-dressed church members. They forgot about the governor and his wife sitting in the fifth row with policemen on all sides of them. Instead the Lord's words rolled through them, and at the end of the service, people stepped out into the aisles to come forward and make decisions for the Lord the same as at every other church they'd been. Even the governor and his wife came to the front to recommit their lives.

The service couldn't have gone any better. Jerry had a great group of actors who might not have been committed to the Lord when they began performing the drama but who now wanted to be a beacon of light to others the same as Jerry did.

As Chaplain Kelley often told them, the Lord didn't

need perfect men. He needed willing men.

That was what Jerry told his mother when she came to visit. He was so excited about how successful the drama had been not only in the governor's church but in all the churches that he couldn't quit talking about it. His mother was happy to listen.

"I've always known the Lord would use you in a powerful way, Jerry." Her eyes glistened with pride. "And this is just a beginning, a warming up for what the Lord has in store for you once we get you out of here."

That sounded good to Jerry.

His mother had her own news. She and his dad had bought a farm in Mercer County. "I know you've been looking forward to coming back to the farm in Shelby County." She looked worried for a moment, but her smile came back. "But this farm will be even better. It's bigger. We can have more cows and just wait until you see how those rich green fields roll away from your eyes."

"You sound practically poetic, Mom. What's so much better about that farm than the one in Shelby County?"

He was surprised when his mother's cheeks flushed pink. "You'll probably laugh at me." She looked down at her fingers tracing a circle on the table. "But when I was younger than you, just out of high school and going to business school in Lexington, we always drove past that farm in McAfee every week when my father took me to catch the bus. I practically held my breath from the time we crossed into Mercer County until I saw the first fencepost on that land. I told my father someday I'd marry a man who'd buy me that farm."

"And you did." Jerry tried to picture his mother so young and already so sure of what she wanted. He'd seen that kind of determination in her eyes often. When it was him she was determined to force into shape, he'd fought her tooth and nail, but all those stormy childhood and adolescent years were in the past. Here in a prison visiting room, they could look at one another and feel love and acceptance. They could enjoy being together.

"I did. I was so young then. It was just a dream, but I've never seen another piece of land I'd rather live on. It'll be a beautiful place for you to make a new start when you're paroled."

"That might be a while. I can't go before the Parole Board until 1976."

"No. That's too long." That same determination filled her eyes that had claimed a farm in Mercer County long before she had any way of owning it. Then after a glance at her watch, she sighed and began gathering up the leftover food. "I'll give the rest of this food to that nice guard that escorted me back here. He said he especially likes my brownies."

"You spoil them, Mom."

"It's nothing. Just a few brownies. I'd bake a million brownies if that would guarantee your safety in here."

"It's not like Reidsville here, Mom. I'm okay."

She laid her hand on his cheek. "You're better than okay. I'm so proud of you. Always remember that. No matter what happens."

"I know. I couldn't have better parents than you and Dad."

"You do have a great father, but I could have done things better."

"That's all in the past, Mom."

The moment she had to leave was always hard for both of them. They wanted to stretch out the time and make it last. "You will write, won't you, Jerry?"

"You know I will or you can call the office. Chaplain Kelley doesn't mind if you call me there."

She hugged him and kissed his cheek. "Take care of yourself and keep depending on the Lord."

"I will, Mom." He walked with her to the exit back out to the free world, a door he couldn't follow her through.

She stopped to hug him one more time. She put both hands on his cheeks and looked straight into his eyes. "Jerry, if it took my life to get you out of prison, it would be worth it."

CHAPTER 40

On September 13th, Jerry got up and prayed the same prayer as every other morning. "Good morning, Lord! Thank you for this new day you've given me. Grant me the courage and strength to do whatever it is you have on the agenda for me on this day. I'm ready, Lord, to serve you. Whatever you give me to do, I want to grab it by the horns and get it done. With your help, Lord. You know I can do nothing without your hand to guide and help me. Thank you for the blessings of yesterday and for the blessings you will be sending my way today."

Jerry was busy. He was happy. He had confidence in his ability to handle whatever came his way. He liked feeling as if the Lord was watching over him and guiding him. He liked going top speed to fit everything in. If the Lord opened doors for him, then the Lord would help him run fast enough to go through all of them.

He was in the dining area wolfing down his evening meal so he could go catch up on his Bible study homework when a guard told him to report to the chapel.

"Why?" Jerry gave him a puzzled look. "Chaplain Kelley left a couple of hours ago."

"Then I guess he came back because he's there now, and he sent for you," the guard said.

A little finger of worry poked Jerry, but he pushed it away. Chaplain Ben might need to catch up on some work.

But as soon as he saw the chaplain's face, the finger of worry turned into a fist that grabbed his heart and squeezed. He pushed out the words. "What's wrong?"

"Sit down, Jerry." Chaplain Ben's voice was quiet. Too quiet.

"I don't want to sit down. Tell me what's wrong." Jerry could barely keep from shouting the words. "Just tell me."

Chaplain Ben put his arm around Jerry's shoulders and guided him to a chair. "It's bad news, Jerry." Tears popped up in the man's eyes.

Jerry let the chaplain push him down in the chair. He couldn't say anything else. He could barely breathe.

Chaplain Ben sat in a chair right in front of Jerry where he could keep his hands on Jerry's shoulders. "It's your mother. Hazel."

"Mom? What about her?"

"I'm sorry, son, but she's dead."

"Dead? What do you mean dead?" He couldn't let the words settle in his brain. He must have heard wrong. His mother couldn't be dead. "She was fine when she was here last month."

"There was an accident. On the farm."

Jerry wanted to jerk away from the chaplain and run away somewhere where he wouldn't have to hear any more. If he didn't let the words into his ears, his mother would still be praying for him to get out of prison and come home. But he sat like stone as his mouth formed the words, "What happened?"

"She was mowing a field with a rotary mower. She was by herself so nobody really knows exactly what happened, but she must have fallen off the tractor." Chaplain Ben hesitated before he went on. "Your father said she went under the mower."

For a second everything around Jerry was frozen. He didn't breath. The tear on Chaplain Ben's eyelash hung suspended and didn't fall on the man's cheek. The clock on the wall stopped ticking. Jerry's hands, still smudged with black where he'd changed the typewriter's ribbon earlier, lay motionless in his lap. His mother had probably already been dead then.

Jerry groaned as if somebody had knocked him to the ground and stomped on his chest.

"Take a couple of deep breaths." Chaplain Ben gave Jerry a little shake.

Jerry did as he was told. Didn't he always try to do as he was told? And now this was how he was repaid. How could the Lord let something like that happen? He didn't think he asked the question out loud but maybe Chaplain Ben knew him well enough to read his thoughts.

"Accidents happen," the chaplain said.

"But the Bible says the Lord has all power. He could stop them."

"He could."

"Then why did he let this happen?" Jerry wanted to hit something. Anything.

"We can't know the answer to that. At least not till we join your mother in heaven, and then we'll know all the answers."

"I don't want to know all the answers. I just want this not to have happened."

"I know, son. So do I." Chaplain Ben blinked back tears. "So do I." His fingers tightened on Jerry's shoulders. When the phone rang. Chaplain Ben looked at it. "That will be your father."

Chaplain Ben picked up the phone. "Chaplain Kelley here. Yes, he's right here." He handed the receiver to Jerry.

"Jerry." His father's voice trembled. "Are you okay, son?"

"I don't know. How about you?"

"Things are bad. I don't think I can stand it. I know I have to, but I don't think I can. She meant everything to me." His dad started crying.

Jerry's heart lurched but no answering tears came to his eyes. Instead he asked, "What happened?" Chaplain Ben had already told him, but he had to hear it from his father.

"I don't know. She was down in that lower pasture. It's flat, no dips or holes, and not the least bit rough, and she was on the Massey Ferguson. The 135. She's driven it thousands of times. You know how she liked mowing the pastures. She wanted the fields to look neat before winter. We were getting ready to move, but she wanted to leave the farm looking good."

Jerry didn't say anything. After a minute, his father went on. "You know the field I'm talking about. The one behind the Robinsons' house. Mrs. Robinson went out on her porch and thought the tractor sounded funny. She walked out to her fence to look and couldn't see anybody on the tractor. Said it was just sitting there running and not moving, so she called me. I'm glad she didn't go over to check herself. It wasn't something a woman should see."

"Was Mom dead when you got down there?" Jerry's words sounded flat and strange as if somebody else was talking through his mouth.

"Oh, son, you don't understand. She went under the bushhog. She was cut all to pieces. It was like I was back in the war, only worse. This was my wife." He started crying again.

"Is somebody there with you, Dad?"

"Milton's here and the preacher and a bunch of others.

I don't know who all. Everything's in a daze right now. But it's you I need here."

"I'd be there if I could, Dad."

After he hung up, he could still hear his father's sobs. He'd never heard his father cry like that. His father was tough. He'd been through the war. He'd seen things nobody should ever have to see, and now he'd seen this.

Jerry's eyes stayed dry as he looked at Chaplain Ben and tried to comprehend what the man was saying. Jerry's ears couldn't take in his words. He was down in the lower pasture hearing the bushhog tearing through the weeds. Tearing through his mother.

Finally a few of the chaplain's words made it through to Jerry. "Is there anything I can do, Jerry? Other than pray for you and your father. You know I'm doing that."

"That's good. Dad needs prayer."

"As do we all. Especially at times like this."

Jerry looked at the chaplain. "I need to be alone for a while."

Chaplain Ben gave Jerry a long, considering look before he stood up. "All right. But if you change your mind and need somebody to talk to, you call me no matter what time of the night it might be."

"I can't talk right now."

"I understand. So what do you want to do?"

Jerry pulled in a long breath. "I want to go in the chapel."

"If that's what you want. You and the Lord can talk it over in there."

After the chaplain left, Jerry went into the chapel, shut the door, and locked himself in. He wanted to be alone. He didn't want anybody sitting beside him filling up the silence with words that didn't mean anything. He walked down the aisle to the front. His eyes were still dry. He was too angry to cry.

The Lord shouldn't have let this happen. It wasn't

right. He and his mother had just begun to understand one another. He sat on the front pew and stared at the wall behind the pulpit while the anger went from a hard knot inside him to a raging storm that engulfed him.

He looked up and yelled. "Why did you let this happen? Mom and I were finally coming together." He jumped to his feet and curled his hands into fists, but there was no one there to punch. "We loved each other."

For a second he felt near tears, but then the anger washed over him again like a tidal wave. "How could you take her from me? It's not fair." He thought of Dave's little boy, Davey. That hadn't been fair either. Or right. Or loving. One of the first Bible verses Jerry learned in Sunday school popped into his head. God is love.

"How can you claim to be a loving God when you take something this precious away from me? After all Mom and I have gone through, what we've been through together, you shouldn't have let this happen. I was going to get out. We were going to start over. We were going to be okay."

Jerry let the words echo around him. Then there was silence. Intensely empty silence. God wasn't speaking to him in the silence. God didn't care about Jerry. God didn't care about his mother. Jerry banged his right hand down on the top of the pew. Pain shot up his arm. That was good. He wanted to hurt.

The anger kept growing. God could stop the anger it he wanted to. God could do anything. Jerry had always been told that. God could have stopped what happened to his mother.

Jerry walked up and down the aisle, first muttering under his breath and then shouting. He hardly knew what he was saying as words spewed out of him like water spurting out of a broken pipe. It didn't matter what he said. God wasn't listening. God didn't care. God had severed the pipeline between them when he let Jerry's mother fall off that tractor.

Jerry stopped in front of a picture of Jesus knocking on a door. "You can just go knock on somebody else's door. I quit!"

Somewhere in the deep of the night when he had no voice left to shout, when his hands were too tired to make fists, when he had no energy left to push it away, his mother's memory tiptoed back into his thoughts. He felt her work-worn hands on his cheeks the last time she came to visit. He saw the love in her eyes as her words echoed in his head. *If it took my life to get you out of prison, it would be worth it.*

"It should have been me, Lord," Jerry whispered. "If somebody had to die, it should have been me."

CHAPTER 41

He didn't want to go to the funeral. He wanted to remember his mother alive, not lying in a casket with all her lifeblood drained away. If he stayed there at the prison, he could still imagine her in the kitchen stirring up some brownies or on her knees weeding her flowerbed. He could hear her banging out her favorite hymns on their old piano. He could see her at the kitchen table paying their bills or even better, standing at the back door staring out the window toward the road where someday she'd see her son coming home. If he went to her funeral, she'd just be dead.

But Chaplain Ben told him he didn't have a choice. "You have to go to your mother's funeral. Your father needs you there. You need to be there."

"I don't have to go anywhere. I'm in prison. I can't go anywhere."

"Prisoners attend family funerals all the time."

"Not out of state. They aren't going to send a guard with me back to Kentucky." Jerry had plenty of reasons he couldn't go. "I'd have to fly."

"I know. I've already booked you a ticket." The chaplain gave him a considering look. "Just one ticket. The warden is giving you special permission to go on your own."

"Without a guard? They're letting me out of here without a guard?"

"You don't need a guard." Chaplain Ben's eyes burned into Jerry's. "We trust you to honor the terms of your leave and be back on the day after your mother's funeral."

Jerry didn't feel trustworthy. He didn't feel anything. He'd come out of the chapel at daylight and gone back to his duties, but he felt as if his very soul had been sucked out of him. His heart had shriveled down to the size of an acorn and he didn't care.

He didn't care about anything. Not that his father was crying or that Chaplain Ben frowned when he looked at him. He didn't care that he couldn't sing. Or pray. The Lord had deserted him, and Jerry had no plans to go looking for him. He kept breathing in and out, pushing food into his mouth and chewing, and doing what he had to do. Chaplain Ben said the first thing he had to do was go to his mother's funeral.

The chaplain drove Jerry to the Atlanta airport and stayed with him until he had his ticket and had found the right gate for his flight.

"I'll be back to pick you up on the sixteenth." Chaplain Ben had already told Jerry that a dozen times. "Your flight leaves out of Louisville early early. Make sure you don't miss it."

"I won't," Jerry said automatically.

"I know you won't." Chaplain Ben's voice softened. "I wish I could go with you. To be there for you and your father. Your mother was a wonderful woman and she loved you very much."

"I know."

"Your uncle will be at the airport in Louisville to pick you up." Chaplain Ben peered at Jerry's face. "You will be all right, won't you, son?"

"I'll be all right." Jerry said the words the chaplain wanted to hear.

Chaplain Ben looked as if he wanted to say more, but instead he pressed his lips together, put his hand on Jerry's shoulder for a brief moment before he turned and left Jerry alone in the airport.

Jerry sat in the plastic covered chair and waited for them to call his flight. Other flights were called. To Dallas. To New York. To Philadelphia. He rubbed his fingers up and down the edge of his ticket and thought about exchanging it for one that went somewhere else. Anywhere else.

He was alone. No one was guarding him. He could do it. Just climb on some other airplane and disappear. Forever. He wouldn't have to go back to prison. He was smarter now than when he'd been caught when he was nineteen. He could figure out a way to stay free. He didn't mind hard work. He could get a job picking oranges or harvesting lettuce out in California or maybe sign on with a shrimp boat trawling the oceans around Florida. He liked Florida.

The announcement for the flight to Louisville came over the speakers. He stood up and moved toward the gate to go into the airplane as if his shoes had lead soles.

Just as he handed over his ticket to the perky lady at the entrance to the airplane, he heard the speakers. "Flight 223 to Miami now boarding at Gate 10."

He stopped moving as he wondered how he could get to that other gate, but the woman was already holding his ticket. The man behind him was pushing forward impatiently, bumping Jerry with his carry-on bag.

The pretty woman smiled. "You are in seat 14A. Someone inside the plane will assist you if you need help."

Jerry walked through the tunnel to the plane. He'd missed his chance. His Uncle Milton would be watching for him at the other end of his flight. So he'd go to the funeral, but after it was over, he'd have another chance in Atlanta to get on a different airplane and go wherever it flew.

◆ ◆ ◆

The casket was open. Everybody who came in to view his mother's body seemed surprised by that. They'd heard the stories about how the mower had cut her body up and how the men had found his father cradling his mother's torso. They had to pry his arms away from her. They told Jerry the stories, but he didn't ask his father if they were true.

Instead he looked at his mother in the casket and wanted her to open her eyes and sit up to tell him what had happened. How had she fallen off? Did she hit a groundhog hole that nobody could find now? Had she had a leg cramp? Had she passed out for some unknown reason? But she didn't open her eyes. She just lay there looking too still and quiet while the bruises darkened under the makeup the undertaker had caked on her face.

She didn't look like his mother. He sat back in one of the folding chairs and studied her profile in the casket while he tried to figure out why. It was his mother. Everybody else kept saying the undertaker had done a wonderful job. That she looked so natural.

It took Jerry a while, but he finally figured it out. It was her mouth. The determination that had always made his mother look ready to bite nails when she was trying to move heaven and earth to get things done was gone. That not only made Jerry sad, it scared him because deep inside where he hardly even dared look he had believed she could make the authorities listen to her and get Jerry released from prison. It didn't matter that she hadn't been able to do it in four years. He'd been sure that sooner or later she would find a way to bring him home.

In one way, he supposed she had. He was home with no guard at his elbow, but he'd have to go back or never have a chance of coming home again. *Flight 223 to Miami is now loading.* The blare of the announcement at the airport kept sneaking back into his head. But he couldn't think about that now. Not with his Aunt Violet telling him how good it was to see him and how bad it was that it had to be under such unhappy circumstances.

He had to be introduced to some of his cousins. He hadn't seen them for almost five years. They had all changed, maybe Jerry more than any of them, but of course everybody knew him. Every eye in the place fastened on him like rubber suction cupped arrows each time he entered the chapel. A momentary hush would fall over the room followed by a rush of whispers.

There's the son. You know the one who's serving time in Georgia. Poor Hazel. She never gave up on him, and he wasn't even really her child. He was Dewey's son by his first wife. You knew Dewey was married before, didn't you? Joletta was her name. I hear she was something else. More than old Dewey could handle anyway.

He didn't actually hear any of that, simply imagined it. He told himself to block out the words in his head. The fact was everybody acted genuinely glad to see him. Nobody looked as though they were worried they might catch something if they shook his hand. Instead they hugged him and cried for him since he still hadn't been able to shed any tears himself. Nobody asked when he might get out of prison. They acted as if they thought he already had.

Some of his buddies from Shelby County High and

Oldham County High came. Jerry was surprised at how many people cared enough about his mother to stop whatever they were doing, put on their good clothes and stand in line to shake Jerry's hand and tell him and his father how sorry they were.

At the first kind word from anybody, Jerry's father broke down. He told everybody how safe the Massey Ferguson tractor was and how he'd have never let Hazel mow that field if he'd believed she had the least chance of getting hurt. When the funeral service was over, Jerry had to pull his father away after his final goodbye so the undertaker could close the casket.

As Jerry walked with his dad to the car waiting to carry them to the cemetery, Jerry turned off his brain. The sunshine heated up his black suit jacket. Sweat slid down his temples as they gathered around the open grave while the preacher said "dust to dust" and talked about Hazel's new body in heaven. Back at the house, he ate the food somebody piled on his plate. The day passed. He lay down on his old bed and slept. It felt too soft after all the prison bunks.

Uncle Milton and Aunt Adele spent the night at the house. Uncle Milton woke Jerry hours before dawn the next morning to make sure he didn't miss his plane. Even though he wasn't hungry, Jerry dutifully ate the sausage and pancakes his Aunt Adele fixed him. Night still ruled when they left for the airport. Some men from church had been doing the milking, so his father climbed in the back seat and rode along with them to the airport. His father and his uncle both felt honor bound to get Jerry back to Georgia. They had no way of knowing how Flight 223 to Miami kept playing through Jerry's head.

Or maybe they did. They stayed with him until his flight was called and watched him get on the airplane. Jerry imagined them rushing to a window to be sure he didn't step back out the plane's door, climb out on the wing, and slide to the ground before the plane took off.

Jerry settled in the seat next to the window. The sky was just beginning to lighten in the east as the plane lifted off the ground, shot up into the sky, and leveled off for the flight to Atlanta. The seat next to Jerry was empty, but a man across the aisle put his head back and started snoring. Jerry hardly noticed as he stared out at the morning shaking off the shackles of night.

Far below in the gray dawn, trees were bushy toothpicks and farm ponds puddles. Specks of bobbing light wound along roads that looked like strings somebody had dropped willy-nilly. A few puffy clouds floated under the plane, and Jerry thought he must be closer to heaven than he'd ever been. All at once the rim of the sun broke up over the horizon and everything exploded in dazzling, golden light.

Plenty of times back on the farm, Jerry had admired a sunrise, but he'd never seen one like this. It was as if the Lord had just been waiting to get his attention, and now that he had it, he escorted Jerry to heaven's front porch, pushed him down in a chair to watch. The sun almost leaped over the horizon, shooting out rays that bounced off the airplane and through Jerry's window.

The sunlight didn't only touch him on the outside, but he felt as if the Lord was wrapping his arms around him, holding him, loving him. Tears slipped out of Jerry's eyes.

"Forgive me, Lord," he whispered. "Forgive me for the way I acted in the chapel. Forgive me for blaming you for what happened to Mom." Jerry paused a moment. "I'm ready to accept that Mom's gone now and to bear it with your help."

Jerry didn't shut his eyes while he prayed. He wanted to see every second of this sunrise and absorb every bit of love the Lord was sending him. The Lord had never deserted him. The Lord had always been there, carrying him along and seeing him through.

Again Jerry whispered a prayer. "Forgive me for all the times I've failed you and for not trusting you to be right there beside me the whole way. Thank you for not giving up on me even when I was acting like an idiot. I know I don't deserve it, but please give me another chance. I want to be your faithful servant and continue serving you in every way I can. Just help me get through this one day at a time and help me find a way to help my dad. Let me lean on thy strength and thy power."

The sun was fully up now and practically pulsing with radiant light. Jerry put both his hands flat against the window. "Here am I. Use me. I'm ready."

CHAPTER 42

He got lost in the Atlanta airport. Jerry couldn't find where Chaplain Ben said he and his wife would wait for him. Flight 223 to Miami wasn't playing through Jerry's head anymore. The sunrise took care of that. He felt renewed, burned clean of all doubts, and ready to stay the course with the Lord.

The first thing he had to do was not let Chaplain Kelley down. The chaplain trusted him. If Jerry didn't show up when he should, Chaplain Ben might think Jerry had betrayed that trust. He might call security. So Jerry had to find him and soon, but the Atlanta airport was huge. Maybe there was more than one main entrance or maybe he hadn't found the main entrance yet or maybe that wasn't where he was supposed to meet the chaplain.

He was walking fast without the first idea of whether it was in the right direction or not when he heard his own name playing on the intercom instead of Flight 223 to Miami.

"Will the party of Ben and Jacqueline Kelley, Jerry Shepherd, proceed to Gate 5." Jerry had just passed gate eight so five had to be close. He picked up his pace.

At the edge of the waiting area, Chaplain Ben and his wife peered anxiously at the passing people. Chaplain Ben was up on his toes, a worried frown on his face. He looked as if he needed a whole pot of coffee. Mrs. Kelley caught sight of Jerry first and grabbed Chaplain Ben's arm. Relief bloomed on both their faces.

"I'm back," Jerry said when he got close enough. "Sorry, I'm late. I got lost."

"Praise the Lord. I didn't know whether you were lost or we were." Chaplain Ben had a big smile now. "But either way, you're a sight for sore eyes."

Back at the prison, some of the inmates looked surprised to see Jerry that night.

"Man, we never thought we'd see you again. We tried to get up some bets about whether you'd be back, but we couldn't find any takers," Jason, the inmate who bunked next to Jerry, told him.

"Which way?" Jerry asked him.

"Which way do you think! Nobody believed you'd come back. I mean you were out there free as a bird. If you'd had any sense, you'd have flown away."

"Don't think I didn't think about it, Jas, but I didn't know what you old boys down here would do without me to sing you a goodnight lullaby every night."

"You're crazy, man." William chimed in from across the room.

"But you love me anyway, don't you, Willie?"

"Like I said, you're crazy," William said.

"Crazy for the Lord."

"Oh no," somebody groaned. "He's gonna start preaching."

The very next night, Jerry did go out to a church to give his testimony. His mother would have wanted him to keep going. She would have told him to use what had happened to her as a way to reach even more people. Getting up in front of the church and talking about how his mother never gave up on him seemed to honor her memory. At the end of the service, he sang "Just a Closer Walk with Thee." Singing one of her favorite hymns seemed to be an added testimony for both of them—for her because she was in heaven starting an eternal closer walk with the Lord and for him because he was praying for a closer walk here.

Things settled back into a routine. He typed Chaplain Kelley's letters. He kept up with the AA correspondence. He went out to schools to do Operation Get Smart. He began a new set of college courses. Everything was the same and yet totally different. Just knowing his mother wasn't at home praying for him made it different.

When he told Chaplain Ben that, he clapped him on the shoulder. "You've got it all wrong, son. Your mother is no doubt up there in heaven standing on the Lord's doorstep demanding he take some action to help you."

After that, every time that nasty sad feeling started welling up inside Jerry, he imagined his mom buttonholing everybody she met on heaven's streets of gold to enlist them in her campaign to get Jerry out of prison. That made him smile.

Down here this side of eternity, Jerry kept her campaign going by writing to Judge Rutherford to tell him why he wouldn't get any more letters from Jerry's mother. It just seemed to be the thing to do. She'd kept the judge up to date on Jerry's progress in prison as though the man was more a concerned uncle than the man who had sentenced Jerry to life in prison.

Judge Rutherford had always responded as if he did sincerely care what happened to Jerry. When Jerry's group had performed *The Challenge of the Cross* at the judge's

Atlanta church, the judge found him after it was over to let Jerry know how much he admired his parents and especially his mother.

Jerry even called Joletta to tell her. He wasn't sure why. He just thought she should know. She had moved back to Tennessee from California and was promising to visit him again.

Still, in spite of all the condolence cards he got from churches all over, prison life somehow insulated Jerry from the grief of losing his mother. He knew she was gone, but at the same time he didn't have to go into the empty kitchen back at the farm. He didn't have to see the empty church pew three rows back where his mother sat every Sunday. He didn't have to see her old black purse missing from the table by the door where she left it so she could grab it quick whenever she needed to run to town.

His father did. He seemed totally adrift without Jerry's mother. When his father called the chaplain's office, Jerry listened and tried to say something comforting. He prayed for his father every day, but what his father needed most, he couldn't do. He couldn't be there to put his arms around him and support him through these hard days. He wasn't there to help him pack up for the move to the new farm in McAfee or help him do the milking the way his mother had. He couldn't be there to help his father find a way to keep living without his wife and helpmate.

Then his father found his own way. In November, his father called Chaplain Ben with news he feared might upset Jerry. Not bad news. Actually good news, Jerry's dad told the chaplain, but he wasn't sure Jerry would understand that.

Jerry didn't. Chaplain Ben broke the news as kindly as he could, but there was no way to make it sound right to Jerry. His father had met another woman. They'd been dating. His father said he and Margaret had already talked about getting married.

"Getting married?" Jerry could hardly believe his ears.

"Now listen, Jerry." Chaplain Ben started talking fast. "I know it may seem a bit soon and it is a bit soon, but everybody handles things like this in different ways. You know yourself what a mess your father has been since your mother died. He can't make it on his own. He said he didn't plan on meeting somebody this soon, but since he did that he doesn't see any reason to keep suffering alone. He claims Margaret understands how he felt about your mother since Margaret lost her husband in sort of the same way as he lost his wife. Her husband was killed in a car crash a few years ago, and of course, she loved her first husband very much. That doesn't mean she doesn't have any love left for now."

"I think the operative words here are a few years ago. It hasn't been three months since we buried Mom."

"I know." Chaplain Ben seemed to run out of words.

Jerry massaged his forehead with his fingers. After a minute, he looked up at the chaplain. "Do you think Mom's death has affected Dad's mind?" Jerry couldn't think of any other reason to explain what the chaplain was telling him. "Do you think he needs to be committed or something?"

"Now, son, let's slow down and think this through. Your daddy's only fifty. That's not all that old, even though it may sound ancient to you. While it may not have seemed like very long to you since your mother died, it probably seems like an eternity to him back there getting up alone every morning, not having anybody to talk to."

"But it's a matter of respect."

"He knows how he respected your mother through their years together. He was a good husband, but his wife died. He grieved for her. You know how much from the calls he made down here. But now he's moved to a new farm, a new house, and he's left the old farm and his old life behind. I think he feels like he's turned the page. He's ready to start a new life."

Jerry shook his head. "I just can't accept it. Not yet."

Chaplain Ben sat back in his chair and took a long drink of coffee before he slowly sat down the cup. "You have to call him. I told him you would after we talked."

"I can't call him and talk about him being with another woman when Mom's not even cold in the grave."

"Yes, you can." Chaplain Ben gave him a look that brooked no disagreement. "And you can try to understand, and if you can't understand, then you can still listen to what he has to say with the respectful attitude of a son to a man who has been a good father to you."

So Jerry called his father and listened to him talk about this Margaret. She was pretty. She was kind. She was lonely the same as he was. She was just what he needed to get on with his life. "You'll see when you meet her, son. She's a fine woman. Kind. Gentle."

"I'm not saying she isn't, Dad, but don't you think you should wait a while? Mom just died in September."

"I know. I never intended to go out and meet someone as nice as Margaret so soon, but I was going crazy at home by myself. You just can't understand."

"But you can't be thinking about marrying somebody already. I mean it's bad enough you're dating, but you're even talking about getting married."

"Well, not till the first of the year."

"But Mom's not even cold in the grave." He'd told himself he wasn't going to say that, but how recently his mother died kept coming back at him. His father shouldn't have even wanted to go on a date yet, much less think about getting married.

"I knew this might upset you, but a man's got to do what a man's got to do," his father said.

Jerry wanted to reach through the telephone wire and grab his father and shake him. He wanted to make him see how crazy this was, but instead he took a deep breath as the silence hummed between them. When he couldn't stand the silence a second longer, he said, "Well, Dad, I don't think it's right, but I can't do anything about it. I'm down here locked up. You can do whatever you want to do. You're going to anyway."

"But I want you to try to understand. Just tell me you'll try. Maybe not today or tomorrow but in a couple of weeks when you get used to the idea."

Again Jerry let the silence hum between them for a minute. "Okay, Dad. I'll try."

"Good. That's all I'm asking."

"Maybe we can talk it out some more when you come down to visit."

"That's another thing. I'm not going to be able to come for a while. I want to. You know I want to, but I haven't found anybody up here in McAfee to do the milking for me. You know how your mother and me took turn about. But we'll still talk. I'll call every week just like before."

"Okay, Dad."

"Things are going all right for you down there, aren't they? Chaplain Kelley says you're still giving your testimony real regular. That would have made your mother proud."

"I know."

"And I got a letter from Judge Rutherford. A real nice letter. He said he hoped he could help us. I think he's going to write to the Parole Board."

"They didn't pay much attention to the last letter he wrote."

"You don't know that. But anyhow, I'm thinking your mother's death might make them take a new look. You know the Lord can make good come from the worst things that happen."

"I didn't want Mom to have to die to get me out of prison." Jerry gripped the phone tighter.

"Nobody says you did, son, but if she'd thought that

would have turned the trick, she'd have given up her life gladly and willingly."

"I know. She told me that the last time I saw her."

"And she meant it. She used to tell me the same thing. So you just remember that the way I feel about Margaret doesn't have any reflection on the years I spent with your mother. But life goes on. We have to go on too."

Jerry hung up the phone on Chaplain Ben's desk. His legs were weak and his chest hurt as if he'd just trudged a few miles through heavy mud. He was alone. The chaplain had left the room to let Jerry talk to his father.

Blinking back tears, Jerry bent his head to pray and his gaze fell on the small cross fashioned out of three nails that Chaplain Ben sometimes held while he was counseling inmates. Jerry picked it up. There was love in those nails. His Lord had let them nail him to a cross. He'd given his life willingly to save Jerry from his sins. With love.

The metal of the nails warmed in Jerry's fingers. He'd never fully understood the love shown by the cross, but now he was getting a glimpse of the kind of love it had taken for Jesus to let them drive nails through his hands and feet. Jerry's mother had had that same kind of love for him.

CHAPTER 43

Christmas was never a good time in prison. No matter how many trees were lit up in the rotunda area, it wasn't Christmas with their families. This Christmas was particularly hard for Jerry. He still got care packages, but each one just seemed to emphasize the ones he wasn't getting from his mother.

Even worse he couldn't talk to his father about missing his mother. His father didn't want to talk about anything but Margaret. Jerry couldn't even get him to talk about the new farm. It was all Margaret, Margaret, Margaret. He was spending Christmas day with Margaret and her daughter and three grandchildren. He had a new instant family. And he was deliriously happy. Delirious at any rate.

Jerry couldn't shake the feeling it was too soon after his mother's death, but at the same time, he didn't begrudge his father this new family. Back in high school,

Jerry used to tell his friends how someday he wanted an instant family. Maybe it was because of the sister and brother his parents had given a home for a while and considered adopting when Jerry was a kid, but for whatever reason Jerry had a tender spot in his heart for children who needed a father. So he'd sometimes thought about marrying somebody who had children, and now his father was doing that very thing.

His father and Margaret set a date in January, but put off the wedding when rumors popped up that Jerry might get an early parole hearing. The rumors were true. The Parole Board had agreed to a special hearing in April about Jerry's early release. Jerry was almost afraid to believe it. He wasn't due for parole consideration until April 1976, still two years away.

He tried not to let it affect his life as he went about his usual routine in the prison. If it happened, it happened. If it didn't, he had survived five years. He could survive two more. But his father decided to put off getting married in hopes Jerry could be at the wedding.

As the date for the hearing drew closer, Jerry couldn't stop thinking about how it would be to leave prison and be part of the free world again. He'd be responsible for his own life.

He wanted that more than anything in the world, but at the same time, he was terrified at the idea. What if he made the same mistakes all over again? While it was true he wasn't the same mixed up kid who had come into the prison system, who knew what might happen to him when he was released? Would he get crazy and mixed up again?

Being in prison was like being in a separate world. He read the newspapers and heard the news on the radio and television, but it really didn't mean that much to him and the other men inside. They had their own world. Somebody told them when to get up in the morning. Somebody told them what to do all day. Food was dished out on their plates. They were ordered lights out at night. That other world was out there, but they weren't part of it.

Chaplain Ben assured Jerry he could make it. "This is what we've been pushing for. You need to be out of here, home with your family, and building a new life with the solid foundation of your faith in the Lord. You can do it, because the Lord will help you do it."

"But it's been five years." Jerry poured Chaplain Ben a fresh cup of coffee and sat down across the desk from him. "I was only nineteen when I came in. I'm nothing like I was then."

"Praise the Lord." Chaplain Ben took a sip of coffee before he sat his cup down. His voice deepened the way it did when he was preaching. "You don't want to be that person anymore just like I don't want to be the person I was five years ago. My knees might not pop and groan so much if I was, but even though this old body gets more worn out with each passing year, at the same time I'm closer to being the man the Lord wants me to be. We live and we learn and we begin to see the Lord's way is not just the best way. It's the only way. We aren't perfect. We never get to perfect this side of heaven, but we strive toward perfection in Christ Jesus for that's how to live for Him. And when we fail—and we all fail—we ask for forgiveness."

"I know I'm forgiven. I've prayed for forgiveness, and I've felt that forgiveness."

"And once you've genuinely prayed that prayer, the Lord not only forgives, he forgets. As far as the east is from the west, so far has he removed our transgressions from us."

"But will the people out there forget?" Jerry looked down at his hands clutched together in his lap.

"Maybe not. That's something you have to live with, part of the cost of what you did. But you said your family accepted you, loved you when you went back for your mother's funeral. They'll do the same when you go out of here. You've paid your debt to society. You've looked deep inside yourself and wrested out the bad, and now you've set your feet on the right path. As long as you stay on that path with the Lord, you will be all right. Even better than all right. You'll do wondrous things for the Lord."

"I want to believe that." Jerry looked up at Chaplain Ben.

"Then believe it. Just think about all the decisions made for Christ because of your willingness to give your testimony. That doesn't have to stop when you get out. You can still stand up and tell what the Lord has done for you." Chaplain Ben pointed across the desk toward Jerry. "Not only can you still do it, you must keep doing it as long as the Lord says do it."

"Everything's going to be different." Jerry leaned forward with his elbows on his knees and stared at the floor. "Everything. Mom's gone. Dad's marrying somebody I don't even know. The farm's gone."

"But there's another farm. A better farm from what your father tells me. And you have a place there. Your father not only wants your help on the farm, he needs it."

"But eventually I'll have to go out on my own. I can't live with my father the rest of my life."

"That's true. You can't."

Jerry sat up and looked straight at the chaplain. "I'm afraid."

Chaplain Ben's face softened. "I know. But you are going to make it, Jerry."

"Will you pray for me?"

"I already do, son. You're always in my heart and my prayers."

Jerry hesitated a moment. "You'll probably think this is half crazy, but did you ever feel like the Lord placed angels along the road to help you do the right thing? To point you in the right direction?"

"The Lord guides us in whatever way He chooses." Chaplain Ben peered at Jerry. "Why? Have you been seeing angels?"

"I have." Jerry smiled a little. "In the crossroads of my life, there have been angels. Some of them I surely missed, but others I've recognized and heeded their directions."

"Then tell me what an angel looks like." Chaplain Ben smiled as he picked up his coffee.

"They come in all shapes and sizes. One was a grandmother type in New Jersey. One was a drawn up old black man at Reidsville." Jerry looked straight at the chaplain. "One looks just like you."

The chaplain put his cup down and blinked back tears. "Son, you have no idea how much I'm going to miss you. I want you free. I want you out there being the man the Lord intends you to be. Maybe a husband and a father. But at the same time, when the Parole Board finally does see that you're ready to go out into the free world, your leaving is going to tear a mighty big hole in my heart."

◆ ◆ ◆

The hearing didn't happen in April. The Parole Board had some kind of backlog and delayed the meeting.

"Governmental red tape, that's all," Chaplain Ben told him. "They'll reschedule it in a month or two and then you'll be out. I know you will." Chaplain Ben fingered the handle of the coffee cup on his desk.

"You want some more coffee? I just made a fresh pot."

"In a minute. First I've got some other news. Good news, but sad too."

"You got your promotion." Jerry tried to sound glad, but the promotion meant Chaplain Ben would be moving to Atlanta where he would be over all the chaplains in the state's prison system.

"That's right. Looks like I'll be moving out of here

ahead of you."

"That's fantastic. They couldn't have gotten a better guy." Jerry had a hard time holding on to his smile. "But you won't mind if I cry a little."

"I'd be disappointed it you didn't. Especially since we'll most likely be crying together. I wish I could take you along." The chaplain shook his head. "But you won't be here much longer. You'll be going home to Kentucky in no time at all."

Jerry's smile slid off his face. "I don't know whether I can make it without you here to help me."

Chaplain Ben smiled but his eyes looked ready to run over. "You'll do fine. Just take it one day at a time and keep your prayer line open to the Lord."

"You'll keep praying for me too, won't you? Even after you move up there with the bigwigs."

"You know I will." Chaplain Ben stood up and threw his arm around Jerry's shoulder. "Every day, and I'll call to check up on you. I won't forget the number here."

"What if I mess up after you leave?"

"You won't. Mr. Cleveland will right here to keep you straight. He's going to fill in here until they hire somebody." The chaplain gave him a little shake. "So stop worrying about yourself and worry about me. I'm the one with problems. I have to go up to the big city where I'll have to try to find somebody who can make coffee just the way I like it."

"Anybody can make coffee."

"Maybe so, but can't just anybody type out a letter the way I want it to be no matter what I actually said."

"You can teach them."

"With enough time, I guess, but what about finding somebody who can sing whatever song I start humming?"

"Two out of three's not bad." Jerry shrugged. "I wouldn't want you to forget me all that easy anyhow."

"Don't worry about that. No way could I ever forget

you. Not after some of the things you've done." Chaplain Ben laughed, then got serious again. "But I will miss you. You're a big part of the reason I got the promotion, because of all the programs you've helped us get started here at the prison. The Lord has his hand on you, Jerry. Let him keep blessing others through you."

Jerry hated seeing Chaplain Ben leave. He was always losing people, but as Chaplain Ben reminded him before he left, the one most important person in Jerry's life would never go away or change. The Lord would always be there right beside him, showing him the way and putting angels in his path. Jerry kept his Bible on the corner of his desk in the chaplain's office so he wouldn't forget that. He put the cross made out of three nails Chaplain Ben had given him on top the Bible. And then he learned to make coffee the way Mr. Cleveland liked it as he waited for news from the Parole Board.

Back in Kentucky, his father couldn't wait any longer and married Margaret in May. So Jerry had a new stepmother he'd never met. He spoke to her on the phone a few times, but neither of them had much to say. He didn't think she could be happy about taking on a convict for a stepson.

Then one morning Mr. Cleveland said Judge Rutherford was working to get Jerry's life sentence commuted to fifteen years. If that happened, Jerry could be paroled at any time.

The letter came the middle of July. There was no hearing. He didn't have to appear before the Board. He was going to be released.

Mr. Gerald Warren Shepherd, D-1902

After careful investigation and deliberation, the Parole Board has decided to release you under parole supervision. This means you will be allowed to serve the rest of your sentence,

*minus credited good time, outside of prison
where you may earn your own living and lead
a normal life.*

There were a couple of paragraphs about the conditions of parole and how he was the only one who could send himself back to prison by not abiding by the conditions of his parole and how his parole officer would be a friend and an advisor.

*You have our best wishes in your efforts to
begin a new life. You went to prison because
you failed to abide by society's rules. We think
you are ready to abide by those rules and be
an asset to your community instead of a
liability. This is why we grant you parole.*

Finally they got to the vital information.

*You are scheduled for release on parole on
July 24, 1974. We wish you success and
happiness.*

July 24th. Less than two weeks away. He let out a shout and did a little jig in the middle of the floor. Then he prayed for courage. And more angels to help him. Lots more angels.

CHAPTER 44

It felt funny walking out of the prison in his free world clothes and knowing that this time he wasn't going to have to go back inside that night. He'd taken off his prison uniform for the last time. He'd told everybody goodbye. The guards good-naturedly threatened him with bodily harm if they ever saw him inside again. The men in the dorm punched his arm and grinned while they asked how much they should wager on his return.

"Better hang onto your cigarettes and not be betting on that," he told them. "As much as I like you old boys, you can be sure I won't be coming back to see you."

Before he left, he went down to the chaplain's office for one last time. He stood in the middle of the floor and let the voices of his past circle around him. Governor Carter and his wife asking him about *The Challenge of the Cross*. All the letters he'd answered from AA groups all over the United States. His mother and father calling him on Chaplain Ben's phone to hear his voice and know he was all right. The fury of the storm when his mother died. And Chaplain Ben. Most of all Chaplain Ben. All their talks over morning coffee. All the advice. All the prayers.

Even though Chaplain Ben had been gone for several weeks, the office was still his, would always be his in Jerry's mind. His laugh echoed off the walls. Jerry could see Chaplain Ben holding up his coffee cup for a refill. He could feel Chaplain Ben's hand resting on his shoulder as they prayed together. He could hear Chaplain Ben telling him he could make it as long as he kept his eyes fixed on the Lord.

Mr. Cleveland came in the office and caught Jerry standing there. "Telling the place goodbye?"

"Yeah. I spent a lot of hours in here."

"You did, but now you're ready to start the next chapter of your life. A better chapter."

"I hope I'm ready." Jerry pulled in a long breath.

"You're ready." Mr. Cleveland stepped closer to him and smiled. "I remember the first time I saw you at Reidsville. I wasn't sure you'd survive prison."

"I might not have if it hadn't been for you helping me get involved in AA and Rinc."

"I had to. Your mother insisted. We either had to send you home so she could take care of you or take care of you ourselves."

Jerry smiled. "Mom was good at insisting."

"That she was," Mr. Cleveland agreed. "Come on. I'll walk out with you to meet your dad. He wants to introduce me to Margaret."

"He'll have to introduce me too." Jerry swallowed hard and tightened his hands into fists. It wasn't going to be easy meeting her father's new wife.

"You'll like her."

"How do you know?"

"A little bird named Chaplain Ben told me when I talked to him yesterday. He said to tell you not to worry about anything and especially not your new stepmother because no doubt she would turn out to be one of those angels you told him about."

"Dad thinks so anyway. It's not her that has me worried anyway. It's me. I've been in here five years. I won't know how to act. What to do."

"You'll figure it out." Mr. Cleveland sounded surer than Jerry felt. "Just trust the Lord and know that nothing can ever separate you from his love. Not tribulation, or distress, or persecution, or famine, or nakedness, or peril, or sword. Nothing. Not even our own fears."

"That's in Romans, isn't it?" Jerry asked.

"Not the last part about our fears, but the rest is. The important thing is do you believe it?"

"I believe it."

"Then rest on that belief. The Lord took care of you in here. He can take care of you out in the world."

When Jerry came out to the release point, his father's smile could have lit up a dark room. Jerry had never seen him look any happier. An attractive dark haired woman stood beside him. Her smile looked a bit tentative, but her eyes were kind when his father pulled her forward.

"This is Margaret. Didn't I tell you how pretty she was?" his dad said.

She blushed but her smile grew surer. "I'm glad to finally meet you, Jerry." She turned to Mr. Cleveland. "And you too, Mr. Cleveland."

And that's all she said. Jerry didn't know whether it was because she didn't know what to say to an ex-convict, especially one going home with her, or whether it was because his dad kept chattering on without leaving anybody else room to get a word in edgewise.

Jerry had never heard his father talk so much. He talked about the surprise he had waiting for Jerry back at the farm.

He talked about how wonderful it would be to have Jerry helping him with the cows. He went on and on about the room they'd fixed up in the new house with all Jerry's old furniture. But nobody mentioned Jerry's mother and what this day would have surely meant to her.

The surprise at the McAfee farm was a brand new two-tone blue 1974 F-100 Ford pickup truck sitting in the driveway. His dad bounced up on his toes with excitement when he handed Jerry the keys. "This is yours."

"Dad, you shouldn't have spent that kind of money on me," Jerry said even as he yanked open the door to breathe in the heady new truck smell. He slid behind the wheel to check out the dials on the dash, hit the turn signal and flash the lights on and off before he jumped out to pop the hood to admire the engine. "Man, this is great."

"You need wheels," his dad said.

"I don't even have a driver's license anymore." Jerry ran his hand along the fender. His own truck. He wanted to climb back in it and drive until his foot got too tired to push the gas pedal.

"You can go apply for a permit tomorrow."

"I'll look cute taking the permit test with all those high school kids."

"You'll just do what you have to do, Jerry."

That was how it was with everything. He needed to get used to not only a new stepmother, but a stepsister and two nieces and a nephew. He would have to learn how to work with a new herd of cows. But first he had to find out if he could sleep in a quiet room in a soft bed again.

That first night as he got ready for bed, Margaret came to his bedroom door to make sure he had everything he needed. After he assured her he did, she hesitated, then said, "I'm glad you're home."

She turned away without waiting for him to say anything. But he knew she meant it. She might not talk much, but she had a gentleness about her. A peacefulness.

As Jerry lay in his bed and stared at the window open to the night air, he felt that same peacefulness in the very air of the house. There would be no yelling in this house. He wouldn't have to be perfect for this woman. She knew he was far from perfect. She knew what he'd done to end up in prison, and she still wanted him there. No wonder his father had wanted to marry her and share that peace and love.

Jerry didn't want to shut his eyes and go to sleep. He wanted to let the sound of the katydids and crickets outside penetrate his very being. A whippoorwill called in the distance and then he heard a screech owl. A car passed by out on the highway. He had forgotten how good those things sounded. He didn't have to listen to the sound of a hundred men settling down to sleep. He was never going to be awakened by a guard running a billy bat along the wall of the dorm again. He had his life back.

In the morning, he could pull on his jeans and go to the barn. He could sit in his new truck, turn the key, and listen to the engine purr. He could throw a stick for Hugo to fetch. He could tell Margaret he wanted three eggs sunny-side up for breakfast instead of a glob of scrambled eggs plopped on his plate. He was ready to work with his father to pay him back for all the years he'd stood by Jerry.

On Sunday, Jerry and his dad got up early to get the milking done before church. His father and Margaret went to Mitchellsburg Baptist where Margaret had been a member for years. The drive wasn't that far.

"You'll get to meet your new sister this morning," Jerry's dad said as he pulled into the church parking area. "She lives just down the road from here in Margaret's old house. Connie is just as sweet as her mama, so I know you'll like her."

"I always wanted a sister," Jerry said.

"Now you have one. And she comes with three of the cutest kids you ever saw. Right, Margaret?"

"I think so, but then they are my grandbabies," Margaret said.

"What are their names again?" Jerry wished for a pen to write cheat notes on his hand.

"Tab's the baby. He's three. Then there's Christy. She's four and as friendly as a little puppy. She made up with Dewey right away. Shayne's seven and it takes a little longer to win her over," Margaret said.

"How about your son-in-law? Will he be there?"

For a minute Jerry didn't think Margaret was going to answer him, but then she said, "Robert doesn't usually go to church."

"Robert's a whole other story," Jerry's dad started.

Margaret stopped him with a hand on his arm. "A story we can tell another day. Not on Jerry's first Sunday home."

Jerry was curious, but he didn't ask questions. He would find out soon enough.

Sunday school hadn't let out when they went inside and found an empty pew. A few people already in the sanctuary came over to shake hands with Jerry and welcome him to the church. They were so friendly Jerry had to wonder if they knew he was an ex-con. Surely they did. The stink of the prison air would take months, maybe years to shake off.

A bell somewhere signaled the end of Sunday school. Jerry watched the people streaming into the sanctuary and wondered if he would recognize his stepsister. Margaret had shown him a picture. A young woman with dark brown hair curled around her face herded three kids into the sanctuary.

Bells started going off, but not back in the Sunday school rooms or even in the church bell tower if the church had one. These bells were clanging wildly in Jerry's head as the woman moved toward him. She was the most beautiful woman he'd ever seen, and she was smiling straight at him. His heart started pounding, and his knees went weak.

He'd heard people talk about this kind of thing, but Jerry had never really believed them. Not at first sight. Not before even knowing a girl's name. But it was happening to him. Not only happening, it was engulfing him. He wanted to take her hand and ask her to marry him on the spot.

And it wasn't just because he'd been in prison. Plenty of pretty girls had made eyes at him when he was playing in the band at Reidsville and some girls at the churches where he'd given his testimony had made eyes at him. Some of them were cute, but none of them had knocked him for a loop like this girl.

He could hardly breathe by the time she got to their pew. The little boy ran straight to hug Margaret. The oldest girl hung back behind her mother and the other little girl stared at him with big brown eyes. Eyes almost as beautiful as her mother's. Jerry pulled in a breath to try to slow his racing heart. He sucked in the smell of her perfume and had to grab the back of the pew in front of him when his head started spinning.

This couldn't be happening. He couldn't have fallen instantaneously in love with his sister. Not only his sister. His married sister.

"This is Connie, Jerry." Margaret's words penetrated his daze.

"Welcome home, brother." Connie's smile was warm as she reached out to shake his hand. "I've always wanted a brother."

Jerry uncurled his fingers from the pew and took her hand. Somehow he managed to stammer a few words. "Yeah, me too. I mean I've always wanted a sister."

She laughed and the bells rang louder in Jerry's head. "How about one with three kids?"

"The more the merrier." Jerry tore his eyes off her face and looked at the children. "I like kids."

Connie put her arm around the oldest girl and pulled

her up beside her. "This is Shayne. That's Christy, and Mama has Tab. All right, guys, say hello to your Uncle Jerry."

An obedient chorus of hello, Uncle Jerry followed. The organist struck up the first chords of a hymn, and they all sat down. Shayne stayed close to her mother, but Christy climbed straight into Jerry's lap and settled in as though she'd known him all her life.

Jerry hardly heard a word of the sermon. All he could think about was the woman sitting next to him. His stepsister. His married stepsister with three children. Being captivated by her wasn't a good thing.

He told himself freedom must have gone to his head. Or maybe he was just crazy. But then every time her arm brushed against his, the bells started going off in his head all over again.

Before he'd left the prison, he had prayed for angels to be in his path, but he hadn't expected to fall in love with the first one he saw.

CHAPTER 45

After church, they went home with Connie and the kids for lunch so they could all get better acquainted.

"Is Robert there?" Margaret asked Connie as they headed for the parking lot.

It seemed a casual enough question, but Connie's smile slid off her face. Then she was smiling again, but not the same easy smile she'd had. "He was when we left for church. You know Robert. He keeps his own schedule."

Now Margaret sounded worried. "Are you sure he won't mind us coming for lunch?"

"Don't worry." Connie waved her hand as though to dismiss Margaret's concern. "I put a roast and some potatoes in the oven this morning. There'll be plenty for everybody. And the kids need to get to know their new uncle." Connie smiled over at Jerry. The good smile again.

Jerry smiled back and managed to keep walking. He

needed to get control of his emotions. This beautiful woman was married. He'd best keep that word front and center in his thoughts. Married.

To Robert. He didn't like Robert even before he walked into his house and that didn't change when they were introduced. Jerry smiled and claimed to be glad to meet him, but he didn't have a smidgen of gladness in his heart. Robert smelled of alcohol as he lay back in his easy chair watching a baseball game. He didn't stand up to greet them, wave them toward a chair, or even turn down the sound on the television.

"Big game today?" Jerry's father asked.

"Yeah, the Reds and the Dodgers." Robert kept his eyes on the screen. Then without looking around at Connie, he asked, "How long before we eat?"

"It'll be ready in a few minutes." Connie hurried toward the kitchen. The oldest girl, Shayne, followed behind her, a shadow almost. She hadn't even glanced at her father. Margaret grabbed the other two kids and headed down the hall to help them change out of their Sunday clothes.

That left Jerry and his father alone with Robert. After an awkward silence, his father said, "Come on, Jerry. I'll take you next door to show you the store Margaret used to run with her first husband. They had a good business going here."

"Still would be bringing in money if Connie hadn't let her mother practically give it away to that lowlife who runs it now," Robert muttered. He picked up an empty glass off the table by his chair and yelled toward the kitchen. "You got anything in there to drink, Connie?"

Jerry's hands curled into fists, but his dad grabbed his arm and pulled him toward the door. "Let's go, Jerry. Can't disturb a man's ballgame."

When they were outside, Jerry said, "He always that sweet or was he just putting on a show for us?"

Jerry's dad shook his head. "I'm not going to talk about a man in his own yard on a Sunday afternoon." As he looked back toward the house, his eyes narrowed. "But I could."

The conversation at the dinner table was strained. Margaret and Connie talked about the people at church and tried to get Tab to eat his green beans. Shayne kept her eyes on her plate while she ate. Now and again she'd steal a glance at her father and then Jerry.

When she looked at him, Jerry smiled and made a silly face. Before dinner was over, he was rewarded with a shy smile. Christy was the only one who seemed totally unaffected by the tension between the adults around the table. She kept stabbing her potatoes with her fork and giggling when the potato chunks shot away from her fork and landed on the table.

They left right after Margaret helped Connie clear away the dishes. Connie told them not to rush off. She was still smiling, trying to make Jerry feel like family, but at the same time she looked tired.

On the way home, Jerry told Margaret what a nice daughter she had. "And the kids are even cuter than you said they were."

"Connie is an angel." Margaret sounded almost sad.

The word angel tickled Jerry's brain. Connie was an angel, but somebody else's angel. The thought pierced his heart. "She does look like an angel. Beautiful like you."

"Listen to you." Margaret smiled, but then her smile disappeared as she looked over at Jerry's dad. "Do you think he was drinking?"

"He's always drinking."

"I should have asked her to come home with us."

"She wouldn't have come."

"I know." Margaret sighed. Her head drooped over.

Jerry's father reached to touch her shoulder. "We've done what we can. We've told her we'll get her out of there.

We've already got an option on that house over on Green Wilson. It's empty. We could move her into it tomorrow, but she has to take that next step. She has to say she's ready for us to help her."

"It's not a good marriage?" Jerry was a little ashamed of the spark of happiness that thought ignited inside him.

"No, I'm afraid not." Again Margaret sighed. "But they have three children, and Connie says she made a vow for better or worse."

"There's worse and then there's way past worse to unbearable," Jerry's father said.

"She's coming around to believing that. She told me she had filed for divorce."

"Well, what's he doing there then?" Jerry's father asked.

"He doesn't know it yet. She's afraid to tell him."

That night when Jerry and his father came in from milking, Margaret was at the kitchen table staring at the telephone with tears running down her cheeks. She'd been talking to Shayne.

Jerry's dad looked at Margaret. "He's been hitting her again."

Margaret nodded. "Poor little Shayne. The other kids were taking a nap, but Shayne heard it all. She had to talk to somebody about it."

"Connie know she called?"

"Of course not. Connie doesn't want us to know how bad it is."

"As if we can't see the bruises," Jerry's father said.

Jerry felt sick. He'd seen a lot of mean things while he was in prison, but he could hardly stand the thought of anybody hitting the beautiful woman he'd met that morning. Not only met, fallen in love with.

"Maybe you should go get them." Jerry forced the words out around the lump in his throat.

"I can't. I promised Shayne I wouldn't tell her mother

she called me, and they're probably okay now. Shayne said Robert left."

"Call Connie and make sure she's all right." Jerry's father leaned down and kissed the top of Margaret's head. "You won't have to say you talked to Shayne. Tell her you thought she looked a little blue today and that the offer still holds about that Green Wilson house. We can make sure she and the children are safe."

Margaret looked up at Jerry. "I'm sorry you had to come home to this, Jerry. But I'm worried sick about her. When Robert's drinking, he, well, he gets mean."

"It's okay, Margaret. She's my sister. I'll help anyway I can."

"As long as you keep a cool head." His dad gave him a worried look. "You can't afford any trouble."

"I won't make trouble, Dad. I'm not that stupid."

"You can't even respond to trouble, son. You have to stay calm to stay free."

They sat around the table and prayed for Connie and the children. Jerry's dad even managed to say a prayer for Robert, but Jerry found it hard to echo the prayer in his heart. What kind of man would hit a beautiful angel like Connie?

The next morning their prayers were answered. Before she went to work at the clothing factory, Connie called her mother to say she'd stayed up all night packing. The baby pictures of the kids and her photo albums were already in the trunk of her car. Before the kids went to bed she made a game of them putting their favorite toys in pillowcases. She told her mother she was praying for forgiveness for breaking up her marriage, but when she looked into Shayne's eyes the night before, she realized she couldn't raise children like this. She knew how a home was supposed to be. She wanted the kind of love and peace for her own children as she'd felt when she was a child.

Margaret couldn't answer her. She was crying too

much. She handed the phone to Jerry's dad.

"It's okay, Connie. We'll take care of everything. You go on to work the same as any other Monday. That way if Robert comes around he won't know anything's going on until it's too late to do anything about it. Margaret will pick up the kids at the sitter's, and Jerry and I will take the truck to get your stuff."

So they drove to the house and loaded up the big truck. They didn't feel bad taking the furniture since most of it belonged to Margaret from the time when the house had been a happy home. Margaret had the kids and was following the truck out when Robert sped past them and veered toward Margaret's car. She swerved away from him off the road into a ditch.

"This isn't good." Jerry's dad pulled the truck over.

"What's he trying to do?"

"Who knows." His dad opened his door. "You stay put and let me handle this, Jerry." As he climbed down out of the truck to confront Robert, he muttered under his breath. "Keep the kids in the car, Margaret." It sounded almost like a prayer.

In the side mirror, Jerry watched Robert jump out of his car and head toward Jerry's dad. Jerry's heart sank when he spotted the bulge in Robert's back pocket. The man had a gun. Jerry quietly opened the truck door and climbed out. Robert didn't see him. He jumped in front of Jerry's father. Jerry very quietly picked up the cattle prod his dad carried in the truck.

Jerry had been out of prison for a week, not nearly long enough. He pulled in a big breath of free air and whispered, "Lord, I guess this is the last of my free time." But he couldn't stand there and let this man shoot his father. Even if it meant he'd have to go back inside for the rest of his life.

CHAPTER 46

Jerry raised the cattle prod. He couldn't let Robert reach for his gun.

Jerry's dad looked over Robert's shoulder at Jerry and shook his head the tiniest bit. The gun was still in Robert's pocket, so Jerry lowered the stick to his side. "What do you think you're doing, Robert?" He made his voice firm the way he'd heard prison guards do.

Robert whirled around. When he saw Jerry, he looked as though he might be remembering where Jerry had been for the last five years. And why. Jerry didn't blink. He knew how to stare down bullies. He'd had plenty of practice in prison. He swung the cattle prod back and forth a couple of times to make sure Robert saw it.

"You can't take my kids." Robert yelled the words even as he backed up a step. His hands were shaking as he held them out in front of him to ward off Jerry. He made no move to reach for the gun.

"The kids belong with their mother." Behind Robert, Jerry could hear the children crying. He wanted to smile over at them to let them know everything was going to be okay, but instead he kept his gaze locked on Robert.

"What's it to you? You just got out of the pen."

"I did, but Connie's my sister now. A brother has to protect and take care of his sister." Jerry kept his voice calm, almost pleasant, but the look he gave Robert held nothing pleasant. "And I plan to do whatever I have to do to protect mine."

Jerry's dad stepped closer to Robert. "Now, Robert, we don't want any trouble. And you know the kids need their mother."

Robert looked over at Jerry's dad and seemed to regain some courage. "They're my kids too. I'm their father."

"More reason than ever for you to get in your car and leave. You do that we won't call the police and tell them how you tried to ram the car your children were riding in," Jerry's father said. "One of your kids could have gotten hurt."

"I wasn't going to hit the car. Just make her stop," Robert said, but all the fight was gone from his voice.

"Just leave, Robert," Jerry said. "Smile and wave goodbye to the kids and leave."

Robert looked back at Jerry. "She can't do this to me."

Jerry stared him down. "It was what you shouldn't have done to her that caused this."

"She didn't tell you I hit her, did she? She's always telling lies about me." Robert spat on the ground. "It's not my fault she's clumsy and keeps bumping into things. And if she told you I shot at her, that's just another lie. The gun went off by accident."

Jerry's grip tightened on the cattle prod. "Leave."

Robert must have heard something in Jerry's voice that made him stop talking and turn toward his truck. He didn't even look toward Margaret's car where his son was screaming and his two daughters watched out the window with wide eyes.

After Robert sped away, they pushed Margaret's car out of the ditch. Then Jerry leaned down to grin at the children inside. "Everything's going to be okay, guys. Your Uncle Jerry will see to it."

They looked as if they weren't sure they could believe him. Then Shayne smiled a little. She'd been the last one he'd expected to smile, but he felt the way he imagined a new father must feel when a tiny baby reaches up and grabs hold of his father's finger. This little girl had grabbed hold of his heart with her shy smile.

"Time to go see what your new house looks like," he said.

They had the truck unloaded by the time Connie got home from work. Two of her co-workers escorted her to the new house, one driving in front and the other behind her. That afternoon after they'd convinced Robert to leave the children alone, he'd shown up at the factory where Connie worked and called her outside. He let her know he had a gun. He told her she couldn't just leave him without giving him another chance to work things out with her. To get him to leave, she promised to meet him after work even though she had no intention of meeting him anywhere ever again. She didn't like lying, but she was scared.

Once Connie and the children were settled in the new house, Jerry took on the task of making sure they were safe. At night after he got through with the milking, he drove over to Green Wilson Street to drive circles around the block to be sure Robert wasn't around. When Jerry passed Connie's house at night, everything about the house looked closed and locked away. She was scared Robert would find her even though she hadn't heard a word from him since that day at the factory.

Jerry started stopping by after he made his rounds of

the neighborhood. The kids called him uncle and she kept saying she loved having a brother. He pretended the same about her as a sister, but what he felt when he looked at her didn't have the first thing to do with brotherly love.

But if she wanted him to be a brother, he'd act like a brother. He didn't want anything to stop her smiling a big welcome whenever he showed up at her door which was almost every night. Often as not, because of how early he had to get up to milk, he would doze off while watching television with her. When that happened, she'd turn off all the lights except the one in the kitchen and leave him sleeping on the couch.

When he woke up, Jerry let himself out the back door to head home. The times he slept till the wee hours of the morning, he crept out to his truck and opened the door inch by inch to keep from waking the neighbors. He didn't want the retired minister next door to think less of Connie for letting him stay so late. Then he'd shift the truck out of gear and coast down to the end of the driveway before he shut the door and started the engine.

When the opportunities to give his testimony started coming in as Chaplain Ben and Mr. Cleveland had assured Jerry they would, he invited Connie and the kids along just so they'd have somewhere to go. At least that's what he told them and his father. The truth was he wanted to be with Connie as much as possible. Every minute of every day wouldn't have been too much time together for him. And the kids already seemed almost like his own. They ran to meet him whenever he showed up and pulled on his hands to come look at this or that.

Still, she thought he was her brother. And his father thought Jerry had embraced Connie as his sister the way he now accepted Margaret as his stepmother. His father had no idea Jerry felt like a giddy teenager every time he looked at Connie. He thought Jerry was in love with a girl back in Oldham County who'd written him now and again while he was in prison. When Jerry drove to Oldham County one Saturday to see Judy and some of his other old friends, his father seemed convinced he was right. Jerry overheard him telling Margaret that Judy would make the perfect wife for Jerry.

But although Judy was a dear old friend, her smile didn't make his heart skip a beat the way Connie's did. He just didn't know how to tell Connie he was in love with her. So he continued to play the part of a brother. He made himself at home on Connie's couch, raided her refrigerator without asking, and teased her about her new hairstyle. But what he wanted to do was put his arm around her while they were watching television. He wanted to run his fingers through her hair. He wanted to feel her head resting on his shoulder.

He prayed for an opportunity to let her know how he really felt, but when she did open the door for him to tell her the truth by asking about his visit with Judy or which girls he thought were cute, he let the chance slip by. Then he berated himself as a coward all the way back to his house and prayed for more courage if he got another chance. The Lord finally took pity on him and threw open the door for him.

Connie and the kids went with him to a church over in Indiana. Jerry didn't know how the church found out about him. He just knew if they invited him, the Lord must want him to go. People responded to his testimony wherever he went, but it wasn't him. He was simply the mouth the Lord was using. Jerry told his story and tried not to get in the way of the message, but on this day, the Lord had a message for Jerry. Or maybe for Connie.

After the service, one of the older deacons came over to Jerry. "That was great, Brother."

The man shook Jerry's hand, then smiled at Connie and the kids who were helping Jerry pack up his equipment. "And we're so glad you brought your beautiful family along. My wife and I got married right here in this church forty-five years ago. Some people don't believe it, but we're just as happy now as we were then. And I can see the two of you feel the same way about each other. It's plain as day how much you and your lovely wife are still in love with one another."

Jerry grinned at Connie. Color bloomed in her cheeks, but she didn't speak up to tell the man Jerry was her brother. So Jerry didn't either. "Well, thank you, sir."

That was easier than going into the family story. It was almost one o'clock and the kids were hungry. Besides he was tired of telling people Connie was his sister. He was ready for people to think they were a beautiful family. He wanted them to be a beautiful family.

They were in the car driving away from the church before Connie said, "It was funny what that man said about us. I guess we should have told him it wasn't true, but it's sort of a complicated relationship."

"You can say that again," Jerry said.

"And the kids are hungry."

"I could go for one of those pimento cheese sandwiches you packed up for our lunch myself."

She pulled sandwiches out of the sack between them on the front seat and handed one to Jerry and some to the kids in the back seat. They were in Connie's car. Her arm brushed against him when she reached over the seat to help Tab with his sandwich. An electric jolt went through Jerry. He tried to make his mouth open to say he thought the old deacon had seen things pretty straight, but instead he took a bite of his sandwich. He didn't particularly like pimento cheese, but he'd never told Connie that.

"Do you want a soft drink? The ice in the cooler has melted, but they're still cold."

"Sure." He needed something to wash down the pimento cheese.

She handed him a drink. "That boy who came up to

talk to you after the service? Were you able to help him? He looked really upset."

"I think so." Jerry said. "He's sort of got off track. Running with the wrong crowd and stuff, but he wants to do what the Lord wants him to do."

"I guess sometimes it's hard to know what that is."

"Yeah." But Jerry knew what the Lord was trying to help him do right then. He could almost hear the Lord saying tell her for Pete's sake.

"You know," he started, but right then Tab spilled his drink and Shayne screamed when the soft drink soaked her Sunday dress. Jerry had to pull over to let Connie clean up the mess, and somehow when they were back on the road again, the moment had passed.

Even so, he vowed that somehow before the day was over, he would let her know his feelings for her were more than brotherly. Much more. All afternoon he would be almost ready to blurt out how he felt, but something would happen. The kids got into fights. Connie dozed off in her chair. He couldn't decide the best words to say. Then he had to go home to help his father do the milking.

He started not to go back to Connie's, but the Lord nudged him, made him remember his vow. The day wasn't over. He drove back to her house where he didn't doze off while they watched television. Too many nervous little ants crawled around inside his clothes. Connie put the kids to bed and he still didn't know what to say. Chaplain Ben would have never believed Jerry could be so at a loss for words. Words usually spilled out of him. Actually he was talking practically non-stop, but he wasn't saying what he wanted to say.

Finally he got up to go home. "We both have to get up early." His feet were heavy as he walked toward the door.

She went with him to see him out the way she did on nights he didn't fall asleep on her couch. "Thanks for taking me and the kids with you this morning."

"It's me that needs to thank you. We go in your car. You fix us a lunch. You help pack the equipment in and out."

"It's no trouble. We like helping you." She smiled at him.

All the nervous ants started biting him. He had to do something. He put his hands on her cheeks, leaned over, and kissed her forehead. Sparks flew. He didn't see them, but he felt them. He didn't stick around to see if he was the only one feeling sparks. He practically ran outside. Once out of sight of the door, he jumped up in the air and clicked his heels together.

"Yes, yes, yes!" he whisper shouted. He hadn't forgotten the preacher asleep in the house next door. He didn't know when he'd ever felt so good. Maybe never. He had no idea what Connie might be thinking. Tomorrow would be soon enough to worry about that. Tonight he'd let the sparks keep burning.

The next morning as they headed to the house for breakfast after milking the cows, Jerry looked over at his father. "Can you marry your sister?"

CHAPTER 47

"Marry your sister? What are you talking about? Can who marry whose sister?" His father frowned. Then his face changed as it dawned on him what Jerry meant. "You mean you and Connie? But what about Judy?"

"Judy was your idea, Dad. Connie's mine. I love her."

His father stopped walking and stared at him. "But what about the children?"

"What about them?" Jerry's heart was pounding in his ears. "I love them too."

His father looked down at the dried cow manure on his boots and then to the east where the sun was rising up above a bank of rose-colored clouds. Finally his eyes came back to Jerry's face. "You haven't known her but a few weeks."

"How long did you know Margaret?"

"Long enough," his father said.

"That's how long I've known Connie."

"What's she say about getting married?"

"I haven't told her yet."

His father looked at him for another long moment. "Then maybe you should," he said before he started on toward the house.

Jerry followed him. "What do you think Margaret will think?"

"I don't know. I guess you'd better ask her yourself, but you might do better to worry about what Connie thinks."

Margaret didn't look as surprised as his father. She hardly paused in stirring sugar into her coffee after Jerry blurted out the same question to her at the breakfast table that he had to his father. "Can you marry your sister?"

She took a sip of coffee and sat her cup down before she looked straight at Jerry. "If you're talking about Connie, technically she's not really your sister. You aren't related at all except by marriage."

"So you think it would be okay?" Jerry hadn't eaten a bite of the eggs and bacon on his plate. He wasn't a bit concerned about food this morning.

Margaret smiled a little. "I don't think it matters what I think. What does Connie think? That's what matters."

"I haven't asked her yet."

Margaret's smile got wider. "Best not tell the whole world before you tell her."

"No ma'am. She's next on my list."

"It could be she should have been at the top of your list," Margaret said. "But you have time. You couldn't get married until her divorce is finalized anyway."

"When's that?" Jerry hadn't thought about that.

"Around the middle of November. A couple of months from now."

"A good month for a wedding," Jerry said.

"You Shepherd men don't believe in long engagements, do you?" Margaret smiled at Jerry's father.

Jerry's father grinned back at her. "We see something good, we go for it."

"Like father, like son." Margaret turned her gaze back to Jerry. "But at least your dad didn't keep it a secret from me."

"I'll tell her." Jerry broke a piece off a biscuit but didn't put it in his mouth.

"Maybe you should consider asking rather than telling." Margaret raised her eyebrows at him. "Now eat your breakfast before I have to warm it back up in the oven."

He did intend to ask, but once he had talked it over with his father and Margaret, it seemed as though it had already been decided. That he'd already asked and she'd already said yes. That all they needed was to decide when and where. And he was more than willing to let Connie do that.

That's what he told her that night. He waited until she put the kids to bed and then when she came back into the living room, he patted the couch beside him. She didn't hesitate. She came right over and sat down beside him. It seemed as natural as morning following night to put his arm around her. She leaned against him as if she'd wanted to do that very thing forever.

"We're getting married." He brushed the top of her hair with his lips.

"Oh?" She sounded a little breathless as if she'd just chased Tab down the hall to make him put on his pajamas.

"Yes." He tightened his arm around her.

"Okay," she said.

"You pick the time and place."

"My divorce won't be final until November."

"I know. Margaret told me."

"They know?" She sounded a little surprised.

"I needed to ask them if a person could marry his sister."

"I'm not really your sister."

"But you always wanted a brother."

"True." She turned to look at his face. "But I guess the Lord decided to answer my other prayer first."

"Which prayer is that?" Jerry wanted to kiss her more than he wanted to breathe.

"The one where I asked him to send somebody to help me raise my children. After I got married and Robert was the way he was, I prayed that he would change." She looked down at her hands clutched in her lap. "I don't know whether Mama told you or not, but I divorced him once before, but he said he'd changed. I thought maybe he had. That the Lord had answered my prayer and he would start being a good husband to me and a father to his children. But once we got married again, he was the same. I tried to be the wife he wanted me to be, but he stayed so angry. So unhappy. He always wanted more. Other women." Tears were running down Connie's cheeks, but she made no move to brush them away. "I know what the Bible says about marriage. I wanted to be married that way. I always intended to be married that way."

Jerry tipped up her face and gently wiped away her tears with his fingertips. "None of what happened was your fault, Connie. He's the one who broke your marriage vows, not you."

"But the Bible says you shouldn't be married but once."

"Maybe so, but what about you praying for a good father for your children, and now here I am? Who are we to fight against what the Lord wants for us?" He kissed the last of the tears off her cheek. "I promise to be the best father Shayne and Christy and Tab could ever have. And that's not all. I aim to be the best husband you could ever have." At last he touched her lips with his.

They talked to the preacher at Connie's church in Mitchellsburg first, but though Reverend Brown had counseled Connie to leave Robert and actually said praise the Lord when she filed for the divorce last May, he nevertheless wouldn't marry them. He feared losing his position as preacher if he performed the wedding ceremony of a divorcee.

When they both changed their membership to the Harrodsburg Baptist Church, a church closer to where they lived, the pastor there told them the same thing. He wanted to marry them, but he wasn't ready to risk losing his pastorate if the powers that be frowned on him performing a marriage where one of the parties was divorced.

Jerry wanted to tell the preacher that the real power that was, the Lord, had been more than understanding. The Lord had brought them together. He'd put the love in their hearts. The Lord wanted them to be married. Jerry had never been as sure of anything in his life.

As November got closer, Jerry suggested they be married at the courthouse by the judge. Nobody was in favor of that. Not Connie. Not Margaret or his father.

Connie looked ready to cry. "I won't feel like the marriage is blessed if a preacher doesn't perform the ceremony."

"But the preachers aren't cooperating." Jerry blew out a frustrated breath. "I know. We can go to Georgia and get Chaplain Ben to marry us."

"I can't go to Georgia. Shayne's in school," Connie said.

"Not only that, but your dad and I want to be there." Margaret spoke up. "And somebody would have to stay here to milk the cows."

"I've got an idea," Jerry's dad said. "What about if we have the wedding here at the house? Church can be anywhere believers are gathered. Where two or more are gathered in his name."

"Sounds good to me," Jerry said.

"But we still don't have a preacher." Connie still looked worried.

"Leave that to me. I'll find a preacher."

So Jerry's father made it happen the same as he'd always done. The same as Jerry's mother would have done if she'd still been living. He found a preacher.

Jerry and Connie didn't ask him if the preacher knew she was divorced. The preacher didn't ask Connie or Jerry about their marital status. Maybe he knew. Maybe he didn't. Either way he promised to come to the farm on November the twentieth to perform the ceremony.

A few aunts and uncles came to witness the event including Jerry's uncle Milton and aunt Adele who had been such help to his parents while Jerry was in prison.

Aunt Adele could hardly look at Jerry and Connie without tearing up. "I'm just so happy for you both, and I know your mother would have been too. I'm sure as I can be that she's looking down on you proud as punch."

It was good to have somebody actually mention his mother. Jerry loved Margaret, had even started calling her Mom, but he hadn't forgotten the debt he owed his mother for her faithful love while he was in prison.

"I always wanted to make her proud," he said.

Aunt Adele dabbed her eyes with a tissue. "And you did. Believe me. I was as close to Hazel as I ever was to any of my sisters. She didn't do everything right. She was the first to admit that, but she couldn't have loved you any more if you'd been her own child."

"I was her child."

Aunt Adele smiled at him through her tears. "Indeed you were."

The day was beautiful, cool but with sunshine streaming down out of a clear blue sky. The children were so excited they were practically spinning in place. While Jerry and his father milked the cows a little early that afternoon, Connie and her mother dressed the kids in their Sunday best. The girls wore matching dark pink dresses and Tab had on a white shirt with a little blue bowtie that kept sliding sideways. Connie kept straightening it until finally Jerry told her it looked cuter crooked.

A few minutes before seven, the preacher knocked on the door. After the proper introductions, Reverend Marksbury stood in front of Connie and Jerry and opened his Bible. "Do you take this woman to be your lawfully wedded wife? Do you take this man to be your lawfully wedded husband?"

They gave all the right answers, and at last the young man smiled and said what they'd been waiting to hear. "I now pronounce you man and wife. You may kiss the bride."

And so Jerry did. Aunt Adele and Margaret cried. Jerry's dad clapped his hands together, and the children squealed.

They were still standing in front of the minister when Tab pulled on the bottom of Jerry's suit coat. "Uncle Jerry, Uncle Jerry, can we call you daddy now?"

The preacher looked a little taken aback. That must have been something else Jerry's father hadn't exactly explained to him. Jerry grinned at the preacher and shrugged a little before he leaned down to pick up Tab. "You sure can, son. I'm your daddy now and I love you."

Things went a little crazy then with Shayne and Christy jumping up and down shouting daddy. Everybody laughed, and the preacher joined in even though he looked as if he wasn't sure he should be laughing. Christy and Shayne pulled Jerry toward the table with the cake and punch. They were ready to finally get to eat some of those little pink and white mints Aunt Adele had brought.

With his eyes wide open because he didn't want to miss a second of the best day of his life, Jerry sent up a prayer from his heart to the Lord. *Thank you, Lord, for not giving up on me. Thank you for all the angels at the crossroads and for the times you opened my eyes so I could see them. Thank you for life. Thank you for my beautiful angel, Connie, and for this wonderful family you've blessed me with.*

He could have gone on forever, and in fact, the praises did keep singing in his heart as laughter rang off the walls while they went through the rituals of feeding each other cake and trying to take sips of punch with arms intertwined.

Later when everybody was busy talking and he thought nobody would miss him, Jerry slipped out onto the porch to get a breath of fresh air. He still felt like doing a little dance of joy each time he opened a door and stepped outside into the air. No guards. No checkpoints. No fences. Just free air. And stars up in the sky. At the prison there were always too many lights to see the stars. He took a deep breath and let the night air wrap around him as he stared up at the sky.

Behind him, the door opened, and Connie came outside. "Oh, here you are. I was wondering where you'd got to." She stepped up beside him. "What are you looking at?" She peered up at the sky.

"The stars." He put his arm around her and drew her close to his side.

"The stars in the heavens." She kept her eyes on the stars.

"My mom's up there watching us."

"And my dad. Do you think they're happy for us?"

"I think they're laughing and dancing with the angels." Jerry held out his hand. "Feel the angel dust they're knocking down on us?"

Connie laughed and put her hand out beside his. "Angel dust." Then she looked at Jerry. "We're going to be happy, aren't we?"

"Yes, we are, Mrs. Shepherd. Yes, we are."

A PERSONAL NOTE FROM
ANN H. GABHART

In early 2004 when the Patriot Quartet was returning to Kentucky from a Gospel Singing cruise with the Eddie Crook Company, the Lord nudged the idea of writing down Jerry Shepherd's remarkable story into my head. My husband sings bass for the group and at that time Jerry was singing tenor with them. While they are extreme opposites in singing ranges and in life experiences as well, both of them have a solid unshakable faith and a sure knowledge of the Lord's will for their lives at this place and time.

The group had been singing together for about three years, but had just gotten a bus to travel in the year before. Gospel quartets become small families as they travel around singing on the weekends even without traveling together on a bus. But once *the bus* enters the picture to let the group travel together in the same vehicle, the family feeling grows stronger. Spending hours bouncing along on an old bus to whatever church has opened its doors for the group, eating together, trying to sleep sitting up on the all night rides to the next singing or home, having intense "road discussions" on where to stop to eat or how often to stop for relief tests the mettle of the fellowship of the quartet members and their wives. And you get to know one another pretty well. Along with the harmonizing, the singing family shares laughter, sorrows, stupid moments, joys, favorite songs, testimonies, and their pasts.

Years before the Patriot Quartet was even a dream, I'd heard Jerry give his testimony while singing with another quartet at a church in Burgin, Kentucky. My husband, who has been singing gospel music for many years, was in a different group sharing the program that night. When Jerry said he'd killed a man and been sentenced to life in prison for murder, it was as if the man in front of me had turned inside out.

I'd started watching him singing tenor in the group with one impression and ended–after his testimony–seeing a whole different man. A man who admitted taking another man's life. A man who thought he would be in jail most of his life. A man who said he was only standing there in the front of that church due to the grace of God and the love of his parents who never gave up on him.

God had a purpose for Jerry's life and no matter what Jerry did against that purpose, God didn't give up on him. The Lord set people down in Jerry's path to help him. These earth angels seemed to appear at every crossroad in his life, but even when Jerry ignored them and chose the wrong forks in the road, the Lord kept loving him and sending new people to guide him back to the true purpose for his life. At times Jerry believed he was beyond help, but the Lord knew better.

It was many years before I met Jerry again, now as part

of the same quartet my husband was in. I remembered his testimony, and as we traveled to singings together, he shared more about his past in bits and pieces. Those stories made me wonder if the Lord had brought us together with a new purpose in mind. I've been writing for many years and had recently had an inspirational novel accepted for publication, but I'd never even considered writing another person's story. I wrote about characters I made up, characters who only found life and breath on the pages of my books.

But the more Jerry talked about his life, the surer I was the Lord wanted others to know this amazing story of how God protected and guided Jerry by sending people to help him. The way Jerry blossomed under the constant, never ending, never changing love of our Lord is inspiring.

I owe a great deal of credit for this story to Jerry's mother, Hazel, who kept every letter Jerry wrote home and made copies of many of the letters she and Dewey wrote on Jerry's behalf while he was in the service and then in prison. The letters quoted in the book are unchanged and word for word just as Jerry wrote them or received them while he was in prison with the exceptions of the letter from Joletta (not her real name) and the one Hazel wrote from the prison parking lot after she read Joletta's letter. Both of those letters were lost in prison transfers.

The story is Jerry's. Although I invented many minor characters to interact with Jerry and came up with my own vision of the actual people who played a part in Jerry's life and then put words in their mouths and in Jerry's, each event is true to either what Jerry told me or what his letters revealed. The names of the people he met along the way, including those earth angels at his crossroads, have been changed to protect their privacy. Surely they will recognize themselves if they should come across this story of hope, redemption and pardon and feel joy to have been a part of this man's journey.

Jerry's journey isn't finished. Over the years since he was released from prison, he has told his story many times in hopes that his story will inspire others to step closer to God. He has been the Youth and/or Music Minister at several different churches. For a few years he traveled around the United States doing Home Mission work for the Southern Baptist Convention. He has sung tenor for several Southern Gospel Quartets including The Joymakers and The Patriot Quartet. He was an Over the Road Company truck driver as well as an owner operator driving long hauls for many years.

Now he and Connie live on a farm in Kentucky. He still sings and tells his story. Shayne, Christy, and Tab have all grown up, and are happily married. They've blessed Jerry and Connie with seven beautiful grandchildren who love their Daddy J.

CPSIA information can be obtained
at www.ICGtesting.com
Printed in the USA
LVHW080602060722
722857LV00014B/902

9 780998 353913